Beyond the Centre

Writers in their own Words

Edited by Declan Meade

NEW ISLAND

BEYOND THE CENTRE
First published in 2016 by
New Island Books
16 Priory Office Park
Stillorgan
Co. Dublin
Republic of Ireland.

www.newisland.ie

Print ISBN: 978-1-84840-573-8
Epub ISBN: 978-1-84840-571-4
Mobi ISBN: 978-1-84840-572-1

British Library Cataloguing Data.

A CIP catalogue record for this book is available from the British Library.

Typeset by JVR Creative India
Cover Design by Kate Gaughran
Assistant Editor, Amy Herron
Printed by TJ International Ltd, Padstow, Cornwall

10 9 8 7 6 5 4 3 2 1

Contents

By Way of an Introduction…

In the summer of 1995, at the age of twenty-four, I came to live in Dublin for the first time, equipped with a degree in European Business Studies and German from the University of Ulster at Coleraine. This course with its focus on international marketing and languages was supposed to prepare students for glittering careers in the new Europe. The European Economic Community had only recently become the European Union, introducing free movement of capital and labour. There were untold fortunes to be made.

I wasn't much interested in making a fortune – and so when I moved to Dublin after a year spent working in a bookstore in Atlanta for under six dollars an hour, I didn't turn to the shiny new International Financial Services Centre for employment but rather to the FÁS office on D'Olier Street. I wanted to work in the arts sector and that meant one thing back then: enrolling on a Community Employment Scheme. These schemes were set up to provide the long-term unemployed with training and work experience but many of them had been set up within otherwise under-resourced arts and cultural organisations and were populated by graduates like myself. Within a month of arriving in Dublin, I had a place on the CE Scheme at the James Joyce Centre, where my initial role was as bookkeeper and office assistant.

I worked nineteen hours a week and got paid eighty pounds. I was also entitled to a small training allowance towards personal and professional development and I used this to pay for a ten-week evening class at the Irish Writers Centre. It was a class in writing for television and radio and

I selected it on the basis that it sounded at least halfway practical and career-orientated. Really, I just wanted to write short stories and this is what I was trying to do with the rest of my free time.

*

The Irish Writers Centre on Parnell Square is about five minutes' walking distance from the James Joyce Centre on North Great George's Street. Once I'd discovered it, up beside the Dublin Writers' Museum (more dead writers!), its presence in the city meant a great deal to me. I remember picking up a copy of the Centre's printed newsletter and scouring it for information – and for affirmation. Yes, I made note of upcoming events and of competition deadlines, but much more importantly the newsletter, taken as a whole, and item by item, provided proof of a busy and robust literature scene. There was a lot going on and an invitation to be part of it.

*

By the end of the ten-week course, I'd written a radio play and I sent it to RTÉ. I'm not sure that I ever heard back from them. I don't remember what the play was about.

*

In October 1997, the late David Marcus spoke at a book launch in the Centre and decried the lack of outlets for publishing short stories. By this time I'd met a good many fellow aspiring writers, many of whom were there with me in the audience that night, nodding in agreement. Within six months, emboldened by Marcus's speech, I was back in the Centre to launch the first issue of *The Stinging Fly*.

*

My last attempt at writing a short story was in 2004.

*

Late last year, I said yes without hesitation when Valerie Bistany asked me to commission and edit this anthology of personal essays to coincide with the Centre's celebration of its twenty-fifth anniversary. The remit given to writers was a fairly open one. They were asked to write about whatever aspect of the last twenty-five years interested them most. They could explore changes in the political, the social or the cultural landscapes, or they could choose to examine the period through the lens of their own work. Writers were also given the option to address matters of concern to them in the here and now.

The broadness of the book's remit is in keeping, I believe, with the open spirit that animates and informs the Centre in its approach to serving the needs of different writers at different stages of their writing lives. The essays that the remit has yielded up provide the reader with an experience equivalent to a fly-on-the-wall documentary, the subject being not just the Irish Writers Centre itself – its achievements and some of the struggles it has endured through the years – but also members of the diverse community of writers that it seeks to represent. We hear first hand from them of their experiences, living and writing through the last quarter century.

Declan Meade, 2016

24

Mia Gallagher

I am in the back of the car and my dad is driving, white-knuckled, up the dual carriageway from Cork. We have two hours – maybe two and a half – to get to Dublin. It's 1991 and Dad has never managed the trip in under three hours. Mum's in the front seat, doing her best *Calm down, G.* voice (she calls my dad 'G.', short for Gerhardt; he calls her 'Mim', short for Miriam). Beside me in the back seat is my sister, Etain. I can't remember if we've exchanged a look of complicity at our parents' goings-on, or if we're already off in our separate worlds. Me stressing about the interview at the other end of the dual carriageway and how am I going to get to the flat in time to change and do I even know what I'm going to say and how will it be with Seán when I see him, while Etain – well, Etain thinks her private thoughts.

I remember this twenty-five years on, and I remember the scene first. The pictures, the context, the anxiety. I don't feel it in my body, though my body is where it happened. I picture it, then I think: wow. That doesn't feel like something out of my twenties. Parents in the front; kids in the back. It's – *abracadabra* – pure childhood.

I was twenty-four, on my way to do an interview for the role of Director of the Irish Writers Centre, newly set up in number 19, Parnell Square. I wasn't sure if I wanted the job. It had come up and my fairy godmother, writer and teacher Phyl Herbert, had suggested I apply for it. I was two and a half years out of college, busy but not altogether fulfilled, working at bits and pieces, mostly under the radar, subsisting on the dole. I had been living with my boyfriend Seán for six months – he was the first boyfriend I'd lived with and we were still navigating the weirdness of that: the constant intimacy, the grown-upness, the routine, the howlongwillthislastness. He was in a band and the band was tipped for greatness. I wasn't sure what I was tipped for.

In the eighties, I'd studied communications in college and loved the course; loved the thinking and ideas, loved the creative side even more. Together with a classmate, Dave, we'd made a film on video as our thesis: it looked at magic, psychoanalysis, body image, gender, identity and madness. Olwen Fouéré and David Heap had acted in it. Fired up on Welles and Sally Potter, Jarman and Greenaway, and the privilege of working with such gifted performers, I'd thought – yes, absolutely, this is what I want to do. Make movies! Then reality landed: funding applications, telephone calls, negotiation. I wasn't sure I'd be capable of that. I'd hated the production side of making our film and had kept trying to shunt it onto Dave until he'd called me on it. So I thought through the dialectic and figured out that if I owned the means of production, making art would be a hell of a lot easier. What means of production did I already possess? A pen, a notepad. I would write.

Since I was a kid I'd been confident of my technical skills as a writer. I read voraciously, I'd written a play when I was eight, in school I loved coming up with stories. I'd had a few fiction pieces published in the college art-lit journal and I knew how to write a persuasive academic essay. In the smoggy winter of 1988, I started writing in my small bedroom in my parents' house – disconnected stuff, a weird faux sci-fi parable, then, in the springtime, a long rambling thing loosely based on a Good Friday piss-up I'd just gone to. Nothing added up to anything, but I kept going in the back garden of my first flat, a damp half-house on Curzon Street, Portobello, where I'd moved with my friend Miriam at the start of the summer of 1989, the second summer of love.

Nineteen eighty-nine is older than the Irish Writers Centre, but I grant myself some poetic license in claiming it as a Then-point. Maybe that was when the germ of the idea first started tickling at Jack Harte? I wouldn't be surprised; it was a magical year. Whatever cosmic blight had shadowed Ireland over most of the eighties was starting to shift. People my age were still emigrating, but enough of them were staying on to make the dole office on Victoria Street an interesting place. Unemployed, we all said. Yes, we said, looking for full-time work. Here's the proof. But we were already working, at our own projects, and our proof was fake *Regretfully We Have No Vacancy* letters drafted by our friends: Simon from the Marx Brothers Café, David from the Coffee Inn. Meanwhile in the queues for their weekly 55 quid stood Ed and Niall and Joey from The Dixons, Conor from The Partisans, Kevin and Fergus the film-makers, Claire and Wendy the artists, beautiful journalist Louise (RIP, my love) and her gorgeous Brigitte-Bardot party-girl friend, Barbara. Music and art were thriving, the film-scene kicking off. There was a strong young activist and queer community and acid house had hit the Dublin clubs.

After college, I'd got some paid part-time freelance work as a researcher/ scriptwriter, some of it interesting, some of it not. On my own time, I'd started working with Ruth, a young director, on experimental film scripts critiquing American-brand capitalism, and I'd also joined forces with Seamus yet-to-become-a-world-famous-cheesemonger on an idea that involved trying to convince David Collins that I'd make a perfect host for a TV chat show exploring politics and art. (Unsurprisingly, that one never happened.) Meanwhile, in the back garden of Curzon Street, during the downtimes between work, friends visiting with coffee, croissants and lumps of hash, hopping down to Galway to the Film Fleadh and our busy nightlife in the Coffee Inn, Kehoe's and Sides, I wrote. Scraps again, slightly more joined up. Some ideas for stories, a novella based – cleverly, I thought – on a quasi-Electra complex, where awful things happened to a kid called Lucy Dolan who lived on a small red-brick terrace a bit like Curzon Street. The stories were, generally, solipsistic. Not much happened. Some were nasty, some were boring. One or two had a germ of something intriguing. The novella was interesting and I did wonder if it could be stretched into something more substantial.

The eighties ended with a bang: a historic New Year's Eve party in three old cottages in Blackpitts Place. The houses, now sacrificed to the Boom, were crammed. People stood on cars. *Welcome to the nineties!* roared someone. Paul Tylak, I think. If you ask anyone from the Coffee Inn/Sides scene about that night, they'll say they were there. It was our

Dandelion Market; our Generation X, grungy, hedonistic, acid-fuelled Woodstock.

A couple of weeks later, I met my own watershed. The flat in Curzon Street was so cold, I often discovered mould growing on my clothes in the small crap landlord-issue wardrobe. One bitter night in January 1990, it happened. I found myself *having* to write. It was different to the usual sit down and churn the story out, or follow a pre-existing idea or line of thought until it – perhaps – brought me somewhere. This time I found myself starting and couldn't stop. As if something was perched on my shoulders, looking on, *willing* me to do it. The story was about a friend who had killed himself. Gregg Gough. It's strange writing his name now. I didn't name him in the story, though when it was published, everyone who'd known him knew it was him.

I wrote straight through and when I'd finished, I felt I had something that made sense; there was a sort of truth about it. I felt weirdly squeamish about showing it to anyone: furtive, almost. Ashamed. Over time, I've learnt that comes when I've hit a nerve, some hidden reality in my own experience that only writing has unearthed. Gregg's story, *Departure* – the writing of it, the furtiveness I felt once it was written – has been my touchstone ever since. I know when I'm off the mark, or coming close. I know those rare times when I've hit it.

By late spring, my circumstances had changed. Dublin – then, like now – was a risky place if you were young and needed support to make your art and didn't want to leech off your parents. In late 1989, the FÁS Stasi had called me up: I would need to train or get a placement. I was sick of training. Much as I'd loved college, I'd had enough by the time I'd started third year, and in my arrogance I thought I knew everything anyway, so I signed up for a placement, as staff writer with the Independent Theatre Association. This was a collective of small independent theatre companies and practitioners who wanted better pay, more platforms, more opportunities. For nine months, I trudged down to Ormond Quay and up the four flights of stairs to the ITA's office at the top of a crumbling Georgian building. There were mice in the attic and all of us in the office were on our own small scavenge-hunt, trying to get away with doing as little as possible during our twenty hours a week – with the exception of inspirational John McCourt, our manager, who was capable of being both kind and effective.

By then Curzon Street was under the hammer and Miriam and I had moved to an equally cold red-brick on the northside, down the road from Mountjoy Prison. I discovered a crystal shop on East Essex Street and began to meditate. I also continued to party, drink and have unsatisfying dalliances with unsuitable men. Then, that summer, during the Italia World Cup, something interesting happened: the River Parade of Innocence. The Parades were large-scale, peaceful protests against miscarriages of justice – specifically the wrongful incarceration of the Birmingham Six and the Guildford Four – organised by a group of artists including Charlie O'Neill from The Graphiconies and writer/actor Declan Gorman. The first, held in December 1989, had passed me by. But in 1990, I signed up to join a drumming group and on a gorgeous July evening, right after Packie Bonner saved *that* penalty, my housemates and I swayed down the Quays with the rest of the River Paradistas. It was huge. We had giant puppets, costumes, placards. We danced, we drummed, we sang, and men with Irish suntans rolled down their windows and cheered. *Olé, olé olé olé!*

Looking back, *that* to me was the 1990s. That evening, it was okay to be Irish, and stand up for other Irish people who'd been targeted because of their ethnicity, and not be ashamed of it or frightened of being called a terrorist. It was better than okay. It was *good.* That Parade – not least because of those boozy, happy, apolitical men and women cheering us on with their *olé's* – felt hopeful and important and *big.* A year and a half earlier I'd been in Nicaragua, watching my compatriots on the Irish Coffee Brigade tear themselves apart over the rights and primacy of stickie versus provo, while the liberals in between, the middle-class doctors and nurses, tried uselessly to preach human rights and compassion. The Nicaraguan experience had soured the idea of becoming politically engaged for me; but through their love and joy and sheer fucking creativity, Charlie, Declan and the other Parade organisers had opened up something that felt like it could be a different way in.

I've felt that way about Ireland and being Irish a few times since. Once watching Riverdance during the 1994 Eurovision – though I feel cringey writing this, and wonder at my own cringing: is that the old collective shame again, the thick-Paddy-we're-never-good-enough stuff that's been projected onto Irish people for centuries? Or is it more personal, my inner thirteen-year-old, frightened of not appearing cool? I felt that pride a bit during the 1994 World Cup, at Anne Enright receiving the Booker, watching Aidan Gillen storm it in *Queer as Folk*. Most recently, most fantabuloso-memorably, I felt it the day the Yes vote won. I didn't feel it as much in 1995 when divorce came through. I felt more relief then – and shock, that so many people had still voted No. I didn't feel it during the Boom; that was more like witnessing an awkward teenager negotiating growth spurts, acne and puppy-love crushes on distinctly dodgy others. And I certainly didn't feel it that awful Saturday in 2010 when the Troika rolled in and a huge crowd of us stood, disappointed to our cold, bitter bones, outside the GPO as the snow began to fall and people booed the SIPTU reps with their – to us – cushy packages, while Fintan told us to get on the phone and ring our TDs instead of proclaiming himself our Václav Havel, our knight in white armour who would lead us, creativity-guns blazing, to a brand new Republic.

In 1990, summer turned to autumn. In my crystal-festooned bedroom I tried to get on with my own means of production, writing more bits. Sometime that year – I've no idea when – I had written another story that made sense. It too was about someone I knew who'd died; not a suicide, but a fatal reaction to penicillin. A stupid death, unnecessary. As with Gregg, Geraldine's story willed itself to be written. I didn't name her either. In both cases, I realised, I had been less than a good friend. I had not been there, I had let the person down. The story willed itself to be written, because the story was the track of my unconscious shame, and shame always needs an out.

In September the *Sunday Tribune* published my story about Gregg. I thought about running away to Galway to chase after a boy who didn't love me; instead, I took a holiday to Greece with my friend Helen. We met an Israeli-Australian woman who lived on kibbutzim, and a handsome German cad and I nearly ran away with him on his yacht. I dreamt of a lagoon, still and magnetic, and, to Helen's relief, came back to Ireland, where I got a job teaching Business English to kids only a few years younger than myself. The Parades held a drumming vigil on College Green. Things were moving with the Six and the Four. I talked to a publisher about developing my novella into a young adult novel, and started the process only to find myself quickly losing steam. How could

I write to an audience? That was what I did in my paid jobs. It seemed *wrong* to try and export that structure onto a process of sense-making that was slowly revealing itself to me as mysterious, dark, and painful.

On the 15th of December, I met Seán. Bruised from my dalliances, I'd forsworn musicians, especially the rhythm section, but Seán was a gentleman and a determined one. We dated platonically for a while, then – bam. By February 1991 I'd moved in with him, abandoning my housemates, my rented television, the furniture and crockery I'd inherited from my grandfather. Some of it I later reclaimed, including my housemates; but the television got stolen, leaving me with the bill.

Nineteen ninety-one was a great year for me, but a tough one too. I was in love and didn't have much energy for other things. Paid work had dried up. I'd been sacked from my teaching job for not being able to control my students. Seán's life – the band, its success, the gigs, the nasty behind-the-scenes politics – fascinated me, occupied me. I was back on the dole. I kept house, in a bedsit that was so tiny that on hot nights we had to sleep in the single bed like sardines, head to toe. I scrubbed the shower, I tidied Seán's art materials. We got tired of being sardines and moved across the road into the top-floor flat of a dilapidated Georgian house. It was huge. We had two rooms and a kitchen and our own bathroom; a view back and front over the rooftops of Dublin. A prostitute lived on the ground floor. She had a child who used to visit her on weekends and a snake she wore around her torso like a scarf. Her name was Yvonne and she was very friendly and didn't look like a prostitute. But there were the cars pulling up every half hour and the sound of the washing machine five times a night and we could see her, through the single lens of my brother's monocular, walking down the canal to Herbert Place, where she would wait with the other girls for a car to stop and a man to lean out the window and call her over. She had a keyboard too and used to play schmaltzy music on it. It made me think of *Quicksilver,* a game show from the seventies that Bunny Carr used to host.

I tried to write. I went back to the novella to develop it in a way that felt more like where it – my unconscious – wanted to go. I decided I would pad everything I had out and see where it led me. It was slow work. I didn't really enjoy it. I felt I was writing for the sake of it. I enjoyed tending house, though. We got a kitten that we couldn't keep. I pulled up the grotty carpet on our landing, sanded the boards underneath. I cooked. I started a quilt. I worried about money.

Our Supplementary Welfare Officer was a guy in his early-to-mid thirties. I still remember his name, the almost-iambic rhythm of it. We'd told him we weren't living together as a couple, because couples got docked rent allowance; they needed less money to live on than two individuals, apparently. We had two beds so we put them into the separate rooms and waited for the welfare guy to come up to the house to check we weren't sleeping together. We used to call him the Gestapo, though I'm sure he was just trying to do his job. After six weeks, we got fed up waiting and moved the beds back in together and the following day – Murphy's Law, or maybe they had some strange analog spyware back then – he dropped by. I remember standing in the front hall and mumbling some stupid excuse about being sick so we couldn't let him upstairs. He docked us a chunk off our rent allowance. The resentment gnawed at me. I'd asked my GP for a letter saying there were reasons why, at the age of twenty-four, I couldn't live at home anymore. The letter had been personal, touching on delicate family issues; I'd felt embarrassed asking for it, handing it in. And for what? This slight man, not much older than me, standing in my doorway, looking at me with such wearied disdain?

My friend Emer has two adult children, one nearly thirty, one twenty-five. Her eldest, her son, is a gifted writer. He was raised by loving middle-class parents, groomed, like his cub cohort, to have high expectations, only to find himself graduating as a screenwriter in the late noughties, deep in the black guts of the recession. Funding cuts. No dole for young people under twenty-five, no choice but to live at home. Crap service jobs. He tried New York, London. Now he's back, living in a bedsit, still writing, and writing better. He's thinking of doing teacher training if he can't fund himself by his practice. Me and Emer talk about him. It's the pain that makes you what you are, I say. The things you don't get. The failure, the rejection. That's how it's been for me. I know, she says, but he's my son.

Look at this, Mia, Phyl said in the summer of '91 and I looked at the ad for the Writers Centre job. Director – that sounded posh. It fit the bill. Well, sort of. It meant working with writers. I was one. Wasn't I? At least kind of one? It involved administration. I'd done that. Hadn't I? It would pay. Real money. Take that, Welfare Man. I wrote my application and was granted an interview.

We are steaming up the motorway, the last time I will ever return from a family holiday in the back seat of my dad's car. We'll just about make it. I won't have time to get to the house with the prostitute to change into my interview gear, but I'll borrow a nice top and culottes from my mum, and I'll remember – somehow – what I wrote in my application. They'll be nice, the interview panel – Cormac Ó Cuilleanáin is the only one I remember, though I'm sure Jack must have been there too. They'll be kind, and attentive. They won't give me the job. They'll honour the eminently more suitable Peter Sirr with the position. And for that rejection twenty-five years ago, and the painful, twisting, strange path it's led me on, I remain a thousand times thankful.

Mia Gallagher is the author of two acclaimed novels: *HellFire* (Penguin Ireland, 2006), recipient of the *Irish Tatler* Literature Award 2007, and *Beautiful Pictures of the Lost Homeland* (New Island, 2016). Her prize-winning short fiction has been published internationally and she has received several literature bursaries from the Arts Council of Ireland.

Early Days in Parnell Square

Peter Sirr

July, 1991, Buswells Hotel.

Well, I've got this far, I think. And there's always Rome, that international school, *la dolce vita*… I'd been living in Italy for the past couple of years and a friend had alerted me to the ad. *Irish Writers Centre, Director*. It seemed like an intriguing idea. A centre for writers, a place that would promote and celebrate writing. It was an idea full of promise. I thought of Poetry Ireland, where I'd worked briefly. A cellar in Mount Street full of books, readings here in Buswells and elsewhere in the city. A sense that poetry could matter.

I walk into the room to be met by the entire board of the Centre, all seventeen of them, along with the Literature Officer of the Arts Council, which has agreed to fund the venture – although to what extent is unclear. I've been interviewed for jobs before, in offices, hotel rooms, schools, hiring fairs in airports, but to see eighteen faces peering curiously at me is new. I'm put through my paces in the two national languages… A while later, I'm offered the job, and take it. The terms are less than spectacular, but I'm taken with the idea of the Centre and after a number of years of living abroad and feeling a bit culturally disconnected, I want to live and work in this city.

The numbers in that interview are a warning, or at least an indication of what might lie ahead. There are a lot of fingers in this pie. The idea of the Centre was initially driven by Jack Harte of the Irish Writers' Union. A few years earlier he had obtained a commitment from the government to make a state building available for a writers' centre, and secured a grant of £100,000 from the National Lottery to establish it. At the same time Matt McNulty of Dublin Tourism was in the process of setting up the Dublin Writers' Museum at Parnell Square and Jack, with the support of the writers' organisations and a wide range of writers, negotiated the use of 19 Parnell Square as the Irish Writers Centre.

It was a big, brave idea, just like John F. Deane's founding of Poetry Ireland, but at the same time, for all its apparent simplicity, it was an enormously complicated idea. The jump from any kind of arts practice to an institution that somehow represents it requires long and careful thought. Who will this thing be for? How exactly will it present and represent the makers of the art and the art itself? What will be its relationship with the makers, in all of their great diversity, from established to marginal, and with the wider public? How should it relate to practice outside this small corner of the world? How, exactly, will it survive and thrive?

In the case of the Irish Writers Centre the different organisations that came together to make this idea real were the Irish Writers' Union, the Society of Irish Playwrights, the Irish Children's Book Trust, the Irish Translators' Association. Each of these had its own core concerns, its own vision of what the Centre might be and of what the Director's role might be. These didn't always coincide. In the early weeks of the job I was invited to attend a meeting of the Irish Writers' Union in Liberty Hall. The first item on the agenda was the expulsion of the Director of the Irish Writers Centre from the meeting. The motion was duly passed, and I was requested to remove myself. It was a trivial incident, but it was a sign of the extent to which the Irish Writers Centre would be contested ground.

And yet, I suppose, how could it not have been? Wasn't it Shaw who described a literary movement as several writers living in the same city and hating each other cordially? It would have been a miracle if we had all agreed on the shape and aims of this new organisation, but of course it made my own relationship with the board necessarily fraught. For some organisations, the primary role of the Centre was in effect to serve them, to be a kind of secretariat. Again this was understandable but not what

I was interested in, or what the brief of the Centre was, or what the Arts Council was interested in funding.

The vision, that thin cloud of aspiration floating above the interests of the constituent members, was that the Centre should be a national organisation with a wide remit, and the aim of promoting Irish writing and Irish writers to as wide a public as possible. There were lots of fights about this. There was a real sense in which the Centre was a minority government within its own oddly calibrated structure and every board meeting was an ideological battleground. Theoretically, once elected to the board, the representatives of the organisations were supposed to transcend their origins and serve the board disinterestedly. Some did this willingly, for others it was a step too far. At one stage in the first year a section of the board seceded and began meeting elsewhere, with my own removal occupying a prominent place on the agenda. This was, inevitably, discovered, the agenda leaked – I felt a little like Brendan Behan being condemned to death in his absence ('well, they can shoot me in my f*****g absence as well') – and a fair amount of rhetorical fisticuffs and resignations ensued at the next meeting of the board proper. The pattern had been set, though, and would continue to enliven the boardroom and nudge those eighteenth-century ghosts awake for the next decade.

And yet, in a very Irish conundrum, these battles about who we were and how exactly to use our resources were almost comically out of proportion with what we actually had. Apart from myself there was, initially, just one other member of staff, Jacinta Douglas, who had, until then, been employed by the Society of Irish Playwrights. Her new role therefore required heroic diplomacy to balance the different sets of expectations. Later, Katherine Moore joined the small team, and later still we were able to create two further positions, but our first grant from the Arts Council was so tiny it was hard to take seriously as a commitment to a brave new project. It was as if, having decided in principle to back the project, the Council wanted to test our mettle by putting us under the severest possible pressure, condemning us to genteel poverty. I still remember the board meeting where I argued for the spending of a small amount of this grant on a computer, a suggestion that was met with scepticism. A clamour of voices instead urged the purchase of an electric typewriter instead and it was only the casting vote of the chairman that allowed newfangled modernity to prevail. A few days later I climbed up the stone steps of the Centre with an Apple Classic in a rucksack. The house didn't complain, though I remember Eavan Boland looking askance at it on a visit to a workshop. 'What processor is in that? It can't be as good as an Intel Pentium.' We stood there for a while arguing processors and operating systems with the fervour of the obsessed.

The house, of course, was our one huge advantage. Sometimes bricks and mortar are not thought of as important or necessary for an arts organisation's progress. But an accessible physical space was always part of the vision of the Centre. You can't have a single home for a community as diverse and dispersed as writers, who are not always social creatures, but an attractive and welcoming place will generate its own small excitements, our thinking went, and be a modest beacon of the creative impulse. Thanks to those early negotiations with government, we were installed in a beautiful, Georgian building in the heart of the city, and that meant that we had a place to put on events. The building was – and is – by no means perfect. It has no disabled access or lift, the spaces are somewhat limited. It was in fact several months before we could get into it. I spent many hours with the late Pat Seager and her team in the Dublin Writers' Museum as we waited to see how the refurbishment of both buildings would turn out, cooking up a mini festival in the meantime, which we held in the Museum's performance space. Dermot Morgan, Garry Hynes, Martyn Turner, Declan Kiberd… I remember – was it then? – Aidan Higgins reading a story; as he reached the end of each page he would lift the sheet up, consider it with a gesture of resigned distaste and fling it from him out in the general direction of the audience. There was a similar, more alarmingly self-critical moment a while later with another writer reading from an early novel with increasing disbelief, pausing after every other paragraph to ask with hurt puzzlement: 'How did I write this drivel?'

As soon as we took possession of number 19 we could feel the power of the place. It might sound sentimental but I always felt that there was something profoundly welcoming and benign about the physical space. Something about the intimate scale of it, maybe, the way it made events seem like conversations. And people seemed to be drawn to it; there was a constant procession to the door, driven by curiosity or the need for information about some aspect of Irish writing or about outlets for new writing. It made us realise that even though literature is a virtual encounter between reader and text or between writer and reader, there is a hunger for a physical space – apart from a bookshop, launch or festival – in which to pursue an interest in writing, writers, the literal impulse. We weren't a museum – that was and is next door – so what we offered was a link to the living tradition. It was unusual in Ireland but was and is common enough elsewhere. Every German city has its *Literaturhaus* and there are similar institutions all over Europe. The Munster Literature Centre in Cork now performs a very similar function to that of the Centre in Dublin.

One of the great advantages for us in the early days was discovering how the combination of the building and the idea acted as a magnet. We were not long open before Frank Buckley arrived one morning. Frank was a former priest turned devoted art collector and, living in a modest house, was keen to find somewhere to display his paintings. Every few weeks he would arrive, a new painting under his arm – Felim Egan, Sean McSweeney, Graham Knuttell, Michael Mulcahy, Thomas Ryan – and we'd figure out where to put it. Frank wanted his art 'to inspire the inspirers', as he once put it. This was the beginning of what would turn out to be an extraordinary collection of contemporary Irish art and it greatly enhanced the visitor's sense of the building as an artistic haven.

Like a lot of things in those early years there was a happenstance quality to the display of Frank Buckley's collection. The idea occurred because the building was there. If it is there, things will come, if I can mangle Kevin Costner. Having a building and some full-time staff, as well as the co-operation and contacts of the writers' organisations, meant that we could set up exchanges with writers from other countries. We swapped writers with Finland, Australia (later adding a Chinese leg to that exchange) and Italy, and developed contacts with embassies and cultural institutes that saw the building regularly hosting German, French, Mexican and African writers. Without a home, and the visible presence it provided, this would have been impossible.

And we set out to make the best use of it, opening it up to other users as well as ourselves: Ireland Literature Exchange, the Irish Copyright

Licensing Association, Children's Books Ireland, so that the building became a hub for different kinds of literary activity.

We developed a programme of writing courses, and secured capital funding to stock a computer room where writers could come and work. Later, we set aside a quiet upstairs room as a studio for a writer. Jointly with Jack Gilligan, Arts Officer of what was then Dublin Corporation, we had a Writer-in-Residence. Later, Jack Gilligan, Poetry Ireland and the Irish Writers Centre came together to set up the Dublin Writers' Festival.

Although as time went on we did organise and fund events and workshops around the island, the heart of the operation was number 19, and the heart of that was the first-floor event space, what was then called the Blue Room. Regular public literary events, as opposed to book launches or often commercially driven festivals, are rare enough these days. Literary organisations and arts venues tend to be wary of them. They're labour intensive, expensive and it can be hard to lure a crowd on wet Thursday evenings to see poets or novelists read from their latest works.

Yet there's something compelling about seeing writers in action and all of my best memories of the Centre are tied up with visiting writers in the intimacy of the Blue Room. Seamus Heaney, Anne Enright, Les Murray, R. S. Thomas, Iain Crichton Smith, Cees Nooteboom, Miroslav Holub; a convention on theatre in Ireland, conferences on critical culture, revolutionary Irish women, writing in Irish, Hans Christian Oeser interviewing W. G. Sebald. We didn't always confine ourselves to the building: with Evelyn Conlon and the journal *Graph* we brought over Grace Paley from New York for a reading in Trinity; with the Writers' Union we brought Alice Munro, also to Trinity. And the Society of Irish Playwrights were active in organising events such as a brilliant tribute evening to James Plunkett. We funded events and workshops, to the small extent we could, all over the country. Another highlight, for the sheer joyousness of it, was a plot hatched with Poetry Ireland that ended up as The Stray Dog Café at the Mint, a laneway off Henry Street where the Project Theatre was temporarily housed. This was a series of pretty unforgettable Sunday night alternatives to *Glenroe*, with, among others, Maighréad and Tríona Ní Dhomhnaill, Fintan Vallely, Dermot Healy, Nuala Ní Dhomhnaill, The Voice Squad,

Ciaran Carson, Rita Ann Higgins, Moya Cannon, Michael Davitt, Liam Ó Muirthile, Jimmy McCarthy, Agnes Bernelle. These were the days when poets and prose writers happily shared the stage, something which rarely seems to happen now.

Or I think of *Dublin Fifteen*, the CD we co-produced with Pat Boran of fifteen poets including Eavan Boland, Paul Durcan, Paula Meehan, Thomas Kinsella and John Montague reading poems about Dublin. When we brought Michael Hartnett to the studio we discovered he'd forgotten his reading glasses and Pat had to blow up the text of 'Inchicore Haiku' to 500% before Michael could read it. Not that you'd guess it from the measured poise of the recording. It's the only recording of that poem, and one of the things I'm very glad we did.

Almost from the beginning, we wanted to have an educational strand, wanted the Centre to become a place where aspiring writers could undertake courses and workshops with experienced ones. The lights burned late with evening courses in poetry, fiction, memoir, children's writing, and it is great to see that the tradition has continued more or less unbroken for twenty-five years. Nuala O'Faolain once wrote in *The Irish Times* about the encouragement she received for the manuscript that would become *Are You Somebody?* in a course with Mary O'Donnell in the Centre and that seems to me a perfect example of the usefulness of this kind of work. We were lucky to have a great pool of talented writers to draw on and their willingness to share their experience of their craft helped many to develop their own work.

It wasn't all brilliance and glitter, needless to say. We often fell flat on our faces, with tiny audiences and cringing embarrassment, compensated for by the envelope with the fee and drinks in the Teachers' Club afterwards. How many hundreds of anxious minutes were spent pacing on the steps or hovering in the hall, waiting to see if enough souls would appear to take the bare look off the room? But the risk was always worth taking simply to create the sense that this was a place where things happened, where you might happen along unexpectedly and go away surprised and a little happier.

And there were the usual difficulties. The eternal shortage of money. The bureaucratic demands and shifting goalposts of funders. Can you please tell us what percentage of your inquiries come from County

Offaly? Tipperary South Riding? Em, not really. Can you tell us what portion of your audience is Muslim, Pakistani, Transgendered? The ongoing wrangles with the board. We even had board therapy, a day in a hotel with a counsellor which ended, inevitably, in tears. I remember the ashen face of the counsellor as much as our own discomfort.

In my last year, a substantial part of our budget was spent on legal fees as the board structure broke up and the unwieldy governance was reformed. The organisational underpinning of the Centre had simply proved too complicated. This was a pity because many people volunteered a lot of their time in good faith and served the Centre generously and it would have been easier for everyone had things been teased out more thoroughly in the beginning. These, though, were teething problems. Anyone who is around at the beginning of an organisation knows that it can take time to get everything right. The power of the original idea is illustrated by the fact that twenty-five years later the Centre is still here and still very active, thanks to Valerie Bistany and her team, and anyone who looks at the plans for the redevelopment of Parnell Square as a cultural quarter can't but be optimistic for the future. I'm glad to have seen it through its first decade, grateful to have had such sympathetic colleagues and supporters, and hopeful that 19 Parnell Square will still be humming with activity twenty-five years from now.

Peter Sirr was the first Director of the Irish Writers Centre. He lives in Dublin where he works as a freelance writer and translator. The Gallery Press has published *Marginal Zones* (1984), *Talk, Talk* (1987), *Ways of Falling* (1991), *The Ledger of Fruitful Exchange* (1995), *Bring Everything* (2000), *Selected Poems* and *Nonetheless* (both 2004), *The Thing Is* (2009) and *The Rooms* (2014). *Sway*, versions of poems from the troubadour tradition, was published in 2016. He contributes reviews and essays to many publications, many of which can be read on his website and blog. He is a member of Aosdána.

The Irish Writers Centre and the Democratisation of Writing

Jack Harte

The appropriation and exploitation of the arts, and access to the arts are twin issues that preoccupied me twenty-five years ago, and preoccupy me still.

When I arrived in Dublin in the sixties from rural Ireland I was baffled by the attitude to the arts. Access was a complex challenge. That may seem strange to young readers of today who are more familiar with open doors than with closed ones. Writing in particular was hidebound by age-old attitudes.

At the time I had many friends who were aspiring visual artists. They were students at the National College of Art and spent up to twelve hours a day in the college studios, working at and learning their various crafts. At night they would continue arguments and discussions over coffee or pints. And I envied them. There was nothing remotely like this for aspiring writers. Academic courses in the Arts departments of the universities specialised in literary criticism and were more likely to smother creative talent than to nurture it.

My reasoning was that if musicians and painters and sculptors saw fit to dedicate years to learning their crafts and developing their artistic talent, why not writers. They did in the era of the *fili* and bards! But my reasoning was out of tune with the prevailing attitude, and I discovered quickly that such reasoning was scorned. All you needed to be a writer was a pen and paper. You were supposed to arrive at your literary departure point fully fledged, master of your art, confident in your ability, certain that you had been fingered from on high for a literary career.

I had none of these traits and my initial inclination was to withdraw from the arena and cede it to those who had the self-belief to bang their shields and proclaim their genius. Yet there was a feeling that I had a right to participate in this area of human activity, that it was the only area in which I had any talent, and above all, that I wanted to communicate and to express myself through writing. Closer analysis convinced me that those who had been fingered from on high almost all came from the privileged stratum of society and they were also almost exclusively male. So whoever did the fingering was partisan in doling out talent. It was nonsense of course. What these people had was confidence, in abundance, sometimes to the extent of arrogance, and an enviable sense of entitlement. If we quantify the privileged stratum at a generous 20 per cent of society, eliminate the half that is female, then the literary crop was being farmed from just 10 per cent of the people. What a waste. But so it had been for centuries, certainly up to the explosion of popular culture from the sixties on.

If access to writing was problematic for a person from a working-class background, or for a woman, how did the exclusion manifest itself? Few unpublished manuscripts written by women have been discovered. It is my belief that any such literary expression was snuffed out before it reached the page. Confidence and the lack of it were at the core of the problem. A snub, a put-down, a disparaging remark, was probably enough to quash the tentative efforts of many an unsure sensibility, enough to guarantee that a potentially interesting voice was silenced.

The statistics of published writers up to the sixties prove my point regarding women. The imbalance in the ratio of men to women is overwhelming, and if we accept the reasonable assumption that artistic potential is distributed evenly throughout society, then the absence of women's voices is a tragic loss. Similarly, the working class has been under-represented in the ranks of writers up to the late twentieth century. This might be explained in terms of low levels of literacy and the lack of formal education. However, I contend that, as with women, working-class men were handicapped by low self-esteem, and, even when they had the aspiration to write, were easily rebuffed and discouraged. There were exceptions of course. No one could claim that Patrick Kavanagh had any advantages of privilege, and yet his dogged self-belief triumphed. He was an exception. However, many of the apparent exceptions were deceptive. Padraic Colum, for example, gained the admiration of his listeners when he dropped references to his having been born in a workhouse; however, he neglected to add that his father was the master of said workhouse, and that placed his family among the elite of rural Ireland.

The writing confraternity, in Dublin as elsewhere, operated like an Old Boys' Club. Personal introductions were the mode of entry. Even the so-called literary pubs operated like clubs whose membership was closed. But by the seventies it was becoming clear that this whole milieu was barren and anachronistic. When I floated the invitation to writers in 1986 to join a writers' trade union, the response was overwhelmingly positive. One negative response reminded me of the antiquated attitude that I have been describing. A very well-known poet of the time declared, '*I do not agree with what you are doing. To suggest that there are more than a handful of worthwhile writers in the country is to muddy the waters for those of us who are really good.*'

The enthusiasm with which the new Irish Writers' Union set about tackling festering grievances and improving conditions for writers demonstrated a massive willingness to embrace and influence change. Step by step we were rapidly professionalising our art. I had experimented with a comprehensive programme of writing workshops in my school in Lucan, and had established there the first Writer-in-Residence in Ireland, under the new government social employment scheme. These became prototypes and were copied around the country, so that writers were being employed and paid as writers. And aspiring writers were being offered workshops conducted by experienced professionals.

Of course the establishment of a national writers' centre was my overarching ambition. Here fortune came to our assistance. In 1987 Charles Haughey was elected Taoiseach and appointed Anthony Cronin as his Arts Advisor. When I approached Cronin with the proposal that the Government hand us over an unused Georgian building for a writers centre, he was immediately enthusiastic, as was the head of the Taoiseach's Department, Pádraig Ó hUiginn, as was the Taoiseach himself. With that green light I applied to the newly established National Lottery for a grant towards realising the project and received £100,000 in the first allocation of funds. By this time a wide spectrum of writers and organisations had rowed in behind the project, many options were examined, and eventually we decided to join Dublin Tourism in the development of 18/19 Parnell Square as the Writers' Museum and the Writers Centre. We invested our £100,000 and Dublin Tourism invested £400,000. The EU provided the lion's share of the cost of refurbishing the two buildings (£1,800,000) under the Regional Fund.

With the Irish Writers' Union we initiated discussion with CLÉ, the publishers' association, to establish a copyright agency on the UK model, and the Irish Copyright Licensing Agency (ICLA) was established as a subsidiary of our partnership. Liam Mac Cóil, who was on the Executive of the Union looking after the interests of the Irish language writers, had an idea for establishing an agency to promote the translation of Irish language books into languages other than English. He and Michael Cronin made a submission to the Arts Council – Micheal O'Siadhail was the Chairman at the time and was extremely enthusiastic: the negotiations broadened to include Irish books in the English language, and Ireland Literature Exchange (ILE) was born. Both ILE and ICLA were housed in the Irish Writers Centre in their incubation period. And so, at the time the Centre opened its doors in 1991 we had one of the best organised literary sectors in the world, having started out five years earlier with one of the worst.

Over the years the Irish Writers Centre has fulfilled many functions; it has been the most important interface between writers and their public; but for me it has been most valuable in providing access to writing for new entrants, through the open door and the workshops within. The welcoming atmosphere and the non-judgemental response to people's aspirations have been a hallmark down through the years.

The snooty conservative attitude to the democratisation of writing was that it would erode standards. With more people writing, the overall quality would be diluted, we would enter a spiral downwards towards mediocrity. Indeed I had these misgivings myself in the early days, but thought that the additional creative activity would elicit a response in the form of a critical apparatus probably spear-headed by academics. Serious criticism as a discipline never really materialised in the form I envisaged. But neither did the erosion of standards. I am less familiar with the poetry that is being written, but for the past ten years I have been reading as much new Irish fiction as possible, and I am astounded at the standard of prose coming from both established writers and new ones. I am convinced that the proliferation of workshops given by experienced writers for the less experienced has steadily raised the standard of prose writing in Ireland. And we are currently experiencing something of a golden age. Even though the Writers Centre may not be directly responsible for the formation of any individual new writer, I feel that the open attitude and the atmosphere of encouragement generated by the Centre have filtered to all corners of the country and to all participants and would-be participants.

The appropriation and exploitation of Irish writing is a different matter. Culture, in every manifestation, has been appropriated by the ruling class in every society since the beginning of time. Usually it has been exploited for the aggrandisement of the privileged. Often it has been incorporated into the apparatus of repression. Think of the connotation of the word 'cultured' – it is not an epithet generally associated with the unprivileged; it is generally appropriated by the privileged class in any society to draw a line of distinction between it and the 'uncultured' mass.

Twenty-five years ago, I was concerned, even incensed, by the way society appropriated the work of writers, dubbed it 'literature', and exploited it shamelessly, according little recognition or reward to the people who created it. The alienation of workers from the product of their efforts is extreme in the case of writing. Back then, in the eighties, Ireland had very few achievements to enhance the sense of national self-esteem, but it could always point to the achievement of our writers as something that the rest of the world could look upon with admiration and with envy. And we flaunted our great literary heritage at every opportunity. We also shamelessly exploited it. For example, James Joyce turned out to be a magnet in attracting tourists to Dublin, and so Dublin marketed itself as the city of Joyce – and of Wilde, Swift, and a hundred more. But what did Ireland as a country, or as a society, do to merit such a rich dividend? The answer is nothing. Less than nothing, in fact. While most worthwhile books were being proscribed in Ireland as 'indecent or obscene', *Ulysses* was never banned. The simple explanation is that it was banned by national consensus: no one handled it, or offered it for sale; bookshops did not attempt to import it; so there was no necessity to ban it officially. And now we celebrate Bloomsday and the millions of euro it generates for the economy without the fear of being struck down by a bolt of lightning!

In the past the attitude was that 'the only good writer is a dead writer'. Dead writers were easier to exploit, easier to consider as 'literature'. That attitude has disappeared to some extent, and nowadays living writers are given recognition at home and abroad for their enormous achievements. Dublin has been recognised by UNESCO as a 'City of Literature', not because of the great writers of the past, but in recognition of the current vibrant literary environment of the city. Living writers are contributing to our sense of national self-esteem in the way we used to draw on the great writers of the past for such a purpose. But we are just as cynical in exploiting our living writers. We have grown so used to the bounty of writing being provided gratis that the idea of even modest recompense never enters the public consciousness. 'Literature' automatically belongs to the public, and the writers who create it are eased out of consideration. It is exemplified for me in the rebranding of the Dublin Writers Festival as a 'literature' festival.

When one considers that literary tourism generates hundreds of millions of euro every year for the Irish economy, it is incredible that government and society generally is so parsimonious in rewarding writers. To me it is a matter of justice that there be a redistribution of earned income, and government is the only agency that can do it. Proper funding of literary institutions and publishing, the proper implementation of Public Lending Right, the funding of libraries for the purchase of books, are a few small ways in which government could start such redistribution. Residencies, commissions, festivals, all are starved of support, especially since the collapse of the economy. We made some progress twenty-five years ago, but have lost that ground, and much more, in the past few years.

There is a logistical challenge of course in how to effect a radical redistribution of some of the wealth generated by our literary sector. The marketplace is not the answer, since only a tiny proportion of writers receive a remuneration that is commensurate with the time and work they invest in their writing. Cynics will dismiss any protestation with the attitude that if a writer cannot sell his or her work to the public, then the public do not value it. But the public patently do benefit from the work of writers and are happy to do so. And the appreciation of a particular writer may not be immediate, as with Joyce, it may come with mature reflection!

Back in the eighties, after I had the Writers' Union on the road, I went to a conference of the European Writers' Congress in Segovia, Spain, in order to get our Union affiliated. One of the hot issues at the time was the extension of the term of copyright from the standard fifty years. I tabled a proposal stating that writers should be recognised as the owners in perpetuity of the rights in their work; however, given the cultural importance of open access to our work by the public, we would accept such open access after fifty years provided there was a standard levy akin to royalties on the sales of all books in the public domain; this levy would be channelled into a fund for the benefit of living writers. The reaction at first was one of bemusement. But I was serious. If Arthur Guinness could continue to assert the rights to his product 250 years after his death, why should a writer have to cede ownership to the public after fifty? And such a mechanism would ensure that writers enjoyed some of the profits of literature generally while they were still living. The Chair decided to refer my proposal to the next meeting of the Congress in Switzerland, two years later. I went there and again tabled my motion. A number of delegates spoke very strongly against – they regarded the proposal as a tax on books. No speaker actually supported me. The Chair asked if I wanted to withdraw the motion. I said no, we had thrashed out the idea very clearly, and I wanted it put to the floor. To my great surprise it was carried with a substantial majority. This meant that it became the policy of the European Writers' Congress in their negotiations with the EEC on the impending copyright legislation. After 1991 I lost track of the issue, but was disappointed with the outcome – the period of copyright was extended from fifty to seventy years, with minimal benefit, to my mind, to writers or the public. I mention this particular experience to illustrate that there are imaginative ways in which a fairer distribution of the profits of literature could be effected to the advantage of living writers.

If there is such a clear-cut case, even stated in crass economic terms, for the better support of the writing community, why are writers not protesting and banging on doors? Writers are not very effective when it comes to collective action. There are a number of reasons for this. Most writers have to work full time at some alternative job or profession to earn a living. On top of that they may have family commitments. They are constantly struggling to find time for writing. So, what time have they available for participating in organisations?

But there is a more fundamental reason why writers are not natural collaborators. Writing like all art is an expression of individuality. The relationship of a writer to his/her work is akin to the relationship of a parent to his/her child. And just as a father is not objective and impartial in relation to his child, neither is a writer impartial in relation to his own work. His protective instinct leads him into a natural opposition to other writers who are equally jealous in their solicitude for their own creations. Writers perform best as individuals. This should be recognised, respected, and not exploited as is the case at present.

The lack of a strong unified voice for writers and for the wellbeing of the whole literary sector is tragic when one witnesses the contempt of Government for the arts at the present time. Whatever resources are made available are channelled without scruple towards the exploitation of the arts for economic purposes. When high-profile residencies are established they are usually attached to the universities, with teaching duties included. At Budget time the allocation to the Arts Council is always examined as the barometer reading of support for the arts, but the annihilation of funding previously channelled through the local authorities is ignored. In these circumstances, the Irish Writers Centre must continue to be a vibrant presence in the arts landscape, with a clear identity as the place where writers express their identity as creators and continue to express their entitlement to a fair return on the contribution they make to society, to the economy, and to the country.

Jack Harte's writing includes two novels and three collections of stories. His work has been translated into twelve languages. Since 2015 he has had two plays staged in Dublin and on tour around Ireland. He founded the Irish Writers Centre and the Irish Writers' Union. More information: www.jackharte.com.

Along the Lane

Evelyn Conlon

There's a party going on all the time and it's called Memory. It's a strange sort of event taking place in an even stranger location, because some of the sedate rooms surely couldn't be in the same building as the raucous, daring spillover down the stairs. It has a mixture of noises in it, music that makes you throw up your arms like you're reaching to the sky in a burst of exquisitely senseless abandonment, followed by a historical warning trumpet sound that conjures up the picture of Lot's wife rigid in salt before she tumbles headlong into oblivion. Poor Lot's wife who never got a name. It's a heartening thing that you don't have to accept every invitation and that if you do, you are free to leave when enough is enough. Of necessity, writing for any kind of anniversary event or Festschrift involves a bit of attendance, so I took down a few of the diaries circling 1991 and that proved to be a very bad plan.

The diaries are full of dangerous reminder flags, flashes that could keep a body riveted to the spot, sleepless for a week. Most of the pages are more like a *What's On* than a *What Happened* and when I take a quick skim I notice that I surely must have been having a laugh with myself, one date says 'Warren Born'. Nothing else. And yes I thought I'd better check and another date, twenty months later, says 'Trevor Born'. I intend to look at these books soon but not just yet, not just yet. Leaving aside my own headlong push through life they are a historical cameo all of their own: *The Irish Women's Diary* in particular, that has everything in it from what to do for cystitis to the history of heroin, abortion clinic details pencilled in, activists' names and numbers, gay discos, where and when. No wonder some eyebrows shot up when during our recent Marriage Equality Referendum a journalist claimed that she felt excluded from her own sense of sexuality in the 2010s. Come on, we shouted at the television. The National Gay Federation was set up in the 1970s, radiating out messages from the Hirschfeld Centre, with the young Mary McAleese as a patron. And indeed she was the lawyer who gave her services free to those of us who were setting up the first Rape Crisis Centre. Sometimes I sadly think that people will always be blind to what they don't want to see.

Writers worth their salt show us what goes on before the clean-up but there's a grave temptation to sanitise one's own life, often with good reason, more so for some of us than others. The leaving of parts of our lives out of focus can be essential to steadiness. There's also the matter of self-preservation from the unbearably poignant smell of hope and mistakes not yet made. But for the purposes of this publication I will lasso some of the amber and concentrate on a few events that were part of my life as associated with the Writers Centre in the 1990s. It is now apparently clear, according to the cryptic snail residue of my diaries, that I began giving workshops in the Writers Centre very early on in Peter Sirr's stewardship, and I can only hope and presume that they grew up from my first night of panic as I wondered how the hell I was going to avoid insulting students if they had a way of looking at life which was completely different to my own. This was a big issue for me at the time; I, like others, was in the middle of writing stories about those of us who did not fit into the status quo. I was smarting from a society which was knee deep in the pretence of homogeneity. (This is why it always comes as such a surprise when I hear commentators say that there was no 'angry' Irish literature. We have had to endure that misrepresentation over and over again as it is tripped out by those who read Irish literature selectively and according to what suits their own agenda. And who used, and still use, their power to make sure that 'angry' literature will have to be painstakingly found by future students, instead of taking its place in lights at front of house.)

On that first night I should have been more worried about whether I could teach, but maybe the rattled-up place I was looking from was enough spur to keep us all engaged and pushing our pens. I don't think there were many complaints, certainly none like the anonymous Listowel Writers' Week participant who moaned that I demanded too much work, s/he hadn't felt cherished. This may have been a result of my determination not to allow classes to become therapy sessions. Remember that the nineties were still suffering from the unfortunate slogan that *If you can talk you can write*, now replaced by an equally vacuous statement, something to do with blogs. Sometimes people came to workshops to find out, with great relief, that they couldn't write, that they didn't want to and that there were much more fulfilling ways to engage with their creative selves. A number of participants in one group set up a local radio programme and when I bumped into them a decade later they were still loving it. I'm not going to do a Ryan Boudinot on it (the man who wrote 'Things I can say about MFA writing programs now that I no longer teach on one'). But I will say that I think we were respectfully delighted with small success, and said so in an appropriate manner, unlike an event recently that I attended where some of the worst poetry I've ever read, other than my own attempts, was introduced as if it had come straight from Stockholm.

Peter Sirr, whom I met outside the portals through *Graph* editorial meetings, ran an interesting ship. He managed a bit of tone raising – he was after all a serious poet, becoming an even more serious one; he was a translator, he read translated works; he practised and believed in literature both with an understanding of what it was and a respectful curiosity if it wasn't his thing, as we say to be polite. Everything he was setting up was of course new, the Centre was at its beginning and workshops were not the stable diet that they now are. In the spirit of this newness, and as a result of my shock at how few books some of the students had even perused, I thought that a workshop on reading might be just the thing and they allowed me to do it. That was a terrific experience, full of surprise and learning. I still remember the wonder and fun of it – one man was there because he had forgotten how to read fiction as a result of his scientific immersion. One woman said that she read too much – that was certainly a new one. She wanted to learn how to go for quality not quantity.

Looking at the diary I see that one evening was given over to discussing Grace Paley, the co-operative anarchist, the combative pacifist and just the best story fisherwoman. There's reference also to Luisa Valenzuela whose mother, Luisa Mercedes Levinson, took to the bed for months, when she had young children, in order to finish writing a book. This anecdote may not be true, it might just have been wishful thinking on my part. Valenzuela wrote avant-garde novels such as *Como en la Guerra* and *Cambio de Armas*, experimental, powerful critiques of the dictatorship in Argentina. We discussed Toni Cade Bambara and Toni Morrison. (I think of Lar Cassidy, the Literature Officer in this context. When Morrison read in Dublin he telephoned and asked if I'd like to meet her, away from the melee, because he knew that I had been speaking about her work before it was profitable to be seen with her.) Of course Alberto Manguel's *Other Fires* is on the list as well, delighted in its own nerve. And that was just the beginning.

It is a measure of how quickly the Writers Centre became part of my landscape that, with my secretive diaries in front of me, I have to re-check because I cannot believe that the lights weren't on there as we trudged home from the Tuesday night committee meetings of the Anti-Amendment Campaign of 1983, and even indeed 1979 when I was hanging a black flag out my window as the pope's helicopter passed over, and refusing people tea who called at my house on the way to the Phoenix Park. My confusion about that must have come about because it was only then that I was working on the story 'The Park', a tribute to those very people who were not part of the horde who trooped to see him – the ones who found pope-free places to be and who don't now have to blame their parents or peers for making them go. I was writing the story for a Serpent's Tail anthology called *God*, to be followed by another called *Bad Sex*. It was remarked at the London launch that the only two people who actually attended to the title were the Muslim man and the Irish woman.

As well as a place of teaching, the Writers Centre was the venue for some personally important nights, including conducting an interview with Leland Bardwell, which faltered for a few minutes when her ex-husband turned up and parked himself in the front row. The Centre was also part of the backing, along with *Graph* review, of getting Grace Paley to Dublin to give an unforgettable reading, and have a weekend that she prized for all of her days, and that those of us who were there remember with serious fondness. But no night was more memorable than the night of the launch of *Zvono*, the first newsletter, with the possible intention of more to come, put together by a group of Bosnian refugee women that I was working with.

This is how it began. I was at a party in the house of Dermot McLaughlin and Ursula Kennedy minding my own business, no doubt, when I was introduced to their neighbour Rita Carson, a social worker who was organising things, lots of things, for the recently arrived refugees from Bosnia. I said that yes, I would 'do something'. I knew once I'd said it that it was going to be a disconcerting experience. This had happened to me before. I could still hear the echo of the Yes when I had agreed to go in to Mountjoy and Wheatfield Prisons. Within a week I was taking wrong turns and driving up and down fifteen cul-de-sacs looking for the Hartstown Community Centre. The minute I met the women I knew that this would not be a one night venture, even though Srebrenica was not a place we had at that time any particular reason to have heard of. Most of them had left in the dark in the clothes they wore, no bag full of books, so I thought it might be useful if I taught them how to say their children's stories out loud, then write them down, so they would have something on paper, in their own language, to read to their care at night. I was not being paid for this but thought it wouldn't do me any harm to give up a night or two away from my safe home. Of course once I got to know them it was impossible to call it a night. And then we fell into the notion of getting them to put together a newsletter, with an idea that there could be more than one issue. And why not, we'd launch it. And maybe it would be nice to go out somewhere to do that? This is where the Writers Centre came in, organising, with quiet class, an extremely difficult emotional event. My erroneous forecasting of what libation would be needed didn't help matters. I want to include some of the simple words of that issue. In my introduction I talk about the courage, the coffee, enough of it for a lifetime, the cigarettes. Yes, of course, we could and did. And, of all the things, the humour.

Rita Carson wrote that a male Bosnian friend had said, 'Oh I know what you're going to do with that Women's Group. You're going to tell them that everything should be fifty-fifty.' Another one said, 'You'll be bringing them to the pub.' And although she wrote that there was time yet for us to do it, we never did get there. One of the most poignant pieces is the interview conducted by the nineteen-year-old Fatima with her mother, whose main complaint about Ireland is that is too cold. She says, 'In essence, Ireland is a good country but my wish is to return to my husband. My only wish is to go back to my garden, my house, and my husband. If I was able to sit at the small wooden table in my garden with my husband, and drink morning coffee, as we used to do, who would be happier than me.' Over the page is the simple front cover, pictures drawn by some of the children.

I have to tell you that of course there was no second one. The date of the launch was 21 June 1995 and the massacre occurred on 11 July, less than a month later. And I am afraid that, yes, husbands talked about in the Hartstown room were found to be dead.

It might seem incongruous to try for a happy note after that but it is important to remember that, astonishingly, lives were reconstructed, both here and back there when some of the women finally got home.

As my work settled into itself and different demands arrived, there came a time when I no longer took the night journey to Parnell Square but I never pass it without checking to see if the lights are on in the teaching rooms.

Evelyn Conlon, novelist and short story writer, co-ordinated a writing workshop for Bosnian refugees in 1995 and edited a newsletter written by them. In 2004 she compiled and edited *Later On*, a memorial anthology of prose and poetry, thirty years after the Monaghan bombing, a collection that was used as the central theme for an Italian-based lecture series titled *The Language of War*. Books Upstairs recently re-published two of her books, *A Glassful of Letters* and *Telling*. Her latest novel, *Not the Same Sky*, was published in 2015. www.evelynconlon.com

Vol. 1, No. 1

June 21st, 1995

ZVONO
THE BELL

Razija Ademovic
Davorka Dragojević
Fatima Ramić
Azra Ramić
Rabija Gogić
Rabija Smailagić
Marion Dragojević

MISLI I REFLEKSIJE BOSANSKIH ZENA KOJE ZIVE U IRSKOJ

THOUGHTS AND REFLECTIONS OF BOSNIAN WOMEN LIVING IN IRELAND

Prepared and Produced by the Bosnian (Dublin 15) Women's Club, Hartstown Community Centre

Volunteers & Interns

Catherine Phil MacCarthy

In early December 2008 at a meeting in the Irish Writers Centre, where I was one of eleven Board members, a crisis erupted. The Board was informed that the Arts Council had withdrawn the grant from the Centre, one that amounted to €200,000 in the previous year. Around the table the response was one of surprise and shock. Why had it been done and what outcome was expected? As well as the Director, there were three other members of staff: a Finance and Admin officer, a Communications Manager, and an Information and Resources Officer. There was also a part-time receptionist/caretaker.

The Director and staff at the Centre immediately worked to rally support among the community of writers. Through Christmas and into the new year, several established writers pledged their support and offered to give readings as a way of raising funds. By mid-January, *The Irish Times* had identified a key angle of the Arts Council's response: 'Value for money is raised in the document under "Key Features": The core staff costs for the organisation are high, at €237,550 for four full-time members of staff…"' The newspaper put the then Director's salary under particular scrutiny.

The Arts Council grant amounted to more than half of the Centre's budget in 2008, the rest being raised mainly from creative writing workshops and renting out rooms in the Centre for events and courses.

Tutors regardless of their seniority were then paid an hourly rate, for teaching two-hour modular courses or workshops over eight or ten weeks, for the preparation and delivery of a course that amounted to about forty hours of work. The rate had barely increased since the first workshop I had given there in 1996. Writers and poets sometimes have no other source of income, and may rely on that income to make ends meet.

An extensive survey undertaken in France by SDGL (*Société des Gens de Lettres*) published in March 2016 and funded by the French Ministry of Culture found that authors' incomes have plummeted since 1990. Double- and multiple-jobbing has become the norm. Established writers with years of success behind them still struggle to make a living: the average income is €17,600. The most shocking finding is that six out of ten authors make less than €1,500 a year. Young writers are regarded as being particularly 'at risk'. It is no longer the blank page that writers fear most, but the constant juggling to make a living. In response to the survey, the *Guardian* commented that established writers' incomes in the UK average €14,000 a year. The French survey found that over-production, as well as a substantial drop in book sales in the last few years have exacerbated the problem.

A report on *The Living and Working Conditions of Artists in the Republic of Ireland* published by the Arts Council in 2009 found that, 'For professional artists in ROI, their average (mean) income from work as an artist in 2008, after expenses, was €14,676. However, 50% of ROI artists earned €8,000 or less from their work as artists in 2008.' This study included professional writers. It focused on members of Aosdána, and did not take account of artists who are not members. A more recent survey by Visual Artists Ireland found that artists' incomes have dropped further between 2008 and 2013. Writers' incomes vary greatly. Many writers have a full-time day job. Others work part time, and balance incomes by 'moonlighting'. Most do this by teaching and lecturing or through work in administration, management or libraries.

I had worked as a tutor at the Irish Writers Centre from 1996 (when Peter Sirr was Director), and also at St Patrick's College, in addition to teaching on a couple of courses and coordinating a series of drama workshops at the Drama Centre, University College Dublin. I had also in 1994–95 been Writer-in-Residence for Dublin City. When the decision to withdraw the Arts Council grant came, I had an understanding of the role the Centre played in the life of emerging writers as well as those who are established, and of its cultural significance for the wider community of readers and writers. The next board meeting following the decision was scheduled for an afternoon in early January. Seven members had already resigned (or were about to) following the Arts Council's decision, and would not attend the meeting. Not only that, from then, the remaining board members were responsible for the Centre's finances: Carlo Gébler, then Chairperson, Nuala Ní Dhomhnaill, Frank Callanan, barrister, and myself. At the December meeting it had emerged that the withdrawn grant meant that the Centre would start 2009 in the red to the tune of €60,000.

What should be done? Should the Centre be closed down, and the keys handed back, along with the fine collection of contemporary art that it houses? The Irish Writers Centre belonged to writers and they had yet to be consulted. When it came to the Director's salary, most of us – including some board members – were in the dark. Yet, the board had created the problem. *In dreams begins responsibility*, Yeats had said. Three of the people left were now writers, two of them poets. In that moment it would have been easy to walk away. I believed, however, that if we could 'hold the fort', and keep the writing workshop programme running, writers would have an opportunity to respond, and the Arts Council might be persuaded to reconsider its decision.

It was difficult to imagine how this might be done and even more difficult in hindsight to describe the cloud of anger, then confusion, suspicion, rumour and uncertainty that engulfed the building and seemed to emanate from its walls. The decision to keep the Centre open was a provisional one, and initially evolved from winter to spring. It was a complex process that meant the Director and the staff were to be made redundant and that redundancy payments had to be found by the end of January.

I was nominated to go see the bank manager in AIB's Upper O'Connell Street branch to let her know about the financial situation. Days later, in the gloom of the downturn, I sat inside the second-floor office with a file in my hands. The irony of the situation was not lost on me. How come this file was now in my lap and the Centre's finances becoming for a short time my responsibility? I was there to let the manager know that the remaining Board members had volunteered to keep the Centre going, and that more flexible overdraft facilities would be needed for a couple of months. Though hardly the kind of news she wanted to hear, it turned out that she was a sympathetic woman, who offered her help and advice.

I felt calm in the face of the unfolding drama, naive as it seems in retrospect. Courage was needed to face the ensuing chaos. The decision was taken by the 'skeleton' board to meet every two weeks, chaired by Carlo Gébler who travelled from Enniskillen. Each of us gave up time from our own work and commitments to help out. Tasks were agreed and I volunteered to oversee the running of the creative writing programme. That February and March, I got used to taking the DART to Tara Street and walking up O'Connell Street, past the GPO and the Garden of Remembrance, to an oftentimes eerily silent building. Most of the classes during that time were scheduled for the evenings.

It would have been impossible to get through the first four or five months, without the cooperation of the former Communications Officer, Ian Oliver, who managed the systems, and the Finance/Admin Officer, Annmarie Wolohan, who continued to look after accounts – both on a part-time hourly basis – as well as the advice of several people, including accountant, David McConnell.

I had workshops elsewhere that spring, and my collection of poems that would become *The Invisible Threshold* was in the process of being written or, as I often think of it, was in the process of writing me. The poems that I had begun to write suggested the idea of 'threshold' or the 'liminal', the boundary between two worlds. The struggle to hold the Irish Writers Centre amounted to an invisible threshold in itself, and the Centre was in a liminal space. There was no way of knowing then if we would succeed in our initiative.

By Easter 2009, the overdraft was falling and the bank manager was beginning to agree that the Centre might clear its debts and survive. The bank imposed new security requirements, however, and three board members were now required to guarantee the Centre's bank account. It was a further stumbling block and would mean that three individuals who were volunteers and already overstretched would be personally liable for any debts in the event of a default.

The spring programme was by now coming to a close – and the summer one enrolling during the second week of April. A man in his middle years walked into the office one morning and introduced himself as Patrick O'Byrne. He was sympathetic to the Centre's dilemma and offered to help in any way possible. He agreed to join the Board. (I learnt some time later that Patrick's ancestors had owned a house on Moore Street, close to the action in 1916.) In addition to that, a meeting with John F. Deane suggested that Jack Harte, the founder of the Centre, might be persuaded to rejoin the Board. As the summer ended, Jack took over the management of the Centre with all his formidable experience and dedication.

Along with Jack Harte and myself, Pat O'Byrne volunteered to sign the bank guarantee. Around the same time, I asked a neighbour to recommend an accountant who might be willing to take charge of finances. Andrew Clarke, a chartered accountant, agreed to oversee finance and to recruit a new bookkeeper, since the former finance officer was moving out of Dublin. There was a ways to go and it would take most of the year to break even, and pay basic running costs that included rent, light, heat, photocopiers, telephone, internet and tutors' fees.

As we were struggling to keep our heads above water, I couldn't help but notice that emigration was on a steep rise. The Working Abroad Jobs Expo at the RDS, which is now an annual event, started in March 2009. It was a shock to see people of all ages – many young men and women in their twenties, and whole families with children – waiting along the footpath, the length of Simmonscourt Road. People stood in the rain and wind with infants in their arms, and teenagers at their side, hoping to be allowed in to find jobs elsewhere. Thousands of Irish workers were recruited to work in Canada, Australia, New Zealand, Switzerland, and Dubai.

It was within this economic climate that Jack Harte recruited young graduate interns to the Centre in September 2009. The first group of seven women and two men had skills in IT, publishing, marketing, design, communications and administration, and several of them – now published authors – had an interest in writing. Gradually they took on the administration of the Centre. One of the findings of the Arts Council's 2009 report is that women are more likely than men to take on voluntary work, and it might be said are therefore more easily exploited. By the end of the year, a full programme of activities was being offered between 10 a.m. and 9 p.m., Monday to Saturday. The Centre was again debt free. The 2008 accounts were audited and those for 2009, being prepared. Both the Irish Writers' Union and the Irish Translators' and Interpreters' Association had representatives on the board and held regular meetings and events in the house. In addition there were book launches, reading nights, literature discussions and a series of benefit readings with established writers organised by John F. Deane and Nuala Ní Dhomhnaill.

In November 2009, Seamus Heaney and John Banville read together to a packed house. Tickets for the event had sold out within a couple of hours of going on sale. The phones were busy again. John Banville's interview with *The Paris Review* had been published earlier that year: '*This is a problem for Irish writers – our literary forebears are enormous. They stand behind us like Easter Island statues, and we keep trying to measure up to them, leaping towards heights we can't possibly reach.*' On the morning of the benefit reading, another Irish writer had made the news headlines: Colum McCann had the previous evening been announced as winner of an American Book Award for his novel, *Let the Great World Spin*.

I returned to the Centre in early 2012 for a naming ceremony. The rooms were each named after a well-known writer: Eilís Dillon, Benedict Kiely, Robert Greacen, Michael Hartnett, Eithne Strong and Mary Lavin. For three years the Centre was kept open by the efforts of young people (including Clodagh Moynan whose internship and invaluable contribution lasted over four years). All were well qualified, guided by a board that now included Jack Gilligan who had joined in January 2010, and brought his considerable experience as Arts Officer for Dublin City to the table. Interns were eventually paid a modest allowance and travel expenses. It would take until the spring of 2013, before a new Director, Valerie Bistany, was appointed, whose dynamism and flair would lead the Centre into a new era. New initiatives include A Poet's Rising, a North–South exchange, the recruiting of distinguished writer-Ambassadors, and the President of Ireland, Michael D. Higgins, as patron. After such valiant efforts by so many, including the current

Director, staff, and board members, should the Centre's grant not now be fully reinstated?

The Centre's experience between 2008 and 2016, and its struggle to cope with the management crisis as well as the impact of the economic downturn, reflects the kinds of difficulties experienced by citizens of the country in those years. The intervention of interns might work in an emergency, if qualified people are available and willing. It is hardly how a writers' centre should be run. It is true to say that people in the arts, both administrators and artists, are expected to work for the love of it. The entire arts budget for a year would be spent before the end of the first week of January in the Department of Health. Ted Hughes has pointed out that 'art is in general the psychological component of the immune system'. What a difference it would make if arts organisations could focus on the needs of the artistic community, as opposed to the struggle for survival?

'What are creativity's needs for full functioning?' Tillie Olsen asked in 'Silences', an essay first published in 1965 that examines the circumstances of the writing life and the effects of those circumstances on the work. The book of the same title was published in 1982. It is true that a few creative geniuses have managed to lead productive artistic lives while working full-time jobs. However, Olsen investigates the testimony of Balzac, Conrad, Flaubert, Thomas Hardy, Emily Dickinson, and a host of others to ask: 'Why most of the great works of humanity have come from lives (able to be) wholly surrendered and dedicated?' From writer after writer the testimony is clear. Rilke and Conrad spoke of 'unconfined solitude' as the 'spaciousness, which puts no limit to vision.' Olsen writes of the importance of time, continuity, a meditative space: when writers have to divide time and energy, the work is diminished.

It is true to say that there has been a proliferation of books published in Ireland and elsewhere in the last thirty years. Many silences have been broken. However, one of the most important features of a writers' centre, and even more essentially, a poetry centre – a place that includes not just the administration office, but a library/reading room, an auditorium as well as workshop spaces – is that it facilitates the building of a community for poets and writers. It allows people to meet, to attend workshops and readings together, and in the process encourages exchanges between artists working within different genres, and with different levels of experience.

Like most people, writers want to make ends meet, put food on the table, spend time making work, as well as bring their poems and stories to an audience through published works. The confidence, security and inspiration developed in the process is hard to quantify and the valuable artworks that develop are culturally, economically, and above all psychologically valuable.

Catherine Phil MacCarthy has published a novel, *One Room an Everywhere* (2003), and four poetry collections: *The Invisible Threshold* (2012), *Suntrap* (2007), *the blue globe* (1998) and *This Hour of the Tide* (1994). She is a former editor of *Poetry Ireland Review* (1998–99).

Reference File No. 72A

Thomas McCarthy

When I think of Ireland in the last twenty-five years, I think of five women and three men, all brilliant, important, central to my thoughts, makers of my own settled soul. Through their work I found doors into other kinds of perception, new ways of looking at the world, and a definite view of what Irish life contains in terms of its human and literary possibilities and limitations. I see the last twenty-five years as an anthology of their works. All three men are poets, Seamus Heaney, Patrick Galvin and Paul Durcan; and three of the women of my era are also poets, Eavan Boland, Nuala Ní Dhomhnaill and Paula Meehan. But the era itself, those silver years, are book-ended by two women whose genius rests in bursts of prose, Kathy Sheridan of *The Irish Times* and Martina Devlin of the *Irish Independent*. I will never forget the extraordinary reports of Kathy Sheridan as she followed Seamus Heaney to Stockholm in the mid 1990s, reporting daily in *The Irish Times*, sometimes on the front page, on the Nobel progress of our Ulster hero. In those weeks, in those days, Heaney became our Winter King, hauling the entire retinue of Irish dreams and fantasies behind him as he turned and spoke to nations. Day after day Sheridan captured those golden, or gilded, moments with fabulous élan and an *Irish Times* thoroughness: 'On a moonlit, snowbound Stockholm evening, Seamus Heaney stepped up to the podium where Yeats, Shaw and Beckett once stood before him … In the blue and gold splendour of the 200-year-old Swedish Academy's Great Hall, he began his Nobel lecture by recalling that as a child in rural Co. Derry in the 1940s he had first encountered the word "Stockholm" on the face of the radio dial.' She reported on that Ulster formation, the vigilance and realism of the North, the putting down of any extravagant aspirations. The decade had opened, remember, with Heaney's influential *Seeing Things* (1991), a collection that included 'Markings', 'Glanmore Revisited' and brief lyrical raids into the *Inferno* and *The Aeneid*: 'I pray for one look, one face-to-face meeting with my dear father/ Teach me the way and open the holy doors wide.' That year of *Seeing Things* was also the year of Heaney's Oxford Professorship, with its sense of an Irish dog winning the Waterloo Cup. It was the holy door of fame that had burst wide open, and all of us, whether Terry Kavanagh writing in the *Irish Independent* or Ciaran Carty writing in the *Sunday Tribune* or Eileen Battersby and Douglas Dunn writing in *The Irish Times*, all looked on in delighted amazement.

But it is Kathy Sheridan, faithful still with pen and perception, who also book-ends these twenty-five years with another perfect piece of prose, an encounter with the dedicated Socialist Joe Higgins. In February of 2016 she wrote in her paper: 'The venue is a suburban house on the edge of Blanchardstown village, headquarters of the Anti-Austerity Alliance's campaign to keep the vote for Ruth Coppinger, in the Dublin West constituency carved out over decades by Joe Higgins.' She describes this tireless Socialist TD at the point of retirement from the fray of elected politics, retiring like a Senator of ancient Rome to the distant sunlit vineyard where he will have time to read the documents, to indulge his love of music and the arts; an honest, still poor man for whom even the hope of modest travel is too expensive. Some lives are exemplary; one thinks of James Connolly or Peadar O'Donnell; and Higgins, retiring, had made the final modest gestures that will, by being lived-out, set a political agenda around what an honest public life might be. The instinct to teach is as deeply felt in a good politician as in a good poet, and Sheridan captures this insight in what is ostensibly a conventional interview for a newspaper. And out of this personal portrait, inevitably, correctly, a description is achieved of something vitally important in Irish politics – an alternative, truly dissenting viewpoint. It was difficult for Joe Higgins, as it was for others, to be socialist during the years of boom, to carve out a socialist identity in a conservative society; a society where there is constant dismissal of any left-wing argument by 'what he calls the financial and political elite as well as the media.' Sheridan's journalism here is a crucial document, a witness document of the moment of transition when the older generation leaves the battlefield and the radical young enter. Her journalism is part of a great feminist intellectual tradition, a tradition birthed and fostered by an august sisterhood that included June Levine, Nell McCafferty, Nuala O'Faolain, Terry Keane and Mary Kenny. O'Faolain's *Are You Somebody?* and Levine's *Sisters* are key texts of that new radicalism among women: for women to claim some public space for themselves was in itself a hugely radical act. Their books should be read by every young Irishman; they are as radically different from the dominant discourse of the South as, say, the Ulster Protestant literary memoirs, Robert Greacen's *Even Without Irene*, George Buchanan's *Green Seacoast* and Forrest Reid's *Apostate*. To read these things is a radical education for any Southern writer; it is a first glance at strange materials. It is not to be sniffed at, as the earliest texts by women writers were either sniffed at or ignored. The omission of women writers from the canonical *Field Day Anthology* was the most public act of episcopal arrogance in contemporary Irish literary criticism. But this was a timely reminder of how things really stood. The *Field Day* lark did a huge public service to intelligence by coming out into the open with egg all over its face; it was the literary equivalent to those TV 'specials' we have to suffer where withered old rock stars and poets seem to be surrounded by females who are clearly younger than their daughters. What are they doing; for God's sake, where are their wives, their sisters? The fact is, this is male power at work, delivering visual fantasies of youth, and in precisely the way Nuala O'Faolain describes it in *Are You Somebody?*

There is a thing called friendship between women. In the last twenty-five years I feel blessed to have seen the fruits of this friendship, a friendship that has *absolutely nothing* to do with men. Working in the public library service for all of these years I witnessed at first hand the empowering spark of creativity in such deep friendships between creative women: time after time I have watched such literary friendships grow at the lending desk, friendships as rich as that of Elizabeth Bowen and Molly

Keane, or Vera Brittain and Winifred Holtby. It was in such friendships, such radicalising power, that Eavan Boland could continue the work of *In Her Own Image,* could extend her enriched consciousness, into three of the key poetry books of the 1990s, *Outside History*, *In a Time of Violence* and *The Lost Land*. Boland is more than capable of writing for herself; and in an era still dominated by maleness, her complex explanations of her female self became an important literary narrative for at least two generations of women writers. As we know from Irish history (the Irish poets in Corkery's *Hidden Ireland*, the fearsome ballad-writing of Young Ireland) excluded groups will eventually create a counter-narrative where they may raise their voices. This is precisely what happened in women's writing in the last twenty-five years and Boland's poetry and essay-making mapped a new territory that had lain outside the Yeatsian core narrative like an Irishtown at the edge of an English city. In all these years Boland has meant what she said and has written what she meant. It has taken us a long time to register the weight of these female voices, as crucial in literature as in politics. One of the further developments of this growing power will be, I hope, an entire generation of female editors who will be given the task of editing not more anthologies of women's poetry, but the future Faber Books and Penguin Anthologies of Irish Poetry. I look forward to this and I expect it to happen: 'My gifts / are nightly, / shifty, bookish' as Boland wrote in 1980 or, as she explained more fully in 1998: 'This is what language is: / a habitual grief…'

Then again, walking to work in Cork in the 1990s, through wet streets and narrow lanes, or even, in lucky moments of bright sunshine, at the Number 6 bus stop on South Mall, I would sometimes bump into him, that towering poetic presence among Cork poets, Patrick Galvin. There he is, carrying a bunch of mixed flowers from Roche's Stores for Mary, holding a glass of red wine at a reading, fidgeting impatiently at his pack of twenty Major, smiling on with a wry, dramatist's eye, a poet of pure instinct and music. The poet Gregory O'Donoghue would shift his willowy frame to offer a seat, the poet Gerry Murphy would think of something provocative to set the poet laughing, a serious young arts administrator would hover anxiously as if something might go wrong, as if something might explode. But the explosions were on the page and on the stage of Galvin's beloved Lyric Theatre in Belfast. Galvin was a poet of the old school, a kind of Southern John Hewitt, left-wing, internationalist, a believer in communities of poetry rather than the individual poet; believing always that good work would come from any assembly of radicals. His voice, his self-assurance, his London-Irish accent, his humour and mischief, there was nothing like that combination in any other poet: Galvin was unique. Our poet-Professor at UCC, Sean Lucy, would stand to attention and recite, in perfect Received Pronunciation:

In Patrick Street
In Grattan Street
In Ireland Rising Liberty Street
The Kings are out.

Along the Mall
The Union Quay
In every street along the Lee
The Kings are out.

There was something timeless, out of this world, poetic, Andalusian, about Galvin; an atmosphere that he knew he had: his was not a cerebral poetry, but an emotion that explained itself by working outward from a feeling about itself; a pure, confident, emotional poetry. He developed this persona further in wonderful articles in 'Rainbows in Evergreen', his weekly column in the *Cork Examiner*. His audience was enraptured. Strangers would find his work in *Cyphers* or *The Tablet*, his two faithful publishing friends. But for us, the truly blessed, we had the company of the man who wrote *Christ in London, Song for a Poor Boy* and *Folk Tales for the General*. If there was goodness in the air in Irish poetry of the last twenty-five years it hovered very close to Patrick Galvin; you only had to stand beside him to feel an effect called poetry. I feel his absence terribly, a kind of narrowing of the air. His life is a reminder that we shouldn't worry too much about creating 'space' for a writer; a writer asserts and claims his or her own territory, a stake is driven into solid ground that wasn't even visible before the poet arrived. Chill, don't worry about it,

Patrick Galvin might say to a worried young poet, you can always take in washing for a living.

I first met Nuala Ní Dhomhnaill on the day that her first book, *An Dealg Droighin*, was published. That must have been in the foyer of the Listowel Arms Hotel in 1981, the year before Caitlín Maude died. Our conversation was about those multi-talented poets, Maude and Hartnett, Maude's pure, clear voice and Hartnett's attempts at acting. I think we spoke about Maude's voice in her Gael Linn recording of 'Dónal Óg', a haunting track, and of Maude's insistent voice in the poem 'Aimhréidh'. The atmosphere of everyone being in love with Caitlín Maude was still very strong. Ní Dhomhnaill herself had just emerged from the drenching surf of exile and family estrangements. Her power was already immense. Her poetry in the following two decades would soar above every other talent of the Gael, transforming her into an Irish Akhmatova with collections like *The Astrakhan Cloak* and *Pharaoh's Daughter*. In the mid 1990s I stood before a class of Seniors at Macalester College, Minnesota, a class of mainly Lutherans, Episcopalians and Quakers with hardly a drop of Irish blood in them, and read 'Fear Suaithinseach' and 'Ceist na Teangan' with their Heaney and Muldoon translations. The students were enthralled by the work, the strange demands of a poetry and a culture that was registering with them for the first time. It was difficult to move on to another text because the questions kept coming, the duality of the poet's existence in Irish and in translation, the Muse-object suddenly become sexually independent, the idea that all one's hope could be placed in a little boat of language, or that a consecration of terrible experience could be embodied in a Communion wafer; such things thrilled them and made them wonder whether all poems are, in effect, an act of translation.

It is a truism that we can be sure a new talent is abroad when something settled is disturbed and when areas of experience that have been locked are picked open. Ní Dhomhnaill's work, following the iconoclastic energy of the Cork *Innti* crowd, unsettled a language culture that was becoming too deliberate, too programmatic, too sanctioned. But her real genius lies in her ability to archaeologically and forensically (she is, after all, the daughter of surgeons) examine hidden areas of sexuality. The human body is her isle of folklore, the poems are the stories her body has told her; her technical instruments are both *dinnseanchas* and Jung.

Hers is certainly a Jungian *dinnseanchas*; as Denise Levertov once wrote, speaking of Ginsberg and Creeley, 'it's one's own body, the primal, the instinctive, and the intuitive basics one started with, that is being spoken of.' Ní Dhomhnaill has never ceased to be amazing in all of the last thirty years and I can't imagine a definition of those years in her absence.

Another poet of this era whose rise parallels that of Ní Dhomhnaill is Paul Durcan, a poet of Dublin and Mayo who also spent a number of de-formative rather than formative years in Cork before he re-collected himself poetically back in Dublin. He had supplemented and later succeeded Patrick Galvin with a regular column in the *Cork Examiner*. Durcan's *Berlin Wall Café* and *Going Home to Russia* are two of the most important collections by an Irish poet in the post-War era. Despite what the idle may think, Durcan is the most unfairly neglected poet of modern Ireland. His voice is distinctive, his genius beyond dispute, his social themes distinctly Irish and utterly crucial, yet one finds very little detailed analysis of his work or his context. His dramatic public readings, marvellous performances in themselves, may have actually worked against his reputation among scholars whilst simultaneously electrifying audiences: scholars find it difficult to forgive a public success. It is difficult to describe the effect of those two earlier books; they are lyrical, tightly structured, vectored against the hostile world, explosive emotionally and heart-rending. They are a kind of crucifixion in verse, or, at least, a long stay at Calvary; the logbooks of an escape from Golgotha, from the place where love was found and lost again. The homestead of love and attachment is set ablaze and a life of wandering begins, a life that continues to produce collections of tremendous power like *Cries of an Irish Caveman* and *Praise In Which I Live And Move And Have My Being*. In the latter work, published in 2012, Durcan writes in 'The Annual January Nervous Breakdown':

Why do Christmas and Epiphany
Always end in tears – in such bile-black, bilges-beige, canary-yellow tears?

I first met the poet Paula Meehan, in the company of Hugh McFadden and John Borrowman, at Joyce's Tower in Sandycove on a blustery day in

June 1984. The occasion was the launch of *Poetry Ireland Review* No.10 and a set of Beaver Row books. Beaver Row, like Co-Op books, seemed to be the future of Irish writing at the time. Little did I realise then that it wasn't to be the publisher, but the poet, who held the future in her young brain. Community-driven, justice-saturated, feminist and maker of perfect lyrics, Meehan was only at the beginning of a crowded busy career. In a photograph of her young self, published next day in the *Irish Press*, the poet seemed guarded and apprehensive. Three decades of writing and political action later, the poet is not only unguarded, but wise and open-hearted, sanguine and deeply centred. I now find an extraordinary calm in her work, a nurturing calm that invites others in; a world created by good grandmothers, by the company of women. In her all the promises of Máire Mhac an tSaoi and Eavan Boland find a lyric confirmation. In *The Man Who Was Marked By Winter* (1991) she wrote:

Didn't I rob you of your eyes, father,
and her of her smile? No dark blood
but the simple need to lose an uneasy love
drove me down unknown roads...

Her journey, like Eavan Boland's, has been a process of mapping while voyaging. The early 1990s volume itself was a mapping and re-ordering gesture as it collected the best poems from her two earliest books. But it is in the most recent books, in *Dharmakaya* and *Painting Rain*, that a prodigious shift from localised inner-city family memory to a travelled communal memory occurs. Here, her focus becomes a Buddhist humanism, a universal anxiety captured in poems like 'On Howth Head' and 'The Following Message Will Be Deleted From Your Mailbox'. In her Zen-like poems, in page after page, it is the one tree of humankind that struggles to survive; and Meehan turns to the world from an altar of poems in communion with, and receiving transmissions from, Rinpoche's *The Tibetan Book of the Dead* or Gary Snyder's *Regarding Wave*. Earth is suddenly frail as a watercolour, and the poet is a poet become watercolourist, painting the rain black and ultramarine. This painter is a wonderful author and her words now have a Pound-like certainty of paint. She has arrived at a point of silence, a kind of hillside shrine from where her climb continues.

Each of these poets, Ní Dhomhnaill in her Jungian boat of language, Boland in her recovered country, Meehan the Zen watercolourist, Patrick Galvin the gypsy Corkman saturated with *duende*, Durcan tempting a father's judgement upon us all, each advances the possibility of the poem by manipulating the materials available to them; each survived by constantly singing inside the capsule of the last two decades. Sometimes, when I worry too much that I left myself too isolated from the swim of things by continuing a day job in a city library for too long, I recall all the books of these authors. I handled all of these lustrous materials, shelving and date-stamping and recommending. Their books remind me that we are not isolated as long as we read; our primary community is a community of readers. We know each other through reading each other; and such reading is not a kind of polemic: it is, rather, a shared meal on the margins of a highway.

We do tend to underestimate the power of great journalism, forgetting that Yeats and Shaw wrote for the papers constantly and that the preoccupations of journalism became the materials of their plays and poems. We live inside a discourse, we add to it in different ways through reading newspapers. Omagh-born Martina Devlin is now best known as a novelist, a successful one at that, with the visionary, futuristic ambition of her latest work, *About Sisterland*, creating a great stir. But it's for her golden journalism that I'm most grateful in the last two decades. Her regular columns in the years when Ireland entered deeper and deeper into crisis were a consolation to me and kept me sane. 'Day Our Bewildered Bankers entered the Twilight Zone' was clipped from the *Indo* and pinned to my kitchen noticeboard in May 2009, and, six weeks later, her narrative of the beginnings of social collapse under austerity 'Cuts mean that writing is on the wall for our literacy rates' was noted and added to the bills and bank letters stuck to the same board. The state of our nation wasn't a sudden obsession with her because she'd been commenting on our divided society for years. Eleven years before the banking collapse she'd written about the dangers of national delusion: 'We're delighted with ourselves' (6 July 1998) and 'Is the Celtic Tiger mutating into the Celtic Ostrich?' (17 November 1998); and in September 2001 she'd ominously written the column 'Wall Street wipeout'.

Few creative writers have been so close to the day-by-day action of society and matters of public concern: I think of Martina Devlin as a writer of the roaring Twenties, a Scott Fitzgerald watching the ticker-tape in mounting horror, and probably planning an escape into the movie business. The best journalists make a journey with you, inviting you into an almost therapeutic attachment to them, creating a mutual narrative day-by-day. It is interesting now to go through what the hurried Devlin wrote, how clear-headed she was, how uncannily intelligent. I'm just glad that the reference cataloguing staff at Cork City Libraries were aware of her too. Here, there are more than eighty catalogued references to her journalism, including the somewhat sinister library Reference File 72A that charts a decade of economic commentary, with Devlin's article of October 2013: 'A night of confusion and drama that left a bitter taste'. She wrote: 'Undeterred, the Government pushed a blanket guarantee through the Oireachtas at ramming speed. And, as Yeats put it, about a different, perhaps equally epoch-defining event in Irish history, "All changed, changed utterly"'.

The fact is that the Ireland of 1991–2016 couldn't have been imagined. It was so dreadful you wouldn't want to make it up. Bankers, from the best families and our most respectable private schools, colluded to misinform Government, not about millions, but about billions. And their laughter, that dreadful, desperate laughter as they emerged from their locker room to ruin a generation of life-long savers, to make families homeless and send our 250,000 educated children into exile. In the end, and for the sake of the people, Ireland must always begin as a task of fearless journalism before it's allowed to become a work of poetry.

Thomas McCarthy was born in Co. Waterford in 1954 and educated at UCC. He worked for many years at Cork City Libraries. His first collection, *The First Convention*, was published by Dolmen Press in 1978, with seven further collections, including *The Sorrow Garden* (1981), *Merchant Prince* (2005) and *The Last Geraldine Officer* (2009) published by Anvil Press Poetry. *Pandemonium (Poems)* is due from Carcanet Press in November 2016. He is a member of Aosdána.

Sinne Muinne Muide Mise

Alan Titley

Is ea, laidhc, táimid ar an tír is measa ar domhan! Ó maigh Gawd, níl aon dream chomh holc linn.

Ar aon chomhdhul le the most distressed country dá raibh riamh ann cheapfá é sin, ach níl léamh ná scríobh ná insint bhéil ar a bhfuil d'fhigiúir ann a chruthódh a mhalairt. Ach ná bac an fhianaise, cad é a dhein an fhianaise riamh dhuitse? Och, ní maith liom fianaise, mar cuireann sí píce trí lár mo dhrólainne. Drochbhuachaill is ea an fhianaise, agus nílim chun dul ina haice.

Bhíodh daoine istigh chun m'athar agus mo mháthar ó bhíos im bhunóic bheag agus chloisinn an t-allagar – 'Ó sea, is tubaist sinn, ó b'fhearr nach mbeimis scartha leis an mBreatain go brách…' agus mar sin de. Is dual do dhaoine a bheith míshásta agus dá réir sin go mbeadh malartú seo is siúd i gceist. Ní hé gur ghéilleas riamh dóibh, mar bhí cnó na ceiste riamh im chroí, ach ó bhíos san bhunóiceacht sin b'fhearr liom fianaise ná a malairt.

Ar an gcuma chéanna chloisinn 'Dá mbeadh eacnamaíocht an deiscirt níos fearr ná eacnamaíocht an tuaiscirt bheadh na hAontachtóirí ar bís teacht isteach linn!' Bíodh nár thuigeas eacnamaíocht san am – ach ní thuigeann duine ar bith eacnamaíocht – cheapas gur bhaoth mar áiteamh é. Dá réir sin bheadh mórán tíortha beaga ar na himill ar bís clasú le tíortha ba dhá mhó ná iad ar bhonn airgid agus pinginí sa phóca, agus ar chúis éigin de réir a raibh léite agam faoi stair an domhain níor mhar sin a bhí. Go deimhin, nuair a bhí an Tíogar Ceilteach in airde láin ní cuimhin liom oiread is aon pholaiteoir Aontachtach a chuaigh amach ag feachtasú is ag blaidhriúch: 'Hé, h'anam an diabhail, is saibhre go mór iad ó dheas. Caithfimid aontú leo!'

Is chuige atáim gur cheapas go raibh an tógáil a fuaireas macánta go leor agus díreach go leor, agus sa mhéid is gur fiú faic é, nádúrtha de réir gnáis go leor é chomh maith. Ní raibh agam aon bhonn comparáide, gan amhras, ach gur cheapas go raibh na daltaí scoile im thimpeall ar thuiscint chomh cothrom céanna, a bheag nó a mhór. Ní dóigh liom gur tháinig aon duine díobh ar scoil agus ocras air, agus ní heol dom go raibh éinne ina chónaí i mbothán stáin. Bhímis ag magadh nuair a deireadh na múinteoirí linn go gcaithfimis ár gcuid lón a ithe mar go raibh páistí sa tSín ag fáil bháis leis an ocras. Ach níorbh aon mhagadh é. Níor thuigeamar go rabhamar ar ghlúin chomh hábharach is a shiúl an chruinne riamh. Níor thuigeamar gur saolaíodh is gur tógadh sinn i gceann de na tíortha ba bheannaithe dár beannaíodh riamh i stair an chine dhaonna.

Tuigim go maith go bhfuil dainséarach seo a rá. Tuigim, ach an oiread is nach maith le daoine fianaise, nach maith leo comparáid ach chomh beag. Bíodh an diabhal ag an gcomparáid! Tá a fhios agamsa go bhfuilimid níos measa as ná gach tír eile ar domhan, agus is cuma liom cad í an fhianaise a chuireann tú faoi mo bhráid, sin é mo chreideamh, agus imítear leat! Is sinne atá go diail ag an gcaoineadh is ag an gcanrán is ag an gcnáimhseáil – ní hea amháin go bhfuilimid ar an most oppressed people ever, is sinne an failed state is mó ar domhan.

Bhíodh an shaight seo ag dul i bhfeidhm orm, óir ní féidir gan géilleadh don aeráid id thimpeall go dtí gur thosnaíos ag machnamh dom féin. Rud contúirteach é sin chomh maith, machnamh a dhéanamh duit féin. Ní bheidh aon duine buíoch díot. Is cinnte nach mbeidh na caoirigh buíoch díot. Is iad na caoirigh ná na daoine a bhíonn ag méiligh anois mar gheall ar fhorlámhas na hEaglaise Caitlicí, ach a bheadh ina mbaill de na Ridirí Columbánais dá mba rud é go raibh siad thuas i dtríochaidí na haoise seo caite. Iad ag líorac na mban rialta is na mbráthar le haoibhneas lena linn go dtí gur dúradh leo gur dream lofa is cáidheach iad is gur chóir a seachaint. Is é is fuiriste amuigh ná a bheith id fhaisinisteach. Faisinistigh is ea formhór mhuintir na hÉireann, go háirithe iad siúd a bhfuil a bheagán nó a mhórán den oideachas acu. Faisinistigh is ea formhór na ndaoine a ghéilleann d'aon phioc a léann siad ar na príomhnuachtáin gan cheist.

Níl a fhios agam cad chuige ar thosnaíos ag machnamh dom féin, dar liom. Bhí col agam leis an reacht simplí agus leis an bhfreasúra saonta araon. Is ea, bhain an reacht simplí Caitliceach leis na meánaoiseanna agus siar síos, ach bhain an freasúra leis na seascaidí agus le gal soip na huaire. Cad fáth nach dtosnódh duine ag machnamh dó féin?

Ba ghairid go bhfuaireas amach gur bheag an buntáiste a bhain leis. Chuir mé in aghaidh an Tómachais ar an ollscoil ach baineadh marcanna go tiubh díom, agus shéan mé an t-eisinteachas go dtí gur diúltaíodh cead cainte dom. Maidir leis an eiseachas féin, bhí an t-ádh liom éalú uaidh óir ní raibh an t-airgead agam caifé nó aibsint a cheannach san Deux Magots. Theip orm sa pholaitíocht in ainneoin gur scríobh mé go líofa mar gheall ar an ainrialachas, rud is féidir liom a dhéanamh fós. Ar éigean go bhfuair mé pas sa Bhéarla ar an ollscoil, mar shíl mé go bhfuil úrscéalta Jane Austen ar na píosaí scríbhneoireachta is mó gáirsiúlacht dar cumadh riamh, agus ceapaim sin fós. Gairsiúlacht maidir le cad tá tábhachtach sa saol atá i gceist agam, óir tá an stíl chomh leamh le tráthnóna fliuch fada i mBuiríosa Léith.

Ní d'aon ghnó a thosnaíos ar gan dul ar an mbealach mór. B'fhéidir go raibh cuileog bheag san intinn ionam i gcónaí a thuirlingeodh in áiteanna nach raibh súil leo. Bhí an t-ádh liom gur chaitheas dhá bhliain san Afraic tar éis dom an coláiste a fhágaint. Is mar sin a d'éalaigh mé ó chúinge na hEorpa, cúinge ar cosúil le bosca beag lasán ina gcoimeádfá cnuimheanna é ach go sílfeá go raibh seoda agat. Léigh mé litríocht na hAfraice, agus an domhain níos fairsinge, agus casadh daoine orm ó gach gné phroifisiúnta agus chúlra ó sheacht gcúinne na cruinne laistigh de chúpla bliain. Bhlais mé de chogadh, chonac buamaí ag titim, daoine á gcur chun báis, léigh mé na bréaga ó na mórmheáin idirnáisiúnta, ach thuigeas fós go bhfillfinn ar Éirinn.

Níorbh í an Éire í a d'fhágas nuair a d'fhilleas.

Bhí sí fós ag cabaireacht léi féin trí phrioslaí dhaoine eile. Chuir mic léinn na n-ollscoileanna 'réabhlóid' ar bun, toisc go raibh réabhlóid ar bun sa bhFrainc agus i roinnt tíortha eile. Réabhlóid chóipeáilte a bhí ann. Thug leabhar beag amháin 'the gentle revolution' ar a raibh ar siúl in UCD ina raibh réabhlóidithe mór le rá ar nós Kevin Myarse and Roaring Quinn (an tAire Oideachais is measa dá raibh againn – níos déanaí) ag iarraidh deisceanna cuaracha seachas deisceanna cearnógacha a bhainfeadh an bonn den saol intleachtúil agus mothála. D'fhan mé ag gáire agus ag urlacan in éineacht, óir ní thuigfeadh oiread is duine den chomplacht deas compordach sin cad is réabhlóid ann dá léimfeadh sé suas is dá mbainfeadh greim as a bprumpa. Bhí an bás feicthe agam féin, agus an bharbaracht, agus na bréaga, bhí mé dulta thar an Eoraip amach, agus go háirithe thar Éirinn bheag na búrgéiseachta bómheabhraí.

B'fhéidir gur dual do dhuine a bheith mar a bhíonn. Bhí amhras riamh orm maidir le saorthoil siar amach. Tugtar claonta áirithe dhuit, agus buanna, ach an t-ádh a bheith leat, agus meon nó éirim nach féidir leat a mhalartú ar cheann ar bith eile. Ar an mórchóir níl aon dul as againn ach a bheith mar atáimid sa seasamh ina bhfaighimid sinn féin sa saol. Bhí scata leabhar taistil sa teach againn sa bhaile, agus bhraitheas mo shamhlaíocht riamh ag foluain amach thar na críocha a bhí i ngar dom.

Ach ní raibh aon dul as agam seachas a bheith im Éireannach, im bhuachaill, im fhear in áit faoi leith ag am faoi leith. Ní fhéadfainn a bheith im Arabach ná im Tierra del Fuegach ba chuma cad a dhéanfainn; agus ní rabhas im Neanderdalach ach an oiread is nach mbeidh mé timpeall chun a bhfuil fágtha den domhan a shiúl sa bhliain 3000 a.d. Ní foláir dul i ngleic lena ndeonaítear duit idir chorp, chaipín is chleite.

Mar sin, níl tuairim dá laghad agam cén fáth nach bhfuaireas aon bhlas ar scríbhneoirí seachas a chéile nuair a leagadh a raibh de litríocht le fáil os mo chomhair. Thaithnigh Dickens liom, bhí a chuid leabhar sa bhaile; bhí fuar agam téamh le Thackerey. D'aithin mé guth Frank O'Connor láithreach agus bhaineas an greann ciúin sin is dual dó as; bhí rud éigin tacair, rud éigin ró-fhórsálta ag baint le hO'Faolain. Mhúscail Shakespeare mé ar scoil; ach chuaigh prós staidéartha aonghnéitheach na n-aistí ag Lamb agus ag Addison sa mhuileann orm; ina choinne sin thall, dá dtiocfadh duairceas de shaghas ar bith riamh orm, phiocainn suas aiste úd Edmund Burke mar gheall ar Mharie Antoinette – 'It is now sixteen or seventeen years since I saw the queen of France, then the dauphiness, at Versailles; and surely, never lighted on this orb, which she hardly seemed to touch, a more delightful vision.' – agus b'eo mé ina rachtanna gáirí ar fud an chlóis.

Is de réir a chéile a dhéanann gach duine a dhíolaim phearsanta féin. Cnuasaíonn tú brobhanna as gach áit, coinníonn cuid acu, agus cuireann an chuid eile chun tine. Níl aon rud is doimhne a mhíníonn cé thú féin ná an litríocht a chuireann lasadh faoid anam féin. Inis dom cé hiad na scríbhneoirí is ansa leat, agus déarfaidh mé leat cé thú. Caithfear mórán froganna a phógadh sula dtagann tú ar an rí coróineach, go fiú más poblachtánach Cromaileach tú.

Is é is aite ar fad ná nár aithin mé mé féin ná an tír a raibh taithí agam air in mórán dar léigh mé. Caithfidh go bhfuil Kickham ar dhuine de na húrscéalaithe is measa riamh dá dtáinig, go fiú as Tiobraid Árann; ba chuma liom dá maistreofaí Matt the Thrasher sa chombaighned harbhister ba neasa dhó. Cheapas riamh gur saghas gallúnaí ba ea Lever agus Lover. Ní fhéadfainn Yeats a leanúint ag lorg na sióg ar Bheann Gulbain, in ainneoin an fhriotail álainn. Bhí fuinneamh in Synge, ach dá mba gur mharaigh Christy Mahon a dhaid dáiríre agus a ghob a choinneáil dúnta mar gheall air, b'fhearrde sinn uile é. Má chuir bó crúb ina bás féin i scéal Uí Fhlaithearta, ba mhó an spéis a bhí agam sna stéigeanna a sholáthródh.

Bhí cúiseanna maithe nach bhféadfainn breith ar scríbhneoirí seachas a chéile. Is fearr a réitigh scéalta déanacha Edna O'Brien liom ná na clasaicí lenar thosnaigh sí, óir is fada óna chéile taithí chailín óig i gContae an Chláir ó thaithí bhuachalla cathrach. Ba bheag duine b'uaisle ina mheon agus ba bhéasaí ina iompar ná John McGahern, ach chuir spéartha liatha dorcha Liatroma sceimhle orm, agus ba bhreá liom beagán éigin den 'little tent of blue which the prisoners call the sky' sin anois is arís agus mé á léamh. Arís agus arís eile tuigeadh domsa nach raibh i bhformhór na litríochta a bhí á scríobh sa tír ach an ghráin agus an ghruaim. De réir a chéile bhí bá éigin le tuairimí Stailín ag fás ionam – cad ina thaobh nach bhféadfaí rud ar bith dearfach a rá mar gheall ar an áit seo a bhfuil ár gcosa tuirlingte againn uirthi?

B'fhéidir go bhfuil sé ginte sa scríbhneoir a bheith gearánach, féachaint roimhe ar an idéal, a bheith míshásta lena bhfeiceann. B'fhéidir go bhfuil níos íogaire ná an gnáthdhuine, cé nach gcreidim é sin. B'fhéidir go bhfuil léirstintí ag an ealaíontóir lasmuigh de ghnáththuiscint an duine mar adeireadh Francis Stuart, cé nár thug sé mórán samplaí é féin. Tá a leithéid de ghéarchúis riachtanach d'aon phobal sláintiúil, d'aon phobal ar mian leis é féin a bhreithniú go mionchruinn.

Ach cén fáth ar shíl mé gurb é mórthéama aonair singilte scríbhneoirí na hÉireann ná fuath a bheith acu don tír agus gach a mbaineann léi? Cad ina thaobh go gceapaim gurb é lousy Irish childhood Frank McCourt, agus lousy Irish teenage years Eimear McBride, agus lousy Irish grownupedness Líon Isteach na Bearnaí príomhphort na héigse? An é nár oscail éinne a shúile agus féachaint mórthimpeall máguaird ar fud na cruinne, féachaint a fheabhas is a phribhléidí is a bhí siad? An é go bhfuil scríbhneoirí na hÉireann i gcónaí faoi chuing ag an gcúngaigeantacht – ní hí an chúngaigeantacht a chuireann siad i leith na hÉireann agus na heaglaise agus na seanóirí agus fianna fáil agus na mba mallaithe *cliché*úla a tharraingítear aníos as ciseán beag caol na tuisceana éadoimhne – ach an chúngaigeantacht nach bhfeiceann an saol ina lánfhairsinge siar amach agus atá faoi smacht go hiomlán ag uathachas staire agus tír eolais?

Ní hé nach bhfuil cúis agat le fearg a bheith ort gach lá dá n-éiríonn an ghrian. Ba cheart go mbeadh. Is í an tsaint mórchuspóir na haicme ceannais; an córas sláinte ina phraiseach; an Garda gan a bheith ró-éifeachtach; cúbláil airgid go rábach i gcumainn éagsúla charthannachta; bochtaineacht dhomhaite gan gá agus an tír lofa le hairgead; BÁC 4 ag riaradh na meán; gan intinn neamhspleách ar bith a bheith ag polaiteoirí; drochmheas ar chogadh na saoirse; lúitéis leis an Aontas Eorpach; na baincéirí ag gáire gach orlach den tslí go dtí a mbainc féin; an córas dlí gan a bheith incheartaithe; craobh na hÉireann go bog ag iománaithe Chill Chainnigh (de ghnáth); éileamh gan chrích ar country an' irish; leisce ar theangacha ar bith a fhoghlaim; sobal le béal nuair a luaitear teaghlach ríogúil Shasana; móráil mhór nuair a chailleann an fhoireann idirnáisiúnta sacair; eacnamaithe nach dtuigeann faic; oiliúint mhúinteoirí a bheith curtha chun báis; éascaíocht slí do phianpháiseoirí Mheiriceá; meon críchdheighilteach ag an mbunaíocht; baothlitreacha chun na nuachtán…liostáil gan áireamh agus níos sia ar aghaidh fós. Is ea, is ceart a bhfuil de ribí gruaige fanta agat a stracadh tuilleadh gach uile lá.

Ach cad leis a raibh tú ag súil? Útóipia? Magh Meall? Tír na nÓg? An Tír Tairngreachta? We never promised you a rose garden.

Is í an cheist mhór, cad chuige an náire náisiúnta? Cén fáth an ceann faoi, an bualadh uchta, an sodar i ndiaidh an fhaisinisteachais, an fuath atá againn dúinn féin?

Mar níl aon chúis leis.

Sa dioscúrsa náisiúnta i mbliain seo chomóradh Éirí Amach 1916 níor thúisce an chéad lá den chéad mhí den bhliain ar a nochtadh dhúinn ná gur chrom tráchtairí agus staraithe agus breallsúin agus amadáin ag caitheamh anuas air mar ghníomh bunaidh a thug saoirse áirithe dhúinn. Ní hé nach bhfuil miondealú agus síorscagadh riachtanach. Mar bheart mhíleata ní raibh mórán dealraimh le go leor de. Níorbh aon naoimh iad formhór na gcinnirí – agus b'fhearr nach mbeadh. Ba dhóigh leat gur chóir Caisleán Bhaile Átha Cliath a ghabháil ar an gcéad dul amach.

Ach níorbh é sin a bhí ag cur as do na gearánaithe – Patsy McGarry, agus Ruth Deadly Edwards, agus Sir John Bruton, agus Sir Bobby Goldoff, agus Kevin Myarse, agus Weasley Boyd agus cúpla diagaire aniar – ach go raibh sé mímhorálta toisc gur bhain sé le foréigean! Más síochánaí go héag agus go bun na gimide tú tá láncheart agat cur in aghaidh an fhoréigin. Ach más glóireánaí leithscéalach tú ar son an chéad chogaidh mhóir bharbartha, tá sorry orm, mar adeir siad i gConamara. Cá bhfuil siad uainn agus féasta fola mór na Somme á chuimhneamh? Cá bhfuil na hailt go híor na spéire ag cáiseamh na híobairte fola? An airíonn tú an ciúnas sin Willy McBride agus Tom Kettle agus Wally Matilda agus all the fine young men? Fuair níos mó daoine bás – sé nó seacht n-uaire níos mó – sa chéad uair an chloig sin ar an gcéad lá de bhlár fuilteach na Somme ná gach duine arna chur le chéile le linn tríocha bliain de 'thrioblóidí' an Tuaiscirt, idir chiontach agus neamhchiontach. Fuair níos mó Éireannach bás san uair an chloig sin ar son na Breataine ná gach Éireannach eile a fuair bás ar son a thíre agus a phobail féin le céad bliain roimhe sin. Ba cheart dom é sin a rá arís, ach ní bhacfaidh.

Is é atá ag cur orainn náire náisiúnta.

Ceist níos gabhlánaí, cad ina thaobh sin?

Ach ar ais chun na fianaise soiléire, níl cúis ar bith leis. Tá Saorstát Éireann/Poblacht na hÉireann ar cheann de scéalta móra buacacha agus éiritheacha na haoise seo caite agus na haoise seo. Tá a fhios agam, arís, ó tá a fhios agam, nach maith le daoine fianaise. Is fearr leo claonta. Cuireann sé as dom nuair a chaithfidh mé fianaise a tharraingt aníos as poill fholaigh chun ár gcás a sheasamh. Cad is fianaise ann i gcoinne an aineolais agus na dúire? Múchann an náire náisiúnta aon fhianaise maidir le cad tá bainte amach againn ó bhaineamar ár gcuid saoirse (theoranta) amach.

De réir gach tomhais, táimid ar cheann de na tíortha is fearr as ar domhan. De réir gach tomhais táimid níos fadshaolaí ná formhór de thíortha an domhain. De réir gach tomhais táimid níos saibhre, níos mó tithe againn, córas oideachais níos fearr againn, cothromaíocht airgid níos fearr againn, córas sláinte níos fearr (dár n-ainneoin) againn, níos mó maoine de réir cloiginn, agus ar aghaidh leat trí na dréimirí cuntais.

Níos suimiúla ná sin, de réir na mbreithiúntas céanna, bímid i gcónaí níos fearr as ná an Bhreatain in aice láimhe, ach cad is fianaise ann in aghaidh na claontuairime? Ní raibh riamh aon fhreagra ar chairde sin m'athar ar lic an dorais adeireadh go rabhamar níos fearr as faoi réimeas na Banríochta saghas Aontaithe, agus b'é freagra go lom, nárbh fhíor dóibh. Ceann de scéalta móra an domhain, ná conas a bhfuil éirithe go buacach le tíortha beaga.

Táimid (sa saorstát/phoblacht) ar an tír is faide daonlathas ar domhan, agus an tír is síochánta sa chruinne le nach mór céad bliain anuas. Muran maith leat seo, bain triail as a mhalairt.

Nuair a thosnaíonn daoine ag gearán (agus an ceart acu) faoi theipeanna na tíre seo, fiafraím go pras – arbh fhearr leat a bheith saolaithe agus id chónaí fós, agus níl seo iomlán ach go neamhthuairimeach – arbh fhearr leat gur saolaíodh tú, och, seachnaímis an tuiseal tabharthach, in aon cheann de na tíortha seo a leanas, abraimis – an Ailgéir, an Afganastáin, an Úcráin, an Bhulgáir, Tímór Thoir, an Indinéis, an Mhalaeisia, an Ghréig bhriste, an Ghraonlainn, an Afraic Theas, Ruanda, Maracó, an Rómáin, Libia gan Ghadaffi, an tSile, Oileán na Cásca, an Phortaingéil, an Mhongóil, an Eastóin agus iad sin, an tSúdáin thuaidh nó theas, an Bhrasaíl, Texas, an Vatacáin, an tSiria, abair Mali chomh maith, nó Senegal, ceann ar bith de na Congóchaí, ceann ar bith de na Guineachaí éagsúla, a bhfuil ann den Chambóid, an Bholaiv drugaí ann nó as, an Éigipt ná bac na príosúin, an tSín gan an pionós báis féin, an Rúis ghúlagach neamhghúglach, an KhasacsUzbecKirghisGenghistáin agus na stainíní go léir … etc. agus aroile, agus ar aghaidh leat … ach féach, níl ionainn ach aon stát amháin as tuairim is dhá chéad sa domhan áirithe seo, agus níl tú ag iarraidh orm dul ar aghaidh tríothu ar fad?

De na tíortha is fearr as ná sinn, ar mhaith leat, lándáiríribh a bheith id chónaí i gcuid acu? An Iorua a bhfuil sé ag báisteach ann gach lá sa bhliain, an Fhionlainn atá níos fuaire agus níos leimhe ná an cuisneoir, Ceanada arb é *aqui nada* an bun-ainm air, an Astráil atá ina shuí ar chnámha na milliún bundúchasach a díothaíodh gan oiread is cigilt choinsiasa…?

De réir gach tomhais idirnáisiúnta (ach cad is fiú fianaise, cad is fiú fianaise in aghaidh an fhaisinisteachais?) táimid níos fearr as de réir gach tomhais sin ar féidir é a thomhas go tomhaisteach ná beagnach gach aon tír eile ar domhan, nó go deimhin, gach aon dúiche dá raibh riamh ann go stairiúil ar an bpláinéad seo nó ar aon phláinéad ar bith eile ó thús phléascadh an bhaing mhóir gus anois. Nach cúis ghairdeachais í sin?

Ní hea in aon chor. De réir ár gcuid scríbhneoirí táimid nach mór ar an tír is measa ar domhan. Is í an fhírinne ná go bhfuilimid ar cheann de na tíortha is fearr as ar domhan dá raibh riamh ó d'fhágamar an Afraic seasca nó ochtú éigin míle bliain ó shin, ceann de na tíortha is fearr as dá bhfuil anois is dá raibh riamh, is sinn ceann de na glúine is lú ar éilíodh obair sclábhaíochta uathu ó aimsir Phádraig agus na ndraoithe.

Ach nílimid ag iarraidh é seo a chloisint in aon chor in aon chor idir idir a chuige ná a chuigint.

Sa mhéid sin féin, fantaisíocht seachas réalachas lom is ea formhór de scríbhneoireacht Éireann.

Bhí riamh mar ghnó ag an litríocht gairdeachas a dhéanamh go rabhamar beo seachas go rabhamar marbh. De réir is mar a chuaigh an saol i bhfeabhas chuaigh an tuairisc in olcas. Ba cheart gurb í feidhm na litríochta áthas agus iontais a chaitheamh ar fhallaing mhíorúilteach na beatha, is é sin, má tá feidhm ar bith léi.

Suas is anuas lena mhalairt, tá Éire go maith, agus tá an saol go hiontach. D'oirfeadh don fhocal scríte an méid sin a aithint – ar a laghad, anois is arís.

Maidir liom féin de, sa mhéid is gur fiú faic é, táim mórálach go bhfuil baint bheag bhídeach agam le ceann de litríochtaí móra an domhain, ceann de ghuthanna na daonnachta nach bhfuil gránna ná gruama an t-am ar fad.

Alan Titley: Is é *An Bhean Feasa* an dán is eipiciúla sa Ghaeilge chomhaimseartha an saothar is déanaí uaidh, fara *Ag Bualadh Clé is Deas*, cnuasach dá chuid aistí óna cholún seachtainiúil san *Irish Times*. Ollamh Emeritus le Nua-Ghaeilge in UCC, agus roimhe sin ina Cheann ar Roinn na Gaeilge i gColáiste Phádraig DCU sular coilleadh litríocht agus smaointe agus samhlaíocht den chúrsa.

This Sceptic Isle

Alan Titley

Ah yes, we are the worst country in the world, we are a failed state, everything is miserable and dilapidated and dead and deadening, and oh my Gawd, we should hang our heads in shame, and we would have been better off staying with the United Queendumb, wouldn't we just...?

There is much evidence, buckets of it, to refute this there sentiment above, but what has evidence ever to do with people whose minds are closed and who exist in a kind of historical and geographical autism? We spend millions and trillions and zillions on education, and yet, despite the evidence ('What did evidence ever do for me?') many of our brightest and best think this country is a crock of crap.

When I was young and I was in my day, friends of my father would toddle in and gabble, as people do. Having waxless ears, words would waft by, most of them without any purchase, others which burred. Sly sentiments passed on, some but not that many which asked, 'What was it all for?' This was a question asked by John McGahern's Moran in that novel of his in which nothing happens. It was a question which he asked himself on the seventy-fifth anniversary of the Easter Rising entitled 'From a Glorious Dream to Wink and Nod' and is included in his otherwise wonderful collected prose *Love of the World: Essays*.

It was actually about a hell of a lot.

The query is often economic. It is as if we were just economic digits. We are if that is what we think we are. The end of life is to eat more and to guzzle more. To consume more, but only to consume more than we have again, to consume and burst because that is the true end of life. We have reached the limits of our imaginations. If this being the case all small little gutty states would be happy to be swallowed up by their better Leviathans. But then a small voice whispered in my ear that when the hairy Celtic Tiger was roaring, those them Unionists weren't exactly screaming to join the rich fatted cows of the Republic of Ireland. It isn't about the economy, you stupids!

What I am trying to say quite simply and humbly is that I wasn't reared all that badly, really, like. I didn't have anything to compare my upbringing with, of course, not then, not until it was impressed on me like Kipling, that what does he of Ireland know who only Ireland knows? I think it was much the same for my peers and pards. Nobody came to school hungry nor did they live in a scruffy hovel. We used to snigger and laugh when our parents or our teachers threatened us to gulp up our gruel and our porridge as the children of China were starving. Our sniggering was the sons and daughters of thickness. We never realised nor knew that we were blessed in being the most lucky people in the most lucky generation during the most lucky time in the most lucky period of the most lucky chance that ever happened in the luckiest country of all in the entire universe for the lucky chance of more than thirteen billion years or whatever.

If you don't believe me, start thinking!

I fully realise that this is a dangerous and subversive statement. I fully realise that many people choke at the idea of comparisons, that any comparison is inimical to their intelligence. But the only way we have of weighing anything is to weigh it against something else. Are we comparing ourselves to some kind of Utopia? To somewhere over the rainbow? I know full well that Irish political discourse and much of Irish moaning literature mark us out as the most awful oppressed church-ridden know-nothing tight-arsed country in the entire universe. To which the only answer is that they should get out more. They should learn a bit about the world.

The idea of being oppressed by a State of ingrowing toenail thought and constrained by a corset of conservative thinking never dawned on me until I was told it was so. Many friends of mine, still friends of mine I hope, never knew they were oppressed by the Church until *The Irish Times* told them so. I never felt it. When the Church said anything stupid I laughed and went my way, as any bright, intelligent, independent person should do. Those friends of my youth if born ten or twenty years previously would have been the greatest stalwarts of that same Church. Such is the power of Fashionism. *Heil* Fashionism! – because it is all that people believe in.

I was always attracted to heresies, for the heretic at least thinks for himself. We constantly hear of the Leaving Certificate and the need for critical thinking. Do you actually think that if somebody writes that John Redmond was a warmonger, and that Yeats had Fascist sympathies, and that Ó Conaire's stories were largely maudlin mush, and that Stalin was the reason that England does not speak German and that Shakespeare's *Macbeth* is psychologically flawed from the outset, do you actually think that your ideas will not be given short or even long shrift in any examination regime? Whatever the Fashionism of the moment is, you better stick to it. Most people are Fashionists down to their nether regions.

I never knew what it was what pricked me to think for myself, as I like to think.

I have to admit that it didn't deliver the goods. I remember resisting Thomism in college, even though it meant that my marks were rightly slashed, and I excoriated essentialism, not that it helped me either. As for the Fashionism of the moment, I had the good fortune not to have enough zlotys or shekels to buy a slurp or even a swig of that absinthe that did not make my heart grow fonder in The Two Maggots. Nor neither did I do that well in politics as my anarchy didn't accord with those answers that landed on all four paws. I barely passed English, maybe not surprisingly, as I cogently argued then that Jane Austen's style was the most class-ridden pornographic in all of English writing, and it is an idea I still hold dear.

I was lucky not to be made to walk on the main highway. I suppose I could have done so if I had been cursed with a midget mind. I was given a path with many byways out and behind and beyond. That is what education does. The road to salvation was broad and wide and tempting and led to a good job and a safe pension and nothing wrong with any of that. Even the wandering paths lead you to wherever the wondering paths did not lead, and you must follow them all. As Yogi Berra said, 'when you come to a fork in the road, take it.'

I was lucky to be given the opportunity to work in Africa during a savage war when I was just twenty years of age. For what does anyone know of Ireland that only Europe knows? I was fortunate to escape the narrow peninsular introverted self-regarding navel fluffstuff that passes for broadmindedness here. I was lucky to get to read African literature before I had to read the existentialist angst of the privileged rich. I saw bombs, and prisons, and executions and read the fat lies from the fat newspapers and magazines, but knew I would be back in Ireland. I escaped from the narrow peninsular preoccupations of Europe.

It wasn't the same Ireland to which I returned, although still pizzling through much of the same dribble as it always had with a dash of the outside world thrown in. The copycat revolutionists copycatted their way into the news on the backs and on the bodies of real student revolutionists in other countries, particularly in France, although it is true that students had been mown down in the US also. Some small book dumbed it 'The Gentle Revolution', and although it went softly and gently it was never approaching even the lip of a pale excuse of a rebellion. Some of the more inglorious revulsionaries of that time were the Somme-time *Irish Times* journalist Kevin Myers, and the worst Minister for Education we have ever had despite great competition, Ruairí Quinn, who not only managed to banish History as a central subject on the curriculum in case it might contaminate young minds, but who also presided over the utter and barbaric destruction of thought and of the arts in teacher education. Check it out.

Maybe we have no choice other than to be who we are. I was always a bit dubious about the wings of freewill. I really had no choice but to be born in Ireland, and to be a male person being, at a certain time and in a certain place. I couldn't have been an Arab or a Tierra del Fuegan even if the sands or the fires of time had moved; and chance also decided that I wasn't to be a Neanderthal boiling bones, no more than I am going to be around in the year 3000 AD all going very well. You have no option but to deal with the hand you have been dealt whether you like it or not.

Thus, I have no idea why I liked or disliked certain authors who passed my way in my youth and childhood, wherein I might have done something good. Dickens was always great, while Thackeray was stodge. I could hear Frank O'Connor's voice in the street and understood his gentle irony; O'Faolain was always a bit forced and when he had a symbol he stuck it out a mile in case it didn't clobber you. Shakespeare spoke the mad creative language of the yard and you couldn't not get him. On the other hand there were boring essays by Lamb and by Addison which could only be digested with huge gobfuls of donkey's gudge, a kind of black cake which was the staple food of the shop next door to the school. On the other other hand our school essays always offered amusement. When I wanted a laugh or even a broad chuckle I went straight for Burke's description of when he first saw Marie Antoinette: 'It is now sixteen or seventeen years since I saw the Queen of France, then the dauphiness, at Versailles; and surely never lighted on this orb, which she hardly seemed to touch, a more delightful vision.' I still crack up in wild abundance of mirth when I read those unintentionally hilarious words.

Bit by bit and row by row everybody makes their own anthology. You gather up the strands and the wisps, what is there in the middle, what has fallen by the wayside, the cockle and the chips, and you make your own Ireland out of them all. Nothing explains one's own soul more than that anthology, the bits that light your fire. Tell me which writers you revere, and I will tell you who you are. You have to kiss many ugly toadish writer people until you get your prince, even if you are a Cromwellian republican.

The main epiphany being that I never recognised the country I knew in much and in most of what I had read. Charles J. Kickham was surely one of the worst novelists ever to scratch a pen in nineteenth-century Ireland, and more saliently to have crawled out of the ridings of Tipperary north and south. I frankly couldn't give a damn if Matt the Thrasher was mashed in a combine harvester. I always supposed that Lever and Lover were some manner of detergent, preferably to clean out our mouths. Despite Yeats's beautiful words and elegant diction his fairy faith and widening gyres always left me a bit dubious. Synge had great energy and great fun, but maybe if Christy Mahon had really murthered his father there were times we would be happier if he kept his gob shut about it. When a cow committed bovicide over a cliff in one of Liam O'Flaherty's stories I was more interested in the rump steak.

There are reasons why there are writers whom we never 'get'. I much preferred Edna O'Brien's later work than the classics she wrote first, because maybe just a city young fella's world was too different from a country girl's. John McGahern certainly captured some of the doom of a certain kind of youth, but the gloomy grey skies of Leitrim often screamed out for just a glimpse of that 'tent of blue which prisoners call the sky.' Why was it that so many of our writers thought that life was shitty? There were days when I began to understand Stalin, why not celebrate and wonder at this patch of land our feet have been plonked upon for a little while? (This is a joke, for people without irony).

Maybe writers are a moany and groany lot because we fall so short of any ideal we might seek. Maybe the writer is more sensitive than the normal person, although I doubt it. Maybe the writer and artist have insights into life that escape the mere mortal, something which Francis Stuart never ceased telling us, although he singularly failed to tell us what exactly they were.

Of course, and undoubtedly, and *ipso facto* a writer must write what a writer has experienced, or even felt. If Frank McCourt had a lousy Irish childhood, he had a lousy Irish childhood, even factoring Limerick in as a large part of that. It would be crass to aver that Irish writers hated Ireland as John Sutherland surmised in the *Guardian* two years ago. There is no one unorthodoxy, the country and its writings are still as catholic as ever, protesting all the way to the ink. On the other hand, if one was to put together a course in modern/contemporary Anglo-Irish literature it is far more likely that those who were worsted in the game and had a good turn of quirky paddy phrase would be included before, let us say, Hugh Leonard or Bernard Farrell or the classy historical novels of John Banville, the purveyors of the more ordinary wonderful. Time cannot wither nor custom stale our indulgence in ourselves as victims, and as being born in a horrible place. Are we to be forever locked in an unburstable bubble of self-regard?

There is ample reason to rage and rage against the wasting of the light every morning that greets you. And so you should: the sheer greed of those at the top, the crooked unrepentant banks, the rickety health service, the charity scandals, the appalling level of homelessness, the destruction of public housing, the crass stupidity of pocket pump politicians, the acceptance of gross inequality, the address snobbery, the class bias of the media, the ownership of what we know, the arse-licking of the European Union, the incorrectibility of the legal system, the popularity of awful country and Irish music, our linguistic ignorance, our drooling self-congratulations when we win an international match, economists who haven't a clue (although we are not alone in this), free passage for American torture flights, a partitionist mentality, stupid letters to the paper, the barbaric destruction of teacher education by the removal of the need to know anything from the curriculum of the colleges … one could go on, I could go on, but I won't go on, not just now. The most hirsute and hairy of us should be baldy and shiny by the pulling of the hair by now.

But what actually did you expect? Some kind of Utopia? Magh Meall? The Promised Land of Youth and Buttermilk and Honey? Whoever promised us a rose garden without the pricks?

In this centenary year of the 1916 Rising which instigated our war of liberation, no sooner had the sun risen on the first day of the first month of the year but we were treated to a barrage of opinion dissing and mocking and pissing on the parade. Of course, it is perfectly right that a foundling act should be interrogated down to the bung of it. If you couldn't take Dublin Castle it wasn't much of a revolution.

But it wasn't this what bugged the anti-brigade: Patsy McGarry, and Ruth Deadly Edwards, and ex-first minister Bruton, and Sur Bobby Geldof, and Kevin Myarse, and Weasly Boyd, and some dicey theologians who still tried to wring some small change from the just war theology, long discredited or ignored. It wasn't the success or lack of it which exercised their wrath, but the violence! Now, while you draw your breath, just pause and even think. There should be no problem objecting, and objecting with savage indignation to the illegal and antidemocratic 1916 rebellion if you are a pacifist. But to the best and the worst of my knowledge I think that none of the above are pacifists; and if they are, it would have been music to all of our ears to hear them explode in horror at the thought of imagining to consider that we should acknowledge the carnage at the Somme without excoriation and condemnation and the necessary added bits that we would never again conjoin with imperialist forces to bomb and clobber the lesser breeds without the law. Poor old Willie McBride and all the fine young men along with waltzing Matilda might have to do it again and again and again for all that they might say.

For that alone, it has been an interesting year, because 'What was it all for?' as McGahern and Moran so plaintively asked.

There is an answer to it, and it is plain enough.

The Irish Free State/Saorstát Éireann, latterly Ireland or the Republic of Ireland is one of the great success stories of the twentieth century.

Och, I'm sorry, *mea culpa*, I shouldn't have said this, but unfortunately the auld evidence jumps up to bite me.

I was cursed with an education that required evidence, while being fully aware that facts are normally useless in what is basically a culture war.

We are one of the richest and best off countries in the entire universe right now! Oh fuck it, I have just said that we live longer, have better education, more disposable income, more houses per skull, and so on and so on through all those economic ladders which the people up there count. This does not mean that things are not crap for many … I am talking about comparisons.

And comparisons should be the stuff of the writer and of the artist. We imagine other worlds and other possibilities. We always ask: 'What if?'

And 'What if?' is the greatest unasked question in Ireland, as I was almost about to say, the elephant in the zoo. What if we were to start imagining, let us say, outside the penalty area? What if we were to start to imagine the other worlds that are, the worlds that could have been, the worlds in which we might have been captured? Isn't this the greatest work of the artist, the alternative worlds of our imaginations?

The only alternative world to an Irish free state/republic was one that was still part of the United Kingkongqueendumb. There was no other choice, no other possibility the other side of science fiction. It is a question rarely asked, and never answered.

Emigration is the single greatest failing of the Irish political project. But hang on … Given that the greatest emigration of any European country in terms of the slashing of its population by a quarter within a decade happened when we were part of that UKrania, we can't seriously say that it would have stopped in the twenties, thirties, etc., can we? And given that emigration from the UK itself was rampant in those same years, we can't imagine that we would have been different, can we? And travel through the north of Scotland some time, and see the deserted villages of the abandoned desert of UQ places and so on …

But the Irish difficulty with the economics was not just that, as is obvious. But if that is the only ground on which you stand, apart from being more stupid than you think, there are the simple crude going-forward inside-the-box temporal facty things that you might want to notice if you live in the real world. In just about every international measurement that is made comparing country with country in purely material things, Ireland comes out away ahead of the UQ. Sorry, again, oh my Gawd, some ugly facts to scrub the ingrown prejudice: check it out, the United Nations Human Development Index, and all the other bitty ones around it. Not only do we come out ahead of the UQ, we come out motorways and autobahns ahead of them. Ah, but fuck it, they're only facts. You have your prejudice, and you're sticking to it.

My own prejudice is moral, not so much economic, even though we have won that one hands down. I don't like any moral crow as I don't believe we are in any way better or superior than anyone else. But I do think, in fact I know by the incontrovertible evidence, that we have done more good and less evil to our fellow beings of humanity by not being part of the UQ than if we had. This may not be of any value to you, but it is to me.

There is the tiny weeny business of that if we had been part of the continuing UQ we would have been partners in some of the most unjustifiable and barbaric wars raged by man upon women and children in the twentieth century – we would have been a militarised colonising force – the most recent being those attacks on countries in the Middle East which have released the demons of the ages. But we don't want to go there now. Suffice to say if we had been there we would have been complicit in the dead of the countless. Don't know about you, but this is important to me.

If we attacked another country in the morning or in the evening in the act of conquest or occupation, I would hand in my passport and abandon my Irish citizenship.

We are in this Free State Republic one of the longest unbroken democratic one-woman one-man countries in the world; we are, in this Free State Republic, more or less the most peaceful place in the universe. If you don't believe me, lift up your eyes, cast them forth, and behold!

So when the moaners and the groaners and the whingers and the begrudgers start moaning and groaning and whinging and begrudging I ask the simple not very difficult straightforward question, would you have preferred to be born in, and lived in, and be raised in, and let us not be too complete in this, say, like Morocco or Bolivia or Bangladesh or the Philippines or Bulgaria or China or Mexico or Greece or Mongolia or Portugal or Argentina or Egypt or Sudan or South Sudan or Panama or Vietnam or Uzbekistan or India or Somalia or Easter Island, or Romania or Nigeria or Tanzania, or Burma or Belarus or Bhutan, or Azerbaijan or Armenia or Angola, or Kosovo or Mexico or Togo, or Uganda or Vanuatu or Tuvalu, or Malawi, or Djibouti or Burundi…? I can add more if you don't get the picture by now.

And of those that score higher than us in this football league of luck and prosperity, would you really prefer to live in Norway where it rains 465 days a year, or in Canada where Sam McGee or his like couldn't be cremated quickly enough, or Australia living on the recent genocide and destruction of lovely decent human people whose only crime was to be born and to live in their own place? It mightn't matter to you, but it does to me.

Of course, much of our good fortune has nothing to do with us. We were lucky to be in this particular peninsula of Gaia in this time riding on the slavery of yesteryear and the domesticable animals that roamed through Eurasia. Insofar as we fucked up, we fucked up small. This is not a bad success.

It is something, I think, that we writers and scribblers should at least acknowledge. You would never think so given the most celebrated of our internationally famous authors. If you own what are called assets amounting to about €500,000, house and car and dog and TV and iPhone and tablet and all, you are in the top 1 or 2 per cent of the richest people in the world. The richest who ever lived ever. Ever. Is this not something? Actually, is not this something unbelievably fantastic and wondrously miraculous? If you have about €12,000 worth of possessions, say an old banger of a car, you are in the top quarter of the wealthiest people on this orbish earth. Aside from the banger, that's probably just about everybody in the country – apart from the truly unfortunate. Not bad either.

I always had this weird belief that literature should celebrate the fact that we are alive and not dead, that we should look to the greater world, and not just to ourselves.

As for me myself, I feel privileged to have a small muted and muffled wee voice in one of the great literatures of the world, a literature that can celebrate life and existence just as much as it finds it miserable when it is. It makes no sense to say you are 'proud' to be Irish. I never understood this any more than I understood the need for 'roots'. Roots are things that vegetables have, like parsnips. We are not carrots or radishes or yams or even good old potatoes. What we have is air. Our literature is the breath of our country, or at least a great burst of the puff of our humanity.

I have been lucky enough to breathe it in Irish and in English; for what does he know of Ireland who only English knows?

Alan Titley is the author of several novels, many plays, countless stories and two works of poetry, including the epic, *An Bhean Feasa*. He is Professor Emeritus of Modern Irish in UCC, and former Head of Irish in St Patrick's College, Dublin City University. His scholarly interests are Irish and Scottish literature. He has been writing a weekly column for *The Irish Times* since 2003.

Enormous Changes at
the Last Minute

Anne Haverty

Every succeeding generation seems to be primed to assume that the preceding one had less of everything – less freedom, less money and definitely less taste. Immediate forebears tend to be viewed with a mixture of pity and condescension for what they didn't have and we do – a natural assumption to make if we view history as a process of steady advancement. But could it be that twenty-five years ago we actually had more? More of what's important to us as people – hope, confidence, trust in each other. More freedom? In real terms, more money. Better taste even? Wasn't that era lighter in spirit, more tolerant and, well, more fun? Take the Writers Centre for example, whose existence for twenty-five years we're celebrating with this book, a building which has hosted many an interesting and convivial literary event and is an extremely valuable resource for literary folk. But is it more orderly a place, more earnest than might have been expected when it was thought of? Had it existed in former days you can imagine writers – more anarchic footloose writers as they were then – considering it as their resort, its couches possibly venues for a lie-down of an occasional morning after a night before. You can envisage them being indulged by the custodians of those times, and the visiting tourists who would be pleased to mingle with them – though tourists weren't quite the point then, nor the herded flocks with defined and managed expectations that they are now. Did the future look more open-ended then, and so brighter?

Twenty-five years on of course one is older – oh lord, a whole quarter of a century older – and naturally inclined to look backwards with increasing nostalgia. A nostalgia which as we know does not necessarily provide a realistic picture of how things actually were. Not to mention that every quarter of a century that passes wreaks some kind of havoc, large or small, in everybody's life. Unless you are very lucky or perhaps just very young, you will have experienced bereavements or illnesses or accidents of fortune, or disappointments of one kind or another, and these are bound to colour one's outlook.

This inevitable process aside, however, in these years we're concerned with, there have been developments that have had a limiting and shrinking effect. These are global, and not only Irish, developments, and this is significant. If I were writing this twenty-five years ago I suspect Ireland would be at the forefront of my musings. Then, it was a more particular and idiosyncratic place with its own particular ways of doing things. Ireland, like everywhere else, conforms to a global standard now. We were more 'ourselves', as a country and as individuals, before. A global perspective is now the dominant one, and it is global forces, whether blind or inexplicably farseeing, that seek to make us all the same.

For what or whose good is it that we all should be the same? It's hard to see how it can be, on balance, for our own. The answer may lie in two relatively recent and crucial developments that might be called revolutions. One of them is insidious and only dimly recognised. In an article I wrote in 2009 (published in the *Sunday Independent*) and attempting to understand the economic crash, I named it – though the concept had been around for years – 'the revolution of the rich'. The other, the internet revolution, is glaringly apparent to all and universally tangible in the most real sense.

But before considering the implications of these developments we should look at where we were, or thought we were, in those pre-revolutionary days.

Back then in 1991, the very year coincidentally of the founding of the Writers Centre, Francis Fukuyama published *The End of History*.

Hegel and Marx as well as Thomas More in *Utopia* had already used the phrase to describe the end point of their particular idealistic philosophies – to Marx, for example, the end of history would be apparent when the advancement of Communism resulted finally in the withering away of the state. For Fukuyama it was the modern liberal democracies of the west that were bringing about the end of history. In these democracies that had evolved since the horrors of the mid-century, principles of freedom and justice had been established that could more or less guarantee a reasonable level of welfare and wellbeing for all, or at least the possibility of it. With the fall of the Soviet empire and the adoption in China of the practices of the free market there would be no more major wars. There would be conflicts but they would be small and localised. The mutuality of respect for borders and liberal principles and aspirations was so strongly embedded in the democratic project that the idea of inter-nation war was by now archaic.

Certainly, Fukuyama's theory had a complacency that made it suspect and the assumptions it contained about the benign character of the free market looked a little naive. And yet it seemed plausible enough. In the 1990s we seemed to have arrived at a state of equilibrium, political, social and cultural, that could only get better. Continuing progress looked inevitable. In the neighbouring island a young, vigorous Tony Blair emerged from Number 10 to greet the cheering crowds, replacing, we presumed, the ravages of Thatcherist policies with better alternatives. Across the other pond the relatively well intentioned, relatively balanced Bill Clinton was president.

In Ireland the wound of the northern province was in the process of healing. After decades of regarding ourselves as retrograde we could regard ourselves as progressive. As members of the European Union we took a share in the postwar prosperity of Western Europe. Our young people were being educated to 'the highest standard', as we were told and believed. If they had to emigrate – and they did because we had recessions then too and periods of 'austerity' though they were called 'belt-tightening' – most of them could embark on their careers abroad armed with well-earned degrees and certificates. The Catholic Church had finally lost the longstanding tussle to maintain its influence over our public and private affairs – the defeat a consequence of the revelation of lamentable aspects in the conduct of its own public and private affairs nearly as much as it was of our new convictions. We were electing women presidents. We had won the personal freedoms enjoyed by other liberal democracies.

There was greater gender equality, divorce, available contraception, freedom of sexual orientation. The removal of any remaining restrictions obviously would follow as inevitably as night follows day.

All in all we were entitled to be optimistic. Our level of public services left a lot to be desired – wasn't it ever so? – but things could only improve since there was no apparent reason why they should get worse. If there were queues – and I dimly remember there were – for hospital beds and hospital tests and procedures, they weren't as numerous nor wait times as long.

This might be a delusion admittedly, hospitals with their trolleys and crowded wards and waiting lists being more peripheral to your concerns when you and your entourage are twenty-five years younger. If Polish and Russian and Italian weren't yet ubiquitous languages on our streets they soon would be. Wow, how cosmopolitan we were getting! Suddenly people seemed to have more money to spend, even if how and where they were getting it wasn't always clear, and they were having grand times spending it.

From a writer's perspective too things were looking good. We had a new wave of writers, more of them than ever before – and this time I was among them. There was a surge in initiatives around arts activities, the Writers Centre being one. New arts centres were rising countrywide, there was a rejuvenated film board. There were supports for writers and artists that suggested the vocation might be workable in practice as an occupation. Books were still books, tactile, faintly aromatic objects made of paper and print, though we had computers to write them more efficiently with.

It was all onwards and upwards though we wouldn't have bothered with the exhortation because it was self-evident that we would. If the big questions of how to run society weren't quite settled, they soon would be. The fireworks and celebrations that ushered in the new millennium seemed on balance to be justified. We had arrived at a state of efflorescence and we kind of believed it would flower forever.

We didn't know it, not with any clarity – or we didn't want to know it – but beyond our ken, seeds of a different future were also flourishing.

Without banners or manifestos or overt violence the 'revolution of the rich' was in train in the cocooned world of high-end golf courses and plush city bars and financiers' dinner tables. Conducted by devotees of the 'new economics', this 'revolution' shared the traditional revolutionary ambition of the redistribution of wealth – but it turned it on its head. To these neoliberals, financial regulation, established since the mid-century for the common good, was stifling ambition. Rid of these constraints, wealth would be liberated, allowed to flow towards the well-positioned few from the pockets of the many. Staid old banking practices were the major impediment. In the seductive culture of 'new economics' the banks were deregulated and indebtedness facilitated. Debt was made easy, attractive, respectable, even a matter of pride. You could put any price on any product from a house to a handbag and cheerfully we ('we' in the general sense and not necessarily applicable to you) paid it because the bank was happy to lend us the money.

It felt like equality, only a levelling up rather than a dreary levelling down. It felt like liberty, the liberty to spend. It even felt like fraternity, the bankers playing the part of benevolent brothers. When the bankers told us they were geniuses and paid each other huge salaries and told us they deserved them, we agreed. After all, weren't they a new breed of chap, with mysterious talents and esoteric knowledge and a magic touch? Everyone was infected with moneymadness. Everyone wanted to join the club and everyone was encouraged to think they could, and should. Acquisition (of apartments in Bulgaria, of those big weirdly ugly handbags) became a matter of pride as much as greed, a symptom of the anxiety to display one's importance in a culture where money had become the only indicator of importance.

I published a novel, *The Free And Easy*, about that heady time and the people caught up in it, many of them enjoying it enormously. It was a novel written with irony – though irony was on the way out – because the potential for comedy in this new version of Ireland was striking and appealing. But when the flimsy and delusory construct collapsed within a year or two there was little irony to be had and a great deal of anger, as well as pain. We realised we had been subject to a gentle form of extortion. Almost overnight there was a switch in the national psyche from buoyancy to fear and a faltering of hope, and the lifestyles that we had been so encouraged to indulge were replaced almost overnight by austerity and frugality.

Having no choice but to cope, by and large we coped. And we have come out the other side, or so we are told by the politicians who led us through the lean years. But what are we left with in the aftermath? In a way nothing has changed and yet everything has changed. The redistribution of wealth has been effected. The chasm of inequality between the super-rich and the rest is now vast and looks likely to continue its increase. There has been no compensatory and annealing alteration in the mindset of greed and entitlement. Governments continue to collude with it and to treat it with a mystifying tenderness. There is no talk of re-regulation. The new economics is in place.

The most obvious legacy is that most of the rest have a lot less money to spend. But they also have a great deal less than they had before of many important things; less security, diminished employment rights, old reliables like education and pensions made unsure. The biggest loss of all may be the loss of trust; trust in institutions, in government, in the idea of the public good; even, reduced as we are to the status of anxious consumers, trust in each other. The mutual perception of one another as little more than buyers and sellers – and preferably buyers – can only produce a culture of cynicism as well as tedium. The ideology of mass consumption, the more passive the better, and the elevation of monetary value to be the only value is about all that survives from that era. Selling everything, we may have sold our collective soul – that amorphous indefinable thing we only recognise by its absence.

The other revolution of these years (leaving aside the chilling Islamist revolution which from the present vantage looks too intractable to coherently consider) is the technological one. It could have been designed to abet passive consumption though this was probably not the motive of the inventors of the internet – this was the idealistic 'then'. It's ominous that we use the word 'feed', as in 'my feed', with its connotations of passive consumption, of baby-nursing, for the constant stream of information we are the 'consumers' of on our personal screens. This isn't to say that the internet, in concept and actuality, is not a most wonderful invention. That anyone with access to a screen has access within seconds to knowledge and information, garnered over millennia of history and from every corner of the globe, from the most arcane to the most mundane, the learned to the banal, is truly extraordinary.

And yet. You have to question the purposes, whether blind or engineered, of an innovation that requires everyone to own at least one personal device which they must use not just to access this information but simply to survive in the world. This online access to services of all kinds is making, or will soon make, daily access to a screen as essential as one's daily bread and water. No other technological product, apart perhaps from domestic electrification, has ever been made to be quite so essential.

Producing our various screenbearing devices has been a huge benefit to the tech industry and, needing as they do to be regularly replaced, will carry on being beneficial, as it has been a benefit and will continue to be for tech workers. And what, you may wonder, can be wrong with that? What are these devices but tools, the contemporary equivalent of the bicycle in the nineteenth century or the radio of the twentieth, only more remarkable? The screen however is a tool with far-reaching implications because it is becoming, has already become a significant as well as an essential mediator – literally a screen – between us and the real world. And the real world, when it's flattened and reduced to the dimensions of a screen, looks predictably diminished.

'We live in an age,' the film director Terry Gilliam said some decades ago, 'where we're just hammered, hammered to think this is what the world is. Television's saying, everything's saying, "That's the world". And it's not the world. The world is a million possible things.'

He was speaking at a time when there was only television, carefully mediated and regulated and easily ignored, to tell us who and what we were. Our screens come everywhere with us, unregulated, clamorous and tyrannical. They give us an image of ourselves we're more or less helpless to refuse. This image, whether reflected through social media or porn sites or the brutalities of unfiltered news sites is mostly standardised and synthetic, or stupid and unforgiving. A consequence is that who and what we perceive ourselves to be is far more circumscribed than it would have been twenty-five years ago. We're better educated than we ever were, taught, as the educationalists' mantra goes, to think independently. But our capitulation to the screen and its laws would suggest that in fact we're less discriminating, more fearful and more herdlike.

When the French philosopher Alain Finkielkraut was elected recently to the Académie he spoke of the tyranny of 'la doxa'. The concept of the 'doxa' has been around since the time of the ancient Greeks. Every society has its doxa, the orthodoxy of the mainstream, the ambient consensus. With old-style French vehemence Finkielkraut described our contemporary doxa as 'sheeplike, dogmatic and automatic memory, stage-memory, memory reviewed, corrected, and spit out by the system'. You don't have to be a right-wing French philosopher (though the old distinctions between right and left are no longer clear which may be considered a liberation) to anguish over the downward lurch of contemporary culture. And the internet has become the vehicle for the purveying of the doxa, far more intrusive and powerful than the pulpits or the television of old. It seems that the more atomised we become, the more conformist we get. The reactions and actions of people threatened by the not-doxa and of those who voice them can be merely absurd; they can also be extreme and even dangerous.

When we shed the old doxas it seems that we didn't, as we thought we would, shed their repressive and pietistic character. Everything is contentious and fractured, everything is changed – and in some ways everything stays the same.

From my point of view as a writer, the result is frustratingly reductive. In the 1990s we were still as mysterious to one another as we had always been. We could invent each other, and this is what we did because it was all we could do. Now, as we eagerly represent ourselves and express ourselves on Facebook or Twitter or Instagram there is less mystery. We are all knowable and we know that we're more similar than we might have believed, with the same need for self-assertion and the same small vanities and prejudices. We accept that, like everything else, we're commodities.

Any writer must regret the loss of more nuanced times. Human nature has come to look rudimentary and darker. The screen is public and we have secret selves still, unexpressed and inexpressible. But they're not easy to access now and are harder to invent.

It's possible that this may be only a moment of infatuation. We'll get accustomed to the technology and get bored with it, and we will learn to use it with the respect it should have, and the carelessness. Another possibility is that we are facing the prospect of being Fukuyama's

– in fact Nietzsche's – Last Man. The Last Man – and Last Woman of course – is the end point of liberal democracy. Stifled by trivial wants, as overwhelmed by the meaningless round of satisfying them as he is by the fear of losing them, his only recourse is an old one; conflict and violence. This note of pessimism aside, Fukuyama was clearly – and sadly – wrong in his attempt at prophetic analysis. The relevant analysis for us appears to be Slavoj Žižek's *Living in the End Times* (2010), a suitably apocalyptic title for Žižek's apocalyptic vision of where we are now. But, unlikely as it looks, he too could be wrong. And we might, just possibly, surprise ourselves as we occasionally have at gateway times in our history.

Anne Haverty's novels include *One Day As A Tiger* (winner of the Rooney Prize and short-listed for the Whitbread/Costa) and *The Far Side Of A Kiss* (long-listed for the Booker). Her poetry collection, *The Beauty Of The Moon*, was a Poetry Book Society Recommendation. Her biography *Constance Markievicz: Irish Revolutionary* has recently been re-issued in a revised edition.

Before I Die

Ian Sansom

London. Twenty years ago. We've hired the upstairs room of a pub, laid on some sandwiches and put a few pound behind the bar, to celebrate, to tell our family and friends that we are moving to Ireland.

There is general agreement that this is a good thing – a nice idea, something to be admired. Backs are generously slapped, hands warmly shaken, and there is the all-round raising of glasses of Guinness, and of stoups of Baileys by the ladies. It's a good party. We are in high spirits. Our friends say they will miss us, but they promise to visit.

'I've always wanted to visit Ireland,' says one friend. 'Before I die.' This friend is a sensible and kind and intelligent person and not someone suffering, as far as we know, from any immediately life-threatening illness. But to visit Ireland before she dies – it's almost as if Ireland were Mecca, or Jerusalem, a place of pilgrimage, to which true believers are required to make Hajj once in a lifetime, to get right with God, and to experience for themselves the craic and the Guinness, and the long winding roads, and the lack of exotic fruit and vegetables in the outlying areas. Only the very lucky or the very devout actually get to live there, in such a sacred place. In deciding to move to Ireland, therefore, it's as if we have become holy. It is a brave decision, and to be respected. And it'll be nice for the children, like a trip to Disneyland.

Ireland in the English imagination remains a place of refuge and fantasy, one of those places – like the south of France and Tuscany – which it is imagined remains unspoilt by the chain coffee-shops and the endless malls and the ring-roads that have ruined Arnoldian England. Our image of Ireland – an image cherished and clutched as tight to the chests of us English as our pints of real ale – allows us to imagine, in the darkness and warmth of that London pub, that our new lives will no longer consist merely of mundane and tiresome work, of the endless domestic tasks of the English suburbs, but of endless banter, of the attending of the weddings and funerals of eccentric relatives, and the wandering of sandy beaches, whilst all the time being able to enjoy the benefits of a growing European economy and the sound of the curlew's song.

But then, before our friends' glasses are set back down to stain the bar, we go and spoil everything.

For the Ireland we are moving to happens to be Northern Ireland.

There is a stunned silence. Time seems to stop. We are no longer holy. And we are no longer wise. The only sound to be heard is of the ripping of cut-price Ryanair tickets.

It's as if we have played a cruel trick on our nearest and dearest, like the mischievous uncle who points out a beautiful bird high in the sky, and then slaps you around the head as you look up: the oldest trick in the book. The question that goes unvoiced in the silence is as clear and as insistent as it is utterly disbelieving. Why?

My wife, who is from County Down, is pregnant with our third child. We live in a tiny two-bedroom flat in west London. Neither of us has any great prospects. We have no savings, no nest egg, no garden, no plan. So we have decided to risk everything and to start all over again, and Northern Ireland seems like a good place to do it. It is a cheap place to live. The worst of the Troubles – surely – is over. I want to write. My wife wants to try something else, somewhere else. There's family.

Things do not get off to a good start.

As far as I can remember the last you see of England as you leave Liverpool docks is a chemical works – you smell bitumen and the sea, and cooked dinners from the boat's kitchen, and there's a huge sign, each letter about the size of a man, the last words you read leaving England. The sign reads HAZARDOUS AREA. Maybe these signs are up all around the coast of England, I don't know. Maybe they are unique to Liverpool.

I'm on the night crossing – it's cheaper. The boat is juddering and my celebratory pint in the bar seems to have completely obliterated my perspective and after the six-hour drive, having left my wife behind with the children – they're coming over later on the plane – I begin to feel a little shaky, and the waves and the currents and eddies down below seem to look like the veins in a vast slab of meat. (In fact, I am uncomfortably reminded of the fatty beef in gravy which constituted the main course of the four-course dinner – included in the price of the ticket for the crossing on the ferry – and which I have just enjoyed down below in the company of my fellow passengers).

We seem to spend an eternity at the lock gates, waiting to leave England, waiting for the levels to equalise, and my Guinness and my stomach to settle, and then finally we're into open sea. I wave goodbye to no one in particular and make my way down to the cabin, where I can't get to sleep and I lie awake, listening to the rushing of blood in my head and the throbbing of the engines.

A man knocks on the door at 4.30 a.m. and tells me to wake up, which is not necessary, I'm awake already. We're in Belfast. We've arrived. I can't face the cooked breakfast – which lacks a little of the crispness that one requires from bacon, or from toast – and instead I have one of the remaining mince pies and a slice of Christmas cake left over from my mum's in England. I eat them staring up at the big yellow Harland and Wolff cranes – my father-in-law used to work here in the shipyard, so the place already feels like home. I'm not a welder myself – my wife always says that I have little girl's hands – but Belfast in the morning light looks so small and so malleable and it glows so red and I am feeling so invincible, fortified by the mince pie, it's as though I could scoop it all up in the palm of my gloved hand, and beat the place into shape.

Then it's down to the car waiting to disembark, and when I start up the engine it stalls. This is never a happy sound but it is a sound particularly unwelcome when you have a couple of hundred Ulstermen riding in white vans queuing up behind you, yelling and honking their horns. Suddenly I'm no longer feeling invincible. Suddenly I'm feeling like a little Englishman stuck at the top of a ramp unable to enter into a country where I don't belong. But, there's no going back now, I have no other home to go to, so I keep turning the engine over and eventually the car starts up and I'm off through the docks, looking for a road out of Belfast, around the coast, and on into County Down. I retune the radio. The Talks – as always – are in crisis.

I've arranged to pick up the keys from the estate agent at 9.30.

'I'm just over on the boat from England,' I tell them.

'Is that right?' they say.

I stop off at my in-laws for a quick cup of coffee, and then it's down to the new house, the keys heavy in my pocket.

This is our first house – it's been flats up until now, and mostly rented accommodation, so I've never really had to give a second thought to things like plumbing, and roofs, and wiring. I own no fuse-wire, and no buckets – we don't even possess a broom, or a mop, or a cafetière, and these are all things I'm going to need over the next few weeks, along with my chequebook, and a large roll of cash, when the central heating packs up, and the pipes start leaking, and the drains block, and there is raw sewage running down the side of the house, and then the starter motor goes on the car, and the exhaust falls off and a joiner turns up and takes our money for materials and never returns.

But on that first morning I don't know about any of that – that's all to come. For the moment, I'm happy just to get the kettle from a box in the car, and make my first cup of tea at home in Ireland. Northern Ireland. I treat myself to two sugars, and the last of my mum's mince pies from England and as I brush away the crumbs I catch my reflection in the glass of the front door – our first, our very own front door – and what's really amazing is that it's me standing there, and I'm still recognisable, even to myself. My wife and children will be arriving in the afternoon. All I have to do now is wait, and maybe unpack a few boxes.

The town where we live is just outside Belfast. It is a typical scabby Irish seaside town, a place that once boasted piers and dance-halls, and bathing booths, and which now boasts its own small ring-road, an ASDA, a Heritage Centre, and mostly charity shops on the two main streets – Main Street and High Street. There are plans, they say, for another multi-storey car-park, to help regenerate the town centre.

It's a place that is good of its kind, but that no one would particularly want to visit, and that sensitive teenagers long to leave, or at least to write graffiti on, the kind of place you might like to start from or end up, but which you wouldn't necessarily imagine yourself spending the years in between. It is everywhere and nowhere. It is perfectly anonymous.

It turns out to have suited us rather well.

My wife gets a job and then I get a job, and the children soon lose their London accents and start to sound like … well, to me of course, raised in England in the 1970s, they sound like Gerry Adams and Iain Paisley. Of course, there are incidents, but nothing nearly as bad as when we were first married in the late 1980s and we were living in Belfast, before we left for London, vowing never to return: all the times I was suspected of being a soldier; the times I was told to '**** off' back to England; the times I was refused service in shops and bars; the time the man in the flat opposite collected all our post for six months, and then returned it to us, opened; the time we visited friends in Derry and we went for a drink and I was worried whether or not I'd be safe and they said 'Sure, you'll be fine – just as long as you don't open your mouth,' and they weren't joking. This time it's all much more normal, much more polite, much more sedate. The only real trouble is when someone rings one night and tells us that he knows where we live and that he's going to come and kill us. My wife – a journalist – says not to worry. If they ring and tell you they're coming to kill you, they're not really coming to kill you, they're just trying to scare you. I don't find this reassuring.

But twenty years on, more or less, and things have worked out okay. Living here has allowed me to become who I am. I left England unemployed and within a few months of arriving I was a published author: exactly a week after we arrived a publisher rang and said they were interested in publishing my book. I'd been trying for years to get a book published: living here seemed instantly to bring me good luck. And it allowed me to cheat my natural fate. The week before we left London I was offered a weekly column writing about film for the *Sunday Telegraph*. I wrote precisely one review and then explained that I'd have to be travelling over from Belfast each week to see the films and they dropped me like a hot potato. I never heard from the editor again. Northern Ireland was just a step too far, a step beyond, and so it saved me from myself: I could have been just a hack, stuck forever in the screening rooms of Soho.

In the twenty years I've been here, Northern Ireland has produced some great writers. I'm not one of them, obviously, and never will be. I wasn't born here. I don't belong. But I have been tolerated, and left alone to go about my business how I see fit – and no writer could ask for more. I'm glad I made it before I die.

Ian Sansom is a novelist and critic. He is the author of thirteen books of fiction and non-fiction, including the Mobile Library series. The most recent book in his latest series, The County Guides (Harper Collins) is *Westmorland Alone* (2016). He is the Director of the Oscar Wilde Centre at Trinity College Dublin.

A Local Row: The Irish Writer as Martial Artist

Pat Boran

Good writing is always about more than it first appears. However fascinating, the purely autobiographical or anecdotal has to connect with a wider, communal experience. Patrick Kavanagh, for one, knew it when he wrote about Homer making *The Iliad* 'from such a local row'.

When it comes to local rows, at the risk of being entirely too literal, my experience in the arena of the literary arts might be said to comprise just two all-too-real physical blows, the first received, the second delivered. These are the anecdotes, the autobiographical details; what I hope to clarify here (for myself as for others) is their wider significance.

The Blow Received…
As Dublin City Writer-in-Residence in 1998, employed by what was then Dublin Corporation, I was one Saturday morning facilitating a workshop of twenty or so participants in a room in a premises on Parnell Square. After what I thought had been a gently provocative exchange of opinions, intended to help one of the participants see further possibilities in something he'd written, the gentleman in question crossed the room to where I sat and, without warning, threw a fist straight at my face, fortunately making only glancing contact.

I had, as the saying goes, touched a nerve. And though I was slightly shaken by the experience and still had the afternoon session to go, I was also secretly pleased that the other participants in the room (some of them only occasional writers) had witnessed the fact that making poems – this doodling on the backs of napkins or shopping lists or beermats, as many of them saw it – was, and should be, at whatever level of commitment or achievement, a serious activity.

Far from exhausting me, facilitating hundreds of writing workshops up and down the country, many of them at the Irish Writers Centre, seemed – in the years before I had kids, at least – a source of energy and gave me at least one of the things I believe every writer needs: a constantly challenged perspective. Reading provides it, of course; but for those of us who know that it is more popular than elements of the media are willing to recognise, seeing people actually rediscover the power of poetry is a buzz and inspiration like few others.

Out of that residency emerged what would become the Dublin Writers Festival. Intended as a friendly interrogation of Joyce's dominance of the literary sphere, on Bloomsday 1998 Dublin Corporation Arts Office, under Arts Officer Jack Gilligan, presented a free event of contemporary poetry and fiction at St Ann's Church in Dawson Street. In truth we were only part surprised when the queue went right down the street and around the corner into Molesworth Street, stopping a number of notable Joyceans in their tracks. It took two years to properly establish the festival – with the support of the Arts Council, the Irish Writers Centre, Poetry Ireland, and a number of other organisations – but when it did take off we determined to keep in mind the success of that early combination of prose and poetry, of homage to and, at the same time, gentle disturbance of the status quo.

… The Blow Delivered

Within a few years, the small festival already had a heady energy all its own. As Programme Director, for much of the year I was making international contacts, corresponding with writers and publishers and agencies, reading (a lot), managing the website, and, when the balloon at last went up, meeting and greeting and, in many cases, introducing the events themselves, a role which I think is one of the signs of a properly curated programme. We had a number of enthusiastic volunteers, and excellent support from the Arts Office team, but, some evenings I inevitably found myself dashing between venues, a small backpack containing the box office takings of the previous events on my back.

On this particular June evening in 2002 I was trying to catch up with former US poet laureate Charles Simic, whom I had just interviewed before an appreciative audience at the Project Arts Centre. (Simic is very much the poet of the witching hour, or, at least, of the uncanny revelation. His poems are often inhabited by loners stopped in their tracks by surprise encounters with what passes for the normal world.) Easy and warm, as he'd been the only other time I had met him at a translation festival in Paris years before, he had gone on ahead to a designated restaurant on South Great George's Street while I helped ensure things were ready in the auditorium for the next event of the evening. As Simic is something of a personal hero, and I was delighted he had agreed to come, I was both walking on air and lumbering in quicksand. My enthusiasm for the festival meant that, in my half dozen years in the driving seat, I ended up seriously ill on three occasions after it, with both pneumonia and pleurisy, before calling it a day. Adrenaline should never be underestimated as a productive force, but those involved in the arts in Ireland know all too well the dangers of overwork and exhaustion. Though I was greatly looking forward to continuing the conversation with Simic, I was also looking forward to getting home later that night and sleeping the sleep of 'The Dead'.

It was at the point where I was just reaching for the handle of the restaurant door that someone grabbed me from behind. I first felt the tug in the straps of the backpack, the almost electric charge of it shooting across my shoulders and into my neck. When I think of it now, all these years later, I find it hard to credit that I did not simply freeze, clench myself against the attack. As it happened, before I even knew *what* had happened, I had spun on my heel and, as I'd learned to do at a short-lived kung fu class twenty years before, threw a rabbit punch automatically to my rear.

My fist connected. In fact, it was already coming back to perch just under my chin, cocked and ready to be launched again, before I felt the impact. And then I saw, too late, the object of my assault. Standing in the street before me was M, one of my closest friends, who had emigrated some years before and was, as I would later discover, home now for a brief sojourn. In the company of my younger brother following half in laughter, half in horror, across the street, M had spotted me there with my hunted expression and absent gaze, and decided to play a trick. Now he stood in front of me, tipsy enough to be shielded from the worst of the pain, blood running from his nose down his face onto his shirt. 'Well, [expletive deleted],' he was saying, 'Howaya, boy?'

It would have been hard to tell which of us was the most stunned. When did he get home? How was the festival going? Was he sure it wasn't broken? I could hardly think. And all of this through a hunk of blood-soaked tissue until I had to follow Simic into dinner and my brother led our wounded friend back to his nearby apartment for a wash and change of clothes.

*

So what does all this tell me then, this odd, long-drawn-out altercation with imaginary enemies, this disjointed exchange of blows over a period of five years in two separate locations in the city, the first before a small group of emerging writers in a house on a square named for an Irish patriot; the second, with one of my literary heroes only yards away, on a public thoroughfare named for a third-century Roman soldier and Christian martyr (and not for one of the former English kings, as would have been symbolically much more convenient). To get to the heart of the matter, it is often necessary to expend a good deal of time and energy rambling unprofitably around the margins of meaning!

It tells me at least that the image many of us have of the writer's life bears little resemblance to the reality; that many writers make a living from activities that take them away from their desks, for better or worse. It reminds me that for every prestigious festival appearance there are rooms full of potential, beginning, fledgling writers – and readers – and that it is writing that unites rather than separates them. It reminds me that we are not all cut out to be writers, or perhaps festival organisers. It reminds me that some of the best events of those early years of the Dublin Writers Festival combined poetry and prose, Irish and international writers, established names and those who found an audience because of proximity, luck, chance or the vagaries of flight connections between Dublin and wherever they'd come from. It reminds me that the best festivals, and publishers, and broadcasters, keep that in mind. (Some of our best events were with Arab writers, Nordic writers,

French writers, writers whose inclusion on the programme had aroused the curiosity of a loyal but highly discerning literary audience ... They taught me that we rely too much on our connections with the UK and the US, that too often we indulge reputation at the expense of experiment and innovation.)

It is hard to ignore the fact that, after twenty-five years of the Irish Writers Centre (and the many improvements in our support for writers and writing in that time), to our shame in this country we continue to undervalue the literary arts. While championing Irish writing on the world stage, we continue to expect small presses for instance to thrive on the equivalent of a single salary in almost any other area of endeavour. And we continue to show so little interest in the vitality of writing that comes from elsewhere in the world, in whatever language it originates.

That proto-festival event on Bloomsday 1998 was intended to remind residents and visitors to Dublin city that literature, as Joyce himself well knew, was not something that happened only in the glorious past but an ever-evolving tradition with which every new generation must wrestle before making its own. Bernard Shaw once quipped about Shakespeare, 'It would positively be a relief to me to dig him up and throw stones at him.' Rather than run and hide away from such robust criticism, I am certain Joyce, if he were around, would have wanted the writers and writers' organisations that have bloomed in his wake similarly to assault him in turn, not as a way to deny his achievement or 'bring him down to size' – that knee-jerk Irish tendency – but as evidence of true engagement. We have an enviable reputation as an island where writing is important, treasured even, a place where – sticks and stones aside – 'words are all we have' as Beckett claimed. Now and then, for any writer worth their salt (a passing nod to the Romans there and their military salaries), that's got to be worth fighting for.

Pat Boran was born in Portlaoise in 1963. He has published a dozen books of poetry and prose, and, as editor at Dedalus Press, edited numerous anthologies. A former presenter of *The Poetry Programme* on RTÉ radio, he has edited *Poetry Ireland Review* and was Programme Director of the Dublin Writers Festival. His most recent book is *Waveforms: Bull Island Haiku*. He is a member of Aosdána.

Then and Now

Joseph O'Connor

My first short story, 'Last of the Mohicans', was published in 1989. It was written in a not entirely attractive suburb of south-east London. New Cross had escaped bombing during the Second World War, probably because the Luftwaffe looked down among the alleluias of sirens and assumed it had been bombed already.

Thither I went in 1986 when I dropped out of a doctorate at Oxford University, where I'd gone after five years studying History and then something calling itself Anglo-Irish Literature at UCD. I don't know why I accepted the place at Oxford, I disliked academia, longed to be writing. I suppose I felt unable to turn down the opportunity. But my heart wasn't in it. I found, once a Friday evening descended on the dreaming spires that I was hopping on the train to London. Monday mornings rarely saw me hurrying back to the Bodleian Library. After six or eight months, I blew.

I moved with my then girlfriend into a flat which actually *was* a garret, 259E Lewisham Way. She worked as a sub-editor for an educational publishing company, and I did freelance journalism, bits of reviewing, whatever came along. It was an era when you could be broke in London and it didn't matter much. Five pounds bought you into the Comedy Store on a Sunday night. A tube journey was forty pence and a gallery was free.

My girlfriend would go out to work in the mornings and I'd sit there concocting literary gibberish all day or waiting for the phone to ring. My desk was halfway up the stairs, on the landing below the kitchen, with no window, no heat, no natural light and no chair. (I sat on an upended beer crate.) If you put a plant on that desk, which my girlfriend sometimes did, it died within a week.

At the time, I was just outgrowing the baleful influence of Magical Realism on my writing. There is no writer I love more than Gabriel García Márquez, but he should come with a government health warning, especially to the young. It was an era in which I felt that any self-respecting novel must contain a fair sprinkling of talking leopards and fifteen-page sentences. You can get up to that kind of auld craic when you're writing about Colombia, but my own early attempts at novels and short stories were set in Dun Laoghaire, where leopards were not among the wildlife. I must have known in my heart that no good would come of this, and it didn't. It was One Hundred Years of Crapitude.

Partly to drive Magical Realism out of my head, and partly because I found them glorious to read, I had become interested in writers like Raymond Carver, Tobias Wolff, Richard Ford and Richard Yates, the so-called Dirty Realists. My stories became peopled with characters who did very little except drinking, getting divorced or conversing laconically in trailer parks. One of the greatest short stories I know, Richard Ford's 'Optimists', became my model. How wretchedly, abysmally bad were my rip-offs of that story. I try hard never to think about anything I wrote in that era, but every time I do, I know it is not possible to die of shame.

Every day I used to traipse down to the post box on Lewisham High Street and send off my envelopes full of short stories about trailer parks, beer and jails. By the time I got back to the flat, last week's mailings would have been returned. They grinned damply up at me from the WELCOME mat, my horrible unwanted children. Daddy, we're home. Abandon hope.

I had no friends who were writers, indeed knew no writers at all, had little idea as to how the whole business of publishing worked, had never met anyone in the book trade. I had spent five years studying literature in UCD but had never met a writer as part of that (or any other) process. The reader will find it difficult to credit, but in all that time in Joyce's alma mater there was never a single reading or author visit, aside from one that my friends and I organised, a reading by the poet Michael Hartnett. Apart from Hartnett, the only other writer I had ever seen was Hugh Leonard, who lived in a mansion with a view of the sea on Coliemore Road, Dalkey, and drove slowly about Dun Laoghaire in his stately Rolls Royce, silently rubbing it in. Even then, I suspected he wasn't typical.

In desperation, I got a job at the Nicaragua Solidarity Campaign in London. Shortly afterwards, because I had been nominated by Colm Tóibín, for whom I had worked at *Magill* magazine in Dublin, I got accepted to go to Annaghmakerrig. I have been fortunate in my career to have won literary prizes from time to time and to have had bestselling books. None of them will compare to getting accepted to go to Annaghmakerrig. I felt I had won the lottery.

Annaghmakerrig was run by Bernard and Mary Loughlin at the time and visiting writers and artists paid what they could afford. I will be eternally grateful to Bernard Loughlin for accepting the very best payment I could offer: thirty pounds for three weeks. The food was delicious and plentiful, the house was austerely beautiful, if a bit draughty in the storms of that November, but most of all it was a place that meant something. Following the terms of its former owner Sir Tyrone Guthrie's will, it had been repurposed as a retreat for Ireland's artists and writers.

During those three dark weeks in a bleak Monaghan November, I think I became a writer. Simply put, given the monasticism there was nothing else to do. With only myself and two other guests (both men), the house was almost empty, the days were long and lonesome, the nights a succession of damp multi-mile walks to the nearest pub, an unattractive establishment, called, unattractively, The Black Kesh. It was all a long way from Hemingway and his buddies quaffing martinis in Venice. You sort of asked yourself, 'Can I survive this life?'

The house was like a Victorian backstage in a dream, full of masks, stuffed animal-heads, bits of theatrical props, dusty paintings, and it was said to be haunted by a lady called Bunty who had been a servant to the Guthries in the old days. Each room boasted shelves stuffed with books, so heavy that the shelves were bowed, and if you pulled down a volume you might find an old letter or theatre programme in its pages. The garden was wild, overgrown, and the surrounding drumlins were stark. You felt what Kavanagh had been getting at about the stony grey soil of Monaghan burgling his bank of youth. As venues for forging a lifetime commitment to writing go, Annaghmakerrig was second to none. Indeed, I can never visit that remarkable place without experiencing the bittersweet tug in the heart that accompanies all memories of transition.

Some years later, I won the Hennessy Award. My first novel, a truly terrible book called *Cowboys and Indians*, was accepted for publication by the heroic Christopher Sinclair-Stevenson. Critics who should have beaten it to death were kind to it, I think because nobody had written about characters like this before. It became a number one bestseller in Ireland and was shortlisted for the Whitbread Prize. I got invited to Listowel Writers' Week, where people were extraordinarily supportive. And I realised something was happening in Ireland.

Growing up, it had always seemed to me that Ireland had no living literary culture and never would have. This was why all Irish writers of my generation looked to London to get published. We realised the homeland was a joke. But suddenly things were changing. Suddenly, there were readings, festivals, book clubs, readers' groups, literary magazines.

Someone should write a doctoral thesis on the massive influence of the Dawson Street Waterstones bookstore on this little renaissance. John Boyne and Paul Murray both worked there, but so did Paul Baggaley and Cormac Kinsella, who turned the space into a regular venue for readings and other events. All a literary scene needs is a nexus to cohere around, and that's what Waterstones provided. It meant you could meet writers, ask them questions, talk. Memory is a seductive and sometimes misleading sweetheart, but in my mind there were events happening in Waterstones every night of the week. You felt you were part of something.

(My all-time favourite reading was in the autumn of 1994, when my book *The Secret World of the Irish Male* was published. Essentially, this is a book about getting drunk and falling over, but it also contained some journalism, if you could call it that, which I had written from that year's soccer World Cup, which happened in the USA. The book went well, and my reading was thronged, after which we all went to the pub. It was a special night, because the Pope was publishing a book the next day, and the marketing people at Waterstones had decided to open the shop at one minute past midnight to cope with the demand. So, after closing time, we all tottered back to the shop at midnight, to see the vast queue of people lining down Dawson Street to buy the Pope's book. You're right. Ireland has changed.)

I think it was easier to become a writer at that time. Advances were healthy to high. London publishing was interested in Ireland. Last September, at the University of Limerick, where I teach Creative Writing, the great Richard Ford came to give the students a reading. Obviously, the first question from the audience was 'what advice would you have for a young writer?' He said, 'If you can possibly talk yourself out of it, do.' It was meant as a joke (I think), but I knew what he meant. The landscape is tougher now.

For all their mendacity, greed, cunning, wickedness, malice, vengefulness, hypocrisy and sharp practice, the dodgy Fianna Fáilers often seemed to think literature was A Good Thing, like dentistry or being kind to old donkeys. They didn't always have a lot of interest in it themselves, but they were happy to know it was going on. Indeed, the existence of Irish Literature dovetailed with the imperiously Stalinist sense of patriotism they had, not to mention their other grandiosities. It was something we were *better* at than the English, like cricket to West Indians. And so, literature went into the place where little fripperies like having rat-free schools should have been, in the nation's conception of itself.

It was a Fianna Fáil idea to introduce tax exemption on creative earnings, the cheapest and most effective form of subsidising the arts that any European government has ever contrived, and it allowed many, many writers, including me, to live and raise a family by their work. Yes, the annual earnings of most Irish writers wouldn't have paid for one of Mr Haughey's handmade shirts, but still, fair's fair, he did *something*. Elements within the recent Fine Gael–Labour coalition, on the other hand, would cheerfully have shut down every artist and writer in Ireland if they thought it would save ten bob.

And yet, it is surely the most exciting young generation of Irish and Ireland-based writers, ever. Think of the debut books we've seen in the last five years. Donal Ryan. Paul Lynch. Gavin Corbett. Thomas Morris, Rob Doyle. Vanessa Ronan. Susan Stairs. Austin Duffy. Colin Barrett. Audrey Magee. What a constellation! How has this happened?

There are a number of factors. *The Stinging Fly. The Dublin Review.* Writing.ie. The emergence and rapid growth of creative writing programmes in Irish universities and other institutions. Tramp Press. Fish Publishing. Liz Reapy's *30 Under 30* anthology. Dublin's annual One City One Book programme. The extraordinary self-reinvention of libraries in Ireland. The surge in indigenous publishing and in the establishing of Irish-based branches of the major London houses. The ongoing rejuvenation and reinvention of the Hennessy New Irish Writing page. More festivals than ever before, and so many of them including teaching. Competitions. Open mic nights. New journals like my current favourite, the magnificent *Banshee*. And of course, that precious, essential, truly special oasis that is the Irish Writers Centre in Dublin. Whenever I bring a group of my students there, they can hardly bear to leave. And I know why: this is a place where writing is valued. I don't exaggerate when I say that if something as wonderful as the Irish Writers Centre had existed when I was a teenager, I probably wouldn't have emigrated.

But there's a paradox, too. For all the increase in literary activity and the remarkable efforts that support it, it's much harder to get published now than it was in my youth and this has led to an intensive raising of work-rates and standards.

Ireland has its cohort of literary readers but this can be (and usually is) exaggerated. Literature is not especially valued by most Irish people, and why should it be? For five years, I wrote a radio diary on RTÉ One's *Drivetime* programme, and the only times I ever received truly hostile emails were when I wrote diaries suggesting greater funding for the arts. I think it's really important that writers realise this. Whole swathes of the public don't care. We in the bubble think they do, or should, or might, or must, but they don't and that's not going to be changing any time soon. One of the little sustaining dishonesties we sell ourselves in Ireland is that we're a fierce literary country. We're not, we never were, and we're probably not going to be. Indeed, when it comes to the general question of writing within our broader society, things are very much worse than they have ever been. My father, uncles and aunts, all of whom left school at thirteen, had been taught to write beautiful, clear, graceful English. As must be obvious to anyone dealing with students, the best-fed, best-clothed, most highly educated generation of Irish people in history find it very hard to write what they mean. That has implications for everything, from politics to happiness.

When I was a young Irish writer myself, major publishers would take a chance on you, long-term. That doesn't happen so much anymore. In order to break through these days, you'd want to be offering something drop-dead special, like Sara Baume, Danielle McLaughlin or Lisa McInerney are doing. It's scary how good you need to be to get noticed now. Yet, somehow new Irish writers keep appearing and getting published and winning prizes, doing their work, telling the story. I don't know where they find their amazing fortitude and courage but, as a reader, I'm thrilled that they do.

Joseph O'Connor is the author of eight novels, *Cowboys and Indians, Desperadoes, The Salesman, Inishowen, Star of the Sea, Redemption Falls, Ghost Light* and *The Thrill of it All*, two collections of short stories, *True Believers* and *Where Have You Been?*, and a number of stage plays and non-fiction books. He is McCourt Professor of Creative Writing at the University of Limerick and is an Irish Writers Centre Ambassador.

Notes on the Manufactory

Mary O'Malley

In a commencement address at Ann Arbor, Michigan, in December 1988 the poet Joseph Brodsky had the following advice for students:

> *The purpose is to enable you to articulate yourselves as fully and precisely as possible; in a word, the purpose is your balance. For the accumulation of things not spelled out, not properly articulated, may result in neurosis.*

This advice bears examination in the light of the fudge and gibberish that became the accepted language of bureaucrats, politicians and bankers over the past twenty-five years in Ireland.

When language is debased, the scale of values is hard to set. Words can mean anything, lose their precision, and become white noise. The situation is exacerbated when there is no context in which to examine, or even name, what is happening, at least not in the public domain. It's arguable that it is the function of the university as well as the artist to insist on informed debate, and I would agree, but at any rate, sometime early in the late nineties, public discourse, or what passed for it, coarsened and Yeats's somewhat high-handed assertion that '*Ireland is ruined by abstractions ... ill-breeding of the mind ... every thought made in some manufactory and with the mark on it of its wholesale origin ...*', which I disagreed with on first reading, seemed now to be disturbingly accurate. It is that prophetic reference to branding that struck me most.

Culture itself is now discussed more in terms of hotel beds than content. Literary festivals are franchises worth millions. There is a 'culture industry' and where you have an industry, you have an industrial mindset, hell-bent on upping the production of widgets. I learned that much in a year spent 'studying' economics.

Let's take an arbitrary year. In May 1997 Mary Harney became Tánaiste and Bertie Ahern became Pope. That was a slip of the pen, but in a sense, felicitous, since money was the new God and Mr Ahern one of its main representatives on this bit of earth.

Later that summer, President Robinson met Pope John Paul II, Orangemen marched down Garvaghy Road and riots followed. On the 10th of October, at the general IRA army convention in Falcarragh, County Donegal, the majority supported the ceasefire. True to Brendan Behan's assertion that the first item on any Republican agenda is the split, the Real IRA was formed in November.

Clare won the All-Ireland hurling final in September, Neil Jordan's film *The Butcher Boy* was released. Based on the book by Patrick McCabe, it was about compassion as much as brutality. Ireland was reeling from stories of abuse of institutional power, particularly in the Catholic Church, which had lost its grip and any authority to discuss ethics or question social policy. On the abrogation of responsibility by the State and abuses of power by the judiciary, there was a disturbing lack of articulation, if not downright silence.

In what was termed 'the real world', the country was on the up, emigration was down, houses were being built, bought and sold, and life was good. Something called a starter home was invented and everybody under the age of thirty-five was expected to have one. Or two.

But something went wrong in the banking hive mind. The regulator didn't regulate. The bankers behaved like kids after too many sweeties. The gold got goldier, the whirligig spun too fast, it was all a bit psychedelic, an economy on acid.

To such money-drugged giants, the little people must have seemed like midges. Sometime around 2001, I heard a woman bedecked in gold on the phone to her friend: '*Oh yes, you'll be down for the Arts Festival. Sure it's grand. We're all going. We're as good as New York now.*' The arts had arrived.

Hospitals were falling apart but according to HSE spokespeople, progress (a dangerous word in the mouth of a bureaucrat) was always on the way. It would arrive when systems were put in place, and programmes were rolled out. The fact that people were dying on trolleys, homeless in streets, being let out of psychiatric units when their relatives begged to have them admitted, let out into rivers, into lakes, onto ropes seemed to have no effect on the those high up on their mountain where neither blame nor compassion could move them. Such a reality was forbidden in their language, and mention of it in ours was met with an aggressive stream of gobbledygook.

I began to re-read Kafka.

People began to believe they could change nothing. They began to lose faith in language because all they were told were lies and, furthermore, lies backed up by the threat of legal action.

Such a world is mad making and Ireland went mad. The middle classes had a nervous breakdown, buying hearse-like vehicles to transport their children, building 'architect designed' McMansions, second or fifth homes 'in Connemara' or Kerry or drought-ridden Cabo Verde, which put houses out of the reach of most locals, who were, in any case, in New York or Australia or, indeed, Berlin.

All sorts of gadgets fed the neurosis, all sorts of drugs were needed to keep it under control. Local pubs closed and rural Ireland had to be driven to drink, and home afterwards. Drinking shops, as Seamus Heaney sometimes called them, became giant Superpubs. There was no room for anything but superlatives in boom-time Ireland.

Ireland had become the perfect manifestation of Guy Debord's 'Spectacle', making a spectacle of itself in the eyes of those it wanted to impress, but the laugh was on us.

This is where I had hoped to hear the dissenting voices of artists crying stop, and there were some. Perhaps it was in the nature of a newly atomised place that we couldn't really hear one another. I cannot say because it was a time of isolation.

Small wonder I found it hard to write. There was an erosion of confidence, a drowning out of the tuning fork a poet needs to produce something other than merely formulaic verse. When the citizen is turned into a consumer, when everything is termed a hundred and one per cent by people making decisions that affect our lives, when prices and value part company, and you cannot get permission for one house but a developer can build fifty in the same field *'in the interests of the environment and current development policy,'* something has to give.

I don't know what any of this gibberish means but we all know what it led to.

History is full of such folly but it hits home when it is our own particular folly. We are all affected by the psychic energy around us. Ireland was in freefall and there was blanket denial. Any suggestion that we were going too far, that we were losing our children, in the grip of national neurosis was met with a very firm reprimand – did you want us back in poverty and failure? Were you, somehow, suspect? That was the atmosphere as I experienced it. It is a truism that when words are robbed of all meaning, something nasty is hiding behind the wall of noise.

Time and again I thought of the true nature of censorship. Section 31 and censorship had only been repealed in 1994. I wondered what damage it had done in terms of trust. I still wonder about the policeman in our heads, whether the one known as the devil hasn't been replaced by one more devious, less obvious. A new, approved plainclothes version, and all the more effective for that.

'You have to listen to thunder,' a boatman said to me on the quay in Roundstone, 'but you don't have to answer it back.' He meant, I think, keep your counsel but also your convictions. I found both very hard, and to write anything meaningful, surrounded by so much static seemed impossible. It became increasingly difficult *'to keep open the imagination's supply lines to the past'*, as Heaney put it. Or to hear a clear note.

But something always happens next.

The State, which has both stymied and sustained the artist in this country for many years now, can come to the rescue not by setting up more systems or festivals or many layered mechanisms, but by a simple gift of unfettered time. If that time is off the island, the better to see it clearly, then in my case at least, that is all to the good.

The artist repays the State by doing his work, by refracting and reflecting back a reality that does not bear the mark of a wholesale nature.

And that is the reason the State values, or should value, the artist. Both should beware the Manufactory.

I was in Letterfrack reading at Sea Week as I had done for twenty years, when John Joyce asked if I'd like to join the Celtic Explorer for a trip. I was delighted. I joined the ship in July 2007.

The big ship manoeuvred out of the docks in Galway, out the bay and down along the Clare coast, the Cliffs of Moher eerie and silent in the early morning. Passing the Skelligs was like seeing a slow-motion collage as they lined up, then coalesced, then separated. We sailed on, close to Carraig Aonair, Fastnet Rock, to work on a grid somewhere off West Cork, out of sight of land. I hadn't felt this safe since I was a child, so certain of being minded.

I loved the monastic rhythms of the ship, the reliance on values I believed in – a crew who did their jobs well and without fuss, scientists from four countries, a man whose father had been in charge of the Blacksod Lighthouse at the time of Dunkirk.

The scientists from all over Europe were searching for dinoflagellates, microscopic creatures, certain species of which could destroy mussels in the commercial beds along the coasts of Europe. A Spanish scientist explained: '*That one, he is red, and bad.*'

Real work. Several of the crew were lads from Donegal, kept from the fishing by EU regulations and Irish bureaucracy. A whole culture has been wantonly destroyed by mindless legislation and nobody in authority wanted to know. It happens to be my culture, but that is hardly the point. I had some interesting conversations with crew members about EU policy and burning boats.

I was reminded of George Seferis' poem 'The Argonauts':

They were good lads, the comrades.
They did not grumble …
…
No one remembers them. Justice.

Early one morning on the bridge, sitting at a little table designated by the ship's Master, secure in the monastic order of the ship, I started the long sequence of poems I would finish in Rue des Irlandais, Paris in what had once been some trainee priest's cell. The subsequent collection would be called *Valparaiso* after the poem, itself a translation into the Irish from the English. It was a meditation on what mattered, on what was left. In some ways, you might say I found my country there, as had Joyce and Beckett before me. The courtyard in the Irish College was full of light. Perhaps it helped to be in a country where art and enlightenment were words that still held currency, where the word 'republic' could be spoken without shame or fear of misunderstanding.

On Sunday, 28 November 2010, members of the Troika took over the seats the Taoiseach and two Cabinet ministers had just vacated. The journalists assembled were shocked. There was, said one, an icy chill. The party was well and truly over.

I was in England that night. I cried with anger and grief, surprising myself, since I had known from the start that hubris was waiting in the wings. But I hadn't imagined this particular triple incarnation.

I wrote one incantatory poem. It was a little *ránta ráiméis* but it was also an invocation. I only mention it because it invoked the constitution which had, in effect, been nullified. What eight hundred years of colonisation had failed to complete, we had managed in less than ten. Of course it was not that simple. It never is but the Barbarians had triumphed and 'we' had invited them in. 'We' had managed nothing: a small circle of gamblers and crooks had taken control of Ireland Inc, as the papers happily termed us, played roulette with our 'futures', and lost. We paid, and are still paying a very high price.

The bank bailout of November 2010 cost us 64 billion, give or take a few experts' oscillations. I have no idea what that means, but it's a lot of fingers and toes. A lot of used-up futures. My own bank, AIB, where one manager said to me, when I went to ask for a stay of execution on my repayments, 'Can you not take in a lodger?' was given 21 billion. Perhaps they should have taken in a few lodgers themselves.

'Articulation,' writes Brodsky later in his Ann Arbor commencement speech, 'lags behind experience. That doesn't go well with the psyche.'

Now, they are telling us it's over, the past. We're on the up again. 1916 is a movie, a TV series. It has been sanitised, marketed, converted into breathless spin. The harm has been taken out of it but this was not some film script.

The proclamation of 1916 was a hot document. All the men who signed it were shot. It was drafted by a poet, who knew the temperature and intention of what he wrote, and signed by men who understood that they were, as Michael Collins is reputed to have said regarding another, very different document, signing their own death warrants.

I honour them, simply and without comment. I am grateful for what they did. This anniversary year could be an occasion for some of that articulation that Brodsky mentions. Surely a hundred years is a long enough lag?

I believe we have a country that was worth the sacrifices that were made a hundred years ago, and the many before that. The best of it is among the best there is, and the worst no worse than most places. I celebrate the sweet accidents that can still happen in Ireland because of the real culture that has survived, the rare moments that can lighten and sustain and cannot be made in any factory, cultural or industrial.

On a Saturday afternoon in late May, in Peig's pub in Collinamuck in Moycullen, Frankie Gavin, Johnny Connolly and his son, Johnny Óg gathered with Brian Bourke and a few friends to play, and listen, to tunes. This was no performance, but a get-together of peers. There is mutual regard on such occasions.

The sun shone, we sat outside, the rugby was on inside the pub. There were several tunes, and reports from the match. Connacht was ahead, still ahead ten minutes later. Earlier, I had noticed a child of about eight listening to the music. She had a grave face, as some children have at that age. She got her little trainer violin to show Frankie. He admired it and asked her would she play something, whereupon she gave her careful rendition of 'Three Blind Mice' and was asked for another tune. So she played 'The Old Grey Goose is Dead', accompanied by Frankie Gavin, got a round of applause from the ten or so people listening and the session went on.

There was a break and we moved inside. One of the musicians said, 'Give 'em all a ball and it'll be over in two minutes.'

After the Connacht victory, we were alone again and moved to a table under the window, asking for a few more tunes and a song. And

Johnny Connolly and his son and Frankie Gavin played a stately version of 'Cherish the Ladies', a lovely rollicking 'Siad a Mhamó' and 'Na Ceannabháin Bhána', Martina Goggins sang 'a bawdy song' which was restrained and made everyone laugh. There were jokes and asides in Irish and English. As the musicians played the last few sets, the sky from the window was darkening, and the light gave their faces the cast of a Rembrandt painting.

A few more tunes, and home.

That is the real celebration of the Rising, plucking *'till time and times are done / The silver apples of the moon, / The golden apples of the sun.'*

Mary O'Malley was born in Connemara and educated at University College Galway. She lived in Lisbon for eight years and taught at the Universidade Nova there. She taught on the MA programmes for Writing and Education in the Arts at NUI Galway for ten years, held the Chair of Irish Studies at Villanova University in 2013, and has held residencies in Paris, Tarragona, New York, as well as in Derry, Belfast and Mayo. She has published seven books of poetry, the most recent *Valparaiso* arising out of her residency on the national marine research ship. She is a member of Aosdána.

Passionate Midnights, Perfect Jars

Lia Mills

Depend on it, somewhere a poet is wasting
his sweet uncluttered metres on the obvious

emblem instead of the real thing.
Instead of sulpha we shall have hyssop dipped
in the wild blood of the unblemished lamb,
so every day the language gets less

for the task and we are less with the language.
Eavan Boland, 'The Journey' (The Journey and Other Poems)[1]

The language gets less for the task. We are less with the language.

i. the task

'The Journey' was published thirty years ago. The world has changed but language is still in trouble. Not because of hyssop dipped in the wild blood of the unblemished lamb – we should be so lucky – but because words themselves are under threat.

Anyone in possession of a mobile phone knows the temptations (and, let's face it, the joys) of SMS/textese, the abbreviations that lead us to compress words or drop them altogether, to import emoji in the interests of speed. What harm? you ask. Here's another crank, resisting

---

[1]Boland, Eavan. *The Journey and Other Poems*, Carcanet Press (Manchester), 1987.

the natural evolution of language, a dinosaur who wants to keep us all on guard against the split infinitive or the wanton deployment of the spliced comma. It's true that I am an apostrophe nerd, that I'm fond of the semicolon and have been known to flirt with subordinate and conditional clauses but that doesn't mean I'm opposed to word play, experiment or change. Language is alive; like the rest of us it must evolve or die. People use emoji as shorthand, punctuation, visual puns and private code and in that sense they are as effective a form of communication as any. Shorthand has its place, and yes, of course it's useful, even efficient, to key in a quick c u l8r (imo). But I'm talking about something more basic, more sinister.

The landscape and travel writer Robert Macfarlane is one of several writers, including Margaret Atwood and Andrew Motion, who wrote a collective letter to the Oxford University Press protesting deletions from the 2007 edition of the Oxford Junior Dictionary. In 'A Word to the Wild', an article written for the *National Trust Magazine*,[2] Macfarlane tells us that the deletions included:

> *acorn, adder, ash, beech, bluebell, buttercup, catkin, conker, cowslip, crocus, cygnet, dandelion, fern, hazel, heather, heron, horse chestnut, ivy, kingfisher, lark, minnow, newt, otter, pasture, poppy, starling, sycamore, wren* and *willow.* Among the words taking their places in the new edition were *attachment, block-graph, blog, broadband, bullet-point, celebrity, chatroom, committee, compulsory, cut-and-paste, MP3 player* and *voice-mail.*

Words relating to the outdoors and the natural are being replaced by the indoor and the virtual as 'blackberry', he points out, gives way to 'Blackberry'. When challenged, OUP explained that they made the changes to reflect the 'consensus-experience of modern-day childhood.'

Whatever this suggests about changes in the lived experience of childhood, which is alarming enough, it is at least equally worrying that tomorrow's adults stand to lose words, images and referents because they

---

[2]Macfarlane, Robert. 'A Word to the Wild', *National Trust Magazine*, Autumn 2015.

don't conform to experiences that today's urban children have access to or preference for.

Such word substitutions have the capacity to impoverish not only language but our ability to think for ourselves. It's not possible to conceive a thought, let alone develop or extend it, without the vocabulary to contain and express it. Words lead to and join forces with other words in grammatical patterns that add meaning. We can form mental images of concrete artefacts and reproduce them visually but they can only be explained – as abstract concepts can only be communicated – in language. Many of the words in Macfarlane's list of OJD deletions are alive with echoes of other words. They reach radicles, tendrils, rootlets towards images, ideas and associations that enrich our understanding. Think of the colour *kingfisher blue*; think of the mighty oak that grows from acorns or what it means to be a minnow in the pond of life. Without the cowslip's bell, where is Ariel supposed to lie? Go back to that list and read the endangered words aloud. Say *crocus*. Say *willow*. Savour their taste and texture in your mouth, the note they strike on your inner ear. *Broadband* and *chatroom* are blunt instruments by comparison. As Macfarlane has pointed out elsewhere, we don't care for (or about?) what we don't know, and on the whole we don't know what we can't name.[3] The implications for ecology and the environment are stark. If we don't know or care about a thing, it's that much easier to lose or destroy – a principle that applies to language as much as to nature or anything – or anyone – else.

Language must evolve, it has to be relevant. But it needs specificity as well as plurality, a specificity that we stand to lose through laziness or indifference or through simply being too busy to key in a whole word or a properly grammatical phrase. Here is one reason why good writing matters to everyone, not just writers – it's in our interest to keep language alive and that's what we do, every day. Language is our medium; not simply in the sense of being the material we work with, as stone or clay is to a sculptor; nor as the instrument we apply to our material/subject-matter, although it is that too. Not only matter and instrument, it is also

---

[3]'The word-hoard: Robert Macfarlane on re-wilding our language of landscape', Alison Flood, *Guardian*, 13 January 2015 (https://www.theguardian.com/books/2015/feb/27/robert-macfarlane-word-hoard-rewilding-landscape?CMP=share_btn_fb).

the suggestive, oracular source of possibility and hidden meaning, of lost worlds and otherness.

A writer's job is to keep language, not only current and meaningful but playful, evocative, suggestive: refreshed, supple, pliant, ready for use. So when you rack your brains looking for a fresh way of getting your character up the stairs or out the door, you can console yourself that you're doing humanity a favour, that you're in the business of preservation. For the duration of that particular, mundane struggle, you are a custodian of one of the most precious resources we have. Do you even want to consider what life would be like without language? This is not an argument for the use of polysyllabic or striking words for the sake of dazzling the reader with your own pomposity; it's a case for freshness and clarity, for the sheer pleasure of a word as it strikes your inner ear, for its precision or its playful powers of suggestion. The function of language in writing is not to keep us on the surface but to lead us on, to take us down. We don't want our attention to be snagged by what's on the page, we want to be swept behind the lines into a world of imaginary forms and meaning so smoothly that we don't notice until we're too enthralled to leave. As the Victorians knew, seduction is harder – or at the very least takes longer – when copious layers of fabric and ranks of fiddly buttons and hooks get in the way.

When the demons of mediocrity cluster around the keyboard whispering sweet banalities, offering trite-size bites of obviousness, a committed writer fights them. In 'Politics and the English Language' (1946)[4] George Orwell writes about 'ready-made' or 'prefabricated' phrases as the resort of a lazy mind: 'They will construct your sentences for you – even think your thoughts for you ... – and at need they will perform the important service of partially concealing your meaning even from yourself.'

'Ready-made phrases' is another way of saying *cliché* or *stereotype*. Writers, clichés and stereotypes are natural enemies. The first option given for the latter in Roget's *Thesaurus* is the verb, *to make uniform*. Follow this path and you will find these synonyms (among others): *homogenize, abolish differentials, regiment, institutionalize, standardize, mass produce, put into*

---

[4]Orwell, George. 'Politics and the English Language' Horizon Vol 13 issue 76, London.

uniform, make conform. It's only fair to include terms such as *equalize* and *assimilate*, which don't have such negative connotations, but you get my drift. The ability to think for ourselves relies on staying awake at the wheel of language.

Like everything worth preserving, language has its dark powers too and can be turned, corrupted and put to use as propaganda, lies, incitements to hatred. All the more reason to work against those trends and to do our best to resist the obvious, to keep the borders open between language and meaning. There is something meditative and revelatory about the way that good writing invites us to think about, to be with, to feel with, to consider propositions, ideas and worlds other than our own, i.e. to be compassionate as well as empathetic. It constructs worlds and invites readers to enter and explore them.

ii. the call

The classic quest narrative begins when the kingdom is in trouble and the hero is offered a chance to ride out in search of whatever saving thing his or her world needs. So it is with writing. The work starts with an initiating idea. It could be character or conundrum, a place, atmosphere, or question – all stories and writers have different starting points. The idea stands up in the recesses of your mind and waves an invitation: do you want to come with me and do this thing? Whether and how you respond is up to you, but if you do it, everything hinges on the quality of attention you bring to the task and whether you can stay with it.

You are in a relationship with that idea until you've finished exploring it in writing. As with any relationship, beginnings are a thrill. While you're still fresh, it sparks flashes of possibility, flares of delight, shocks of revelation. You're wide open to it, as it is to you. At that point you'll make time for it, you'll drop everything and run when it beckons. The trouble starts when the daily grind, the continued presence and demands you make on each other begin to pall. It can be hard to stay focused and alert, to be fully present with this cranky stubborn fossil – it's only a lump of rock after all, it will never yield its secrets, you don't know what you ever saw in it – what were you thinking? Things can turn ugly, violent. There'll be days when you loathe each other. Other ideas will try to come between you. They're younger and brighter. Ditch that old yoke and come with me, they'll say. That's when you need faith in what you can realise together – if you stick it out.

If you don't commit yourself to the long haul, if your attention strays, if you hold back or hide from the deeper implications of what you're doing, neither of you will be satisfied. If you lie, cheat, evade – you're going nowhere, fast. You need to attend to your idea in every sense: care for it, nurture it, bring it what it needs, feed it, wait for it but above all give it your very best attention. There's nothing like the rush that comes when the work suddenly ignites and you're there – ready – and let yourself go with the sheer intensity and power of it.

iii. being-with language (the labyrinth)

Naming an experience, calling it for what it truly is, offers an anchor for the self when experience threatens to overwhelm us. Writing it as it happens is a way of standing up inside it, looking it in the eye, engaging with it. Writing it says: I know you.

I came to understand my own primal need to write while undergoing treatment for a serious illness ten years ago. Oh, here we go, you'll think. Another 'cancer is the best thing that ever happened to me' merchant – but that's not what I mean at all. It's not what happens to us that matters but how we get through it. My threatened self became a single, powerful organ of apprehension. In roughly equal measure I was both terrified and hell-bent on experiencing everything to the full, even though the experiences I faced were not likely to be pleasant. The best way for my self to be in, to apprehend, test and engage with the experience, was to find a way to express it.

Writing – in a proliferating pile of notebooks that recorded everything and later grew into a book (*In Your Face*) – was the thread that both anchored me and guided me through the labyrinth of the experience of diagnosis and treatment. It steadied and reassured me; it was my way of engaging with everything that happened on my own terms. I had never tried so hard, never concentrated as intently, never been so focused and so open, both at once. And I found something in that contradictory stillness, a key. Summoning words to the task of witness felt like the most important work I'd ever done, urgent and necessary; it would only work if I stayed with it, held nothing back.

111

Anyone can pick up a pencil and make shapes with words. Those shapes may or may not have meaning for a reader other than yourself, but that's where you start. The more you do it, the more easily words will come. You may have three readers in mind or three million. You may not ever want to look for a reader other than your own most private self. The potential value of what you write depends on what you have to say and the skills you develop through practice.

Some working writers shudder at notions such as 'writing is for everyone'. When writing-as-therapy appears on the horizon we turn and flee. This isn't the place to air the arguments between art and popular culture, or between literature and commercial fiction, or between either of those and writing for self-expression or self-help. Our interest here is in the *doing* of the thing, not in ambition or conditions of production, reception, or evaluation.

In an essay on the value of teaching creative writing, the American poet Richard Hugo says of the student who is 'not good', or who is not likely to write much, who may never even want to get into print, that writing a single story or poem that exceeds whatever hopes the student had for it matters.

> It may be of no importance to the world of high culture but it may be very important to the student. It is a small thing, but it is also small and wrong to forget or ignore lives that can use a single microscopic moment of personal triumph. Just once the kid with bad eyes hit a home run in an obscure sandlot game. You may ridicule the affectionate way he takes that day through a life drab enough to need it, but please stay the hell away from me. (*The Triggering Town*)[5]

Hugo's is a valuable reminder that writing is not all gloom and doom, that language, being alive, celebrates life. It is a container for what happens to us, a place to hold it while we assimilate and question it, from all possible sides and angles. Articulation establishes presence and

---

[5]Hugo, Richard. *The Triggering Town: Lectures and Essays on Poetry and Writing*, WW Norton & Co. (New York), 1979.

is an assertion, even a preservation, of self – but who's to say that the process of discovery is not its own treasure, its own source of knowledge, its own power?

iv. what is found there

The quest storyline – a journey to an unfamiliar world, an encounter with a figure who possesses mysterious knowledge and/or power and the transfer of that knowledge or power to the hero, who overcomes obstacles, finds a treasure and returns to enrich the community with its transformative capability – sounds uncannily like a description of reading. It's even more suggestive of the process of writing. The writer might start out on familiar ground but the task is to bring your attention somewhere else, somewhere new and deep, lit by curiosity. That attention is simultaneously open and fixed; the surface world of pen and page or keyboard and screen, cervix-like, undergo a process of stretching, thinning, opening and effacement; the questing mind slips through, unspools threads of language and follows them in and down. The quality of what we find depends as much on the quality of attention we are able to bring to the task as the angle of incidence of the light we shine on it.

It has to be acknowledged that the quest structure has its origins in oral cultures and traditions later displaced by script and print but that's all the more reason to be on our guard now, to be aware of what we stand to lose as new technologies and practices change the patterns of our reading.[6] Screen life, networking, the prevalence of social media – all compete for our attention, calling our eyes this way and that with running heads, sidebars, moving images, split-screen viewing and infographics, directed advertising and prompts that use our own names, as though the machine itself is calling us. Where eyes go, mind follows. Concentration cracks and thought leaks out, formless, like a fracking of our attention that spills our thoughts across the screen of whatever device we are using before they're fully formed. In a proliferation of font types, sizes, colours and formats the

---

[6]This idea is raised in my review of Ali Smith's *How to be both* in the *Dublin Review of Books*, http://www.drb.ie/essays/pay-attention, 1 March 2015.

eye is drawn up and down and side to side as it scans for information; it hops and skitters as one screen fades and is replaced by another – this bears little resemblance to the calm and orderly progress of a reading eye across and down a page in whatever pattern your culture happens to favour. Left to right or right to left, top to bottom or the inverse, there is a pattern to follow, a logic to the cultural codes you adhere to. That is why text is comprehensible – and subvertible. The reading eye knows what to do and how to do it. Left to its own devices it connects text to mind, reader to idea, argument or fictional world, reading mind to writing mind.

As reading pathways change there are likely to be corresponding changes in the human brain. Yes, this could be an inevitable process of evolution but it's alarming to think that our ability to stay with a sentence from beginning to end, to develop a thought or work an idea through to the point of articulation is under attack. If you add that proposal to a general contraction of language and the substitution of cutesy symbols, it's not much of a stretch to suggest that the ability to think for ourselves may be edging towards extinction. Pulled by a flash of colour here or a moving image there, our attention fractured, there is nowhere for an idea or a story to take root. Meaning slides away. Pour water on a glassy convex surface, watch it spill, see what I mean. How vulnerable this makes us – to governmental controls; to power shortages; to commercial interests and lobbyists; to casual temptation and the ease (and dissociation) of consumerism. We need to be able to stay with a thought, an idea, a sentence. We need the ability to focus and to know what we are doing while we are doing it. In other words, we need to be conscious. Is consciousness itself under threat if traditional reading declines?

Psychologists are already suggesting that we retain less of what we read onscreen than from a printed page. If our ability to memorise complicated stories and epic poems was compromised when oral traditions gave way to print, memory could be about to undergo another seismic shift as we outsource it to hard drives, digital passports, the cloud. The question then becomes: who controls the cloud and the systems that store that memory? How might it be abused and to what end?

vi. returns

Here's a question to ask yourself as you approach a piece of writing: if this was to be the last thing you do, would you be satisfied?

It's an invitation to derision to say such a thing. It sounds grandiose, laughable, more than a little needy. Of course the question doesn't apply to Twitter or a Facebook post or even an email (or does it?). And of course the Beckettian principle of 'Ever tried. Ever failed' applies – no one is ever more aware of the flaws and limitations of a piece of writing than the writer; see above about the stages of loathing and disillusionment that follow the initial spark of attraction. When it's over, it's over. It may be years before you can bear to look at it again and then you'll often find it's neither as brilliant as you'd hoped nor as bad as you imagined. It's just itself. The question is not a claim for brilliance or even talent, it's about intention and honest effort. It's about the wild, stubborn, life-enhancing belief that being a writer is a lifelong apprenticeship, that everything you write teaches you something, that you can learn from every mistake. It's about the urgency of your questions, about staying wide awake and being fully alive in the work while you're doing it rather than sleepwalking through it. It's about not sticking to the broad highway but taking detours through the Dark Woods.

What kind of writer are you, passive or active? Engaged or disengaged and with or from what? What we choose to write about, who we choose to read, all matter. Writing matters because reading matters. Reading matters because writing does and so on. They feed each other. If a book is a door, the page is a lit window between one mind and another, one world and another. So is a screen, but there in particular we have reason to be wary of what might lurk behind it.

Writing opens borders in our minds and admits us to the alternative universe that literature is, already thronged with characters and fabulous creatures going about their business as though they don't need us at all. But language is the key, the life-supporting element, the earthy, unearthly flesh and bones in which those characters appear. If it withers, so will our ability to reconstruct their mysterious world and bring them back. Let's not forget that *character* refers not only to a representation of – or an actual – person but also to a graphic symbol. The characters we write,

both figurative persons and the letters we use to evoke them, are bound at the root.

But how do you do it? people ask. You start with words. The world, life, the universe and everything is happening all around you – loud and busy, infinitely multiple. It's happening all at once but it can only be told one word at a time. Choose your word, choose it carefully. Choose another. Go where your sentences take you.

> … Now come
> the passionate midnights in the museum basement
> when out of that random rubble you'll invent
> the dusty market smelling of sheep and spices,
> streets, palmy gardens, courtyards set with wells
> to which, in the blue of evening, one by one
> come strong veiled women, bearing their perfect jars.
>> Katha Pollitt, 'Archaeology' (*Antarctic Traveller*)[7]

Lia Mills writes fiction and literary non-fiction. Her most recent novel, *Fallen*, was the Dublin/Belfast: Two Cities One Book selection for 2016. www.liamills.com

---

[7]Pollitt, Katha. *Antarctic Traveller*, Knopf (New York), 1982.

Distortions in a Writer's Mirror: Changing Perspectives 1991–2016

Mary O'Donnell

Writers are sacrificial lambs to the prevailing zeitgeist. No matter how radical we consider ourselves to be, we can only interpret the world we have experienced or are experiencing. We can, of course, reinvent and dream of the might-yet-be, and often we speculate in versions of a future subjunctive mood through our fiction.

But people pass through places, we arrive, live and die, and our response to the questions underpinning this passage has a great deal to do with shaping the society in which we are placed. Often, we are not thinking about philosophical issues such as the difference between what we as individuals consider to be 'right' or 'just' and what our society considers to be 'right' and 'just', although, in the most practical of senses, we are affected by what society (and sometimes the underlying moral code) prescribes. For example, a woman having an affair in an Irish short story in the early nineties is a very different creature to a woman having an affair in a story set in 2016. The question of paedophilia is openly discussed now (and usually criminalised), as opposed to the whitewashing that hovered in the air twenty-five years ago. 'A Beast of a Man', a short story from my first collection *Strong Pagans* (1991), owes something to Nabokov in its depiction of a paedophile:

Absinthe, Heloise, Angele, Cleo, Leonora, Lolita. And Brigid. Who were the people who wrote about such girls, who were they really? His body had frozen in the manner of most people in audiences faced with titillation, secretly awakening to fullest attention. Detachment was impossible. The air in the cinema flickered with colour, the spectra of shifting scenes, light, broken prismatically across the broad screen. Yet it was blue, the bluest, most beautiful light he had ever seen, his every muscle tensing, catching the density, the exquisite bloom of Humbert Humbert's desire, and then the attenuation, the gradual dissolution of the world he had dared to enter.

The fact that this story went completely unremarked, of all the stories in the collection, reflects for me the fact that we had scarcely grasped the language necessary to discuss such subjects at that time, and indeed I hardly understood it myself.

Also in the early 1990s, a couple undertaking a foreign adoption was very different to a couple doing the same thing in 2016, and a cross-dresser was certainly out on the edge, compared to a cross-dresser in 2016, in an Ireland that attempts to provide equal recognition to the rainbow of fluid expressions that represent being human. These scenarios appeared in my first book and, at my request, the title story was reprinted seventeen years later in my 2008 collection, *Storm Over Belfast*. I felt that readers would follow, with greater understanding than before, my exploration of a happily married heterosexual man who likes to dress in women's clothes.

I think several of the characters in my first collection, if transplanted to 2016, would be baffled, but not displeased by the changes that have occurred. They would find themselves more at ease in a society that is a lot calmer about how people conduct their private lives. In contrast, the characters in my later collection, if forced to stare down the tunnel to 1991, would find themselves bemused by the sense of covert activity that to an extent defined some of my characters. They might actually not understand the repressive conventions of being female and married, single, or childless at that time, or of being gay, of being a priest in love with a woman (or man).

But the transition from there to here, from what preceded my 1990s' 'there', to the 'here' of 2016, has been rapid, conflated and hard-won. Nobody expected the Irish economy to transform itself into something of Brobdingnagian dimensions, before it sank like the witch in *The Wizard of Oz*, in the humiliating vapours of a quenched fire. Wealthy though many became, we also lived in a land of injustice and massive corruption, frequently an inspiring theme for writers, offering as it did the chance to turn our attention to the things that broke so many lives.

While the stories of my 2008 collection were being written, Ireland was on the rise economically, and it was impossible not to notice the sense of economic freedom enjoyed by many – a new confidence and self-belief that at its worst became arrogance. And for me as a writer working during the past twenty-five-year period, I think I wanted an antidote to the stories of my youth, which included work by Sean O'Faolain, Michael McLaverty, Liam O'Flaherty, Frank O'Connor and Muiris Ó Súilleabhán's marvellous novel *Fiche Bhliain ag Fás*. I can't say I didn't love these stories at the time, because I was charmed by them. But as I went through my teen years and carried on as a young woman in my twenties in a very repressive Ireland, I looked to something identifiably more forward-looking for inspiration. Often, the voices came from German literature, where I found waywardness of a different brand, time turned on its head, and the strangest of characters fighting it out for expression in stories which reflected the hypocrisies but also the un-Irish *freedoms* of pre-World War II Germany and beyond. In such literature, one found a sense of progressive personal outlook that did not always exist in Ireland even in the 1970s or 1980s.

But there was one Irish writer who continued to inspire my sense of fictive justice. The short story 'Janey Mary' by James Plunkett, set in post-World War II Dublin, bit more deeply into my consciousness, and I have often remarked how it would still speak to the Ireland of today. Janey Mary is sent out by her widowed mother onto the cold streets to beg for food. In her desperate search she joins a large crowd of people queuing outside the Augustinian Church, awaiting bread rations. In the scramble, Janey Mary is trampled on, but the good priest Father Benedict intercepts her – and, no, he does not molest her. The story has religious overtones, with its final image of her feet, marked (Crucifixion-like) by the nails of the boots that crushed her.

Sounds quaint? Anachronistic, even? But hey – surprise, surprise – hunger hasn't gone away from our cities, and children are still sent out to beg.

It's important to point out, when we refer to writing earlier than twenty-five years ago and use the word 'traditional', that this word is not in fact accurate. Writers were addressing society's edges and awkwardnesses, suppressions and hypocrisies – from Sean Mac Mathúna to Ita Daly, a young Dermot Healy and indeed a younger Éilís Ní Dhuibhne. But our society was perhaps outwardly more homogeneous. The break with this homogeneity is what signalled coming change. The first hints of a departure from earlier writing norms came when many writers of my generation moved towards Europe and away from traditional narratives, which were regarded by some commentators as too rural, too pastoral, too reflective of an outwardly unchallenged country. But surely the writing should not be blamed for the society from which it emerged!

As I never emigrated I've experienced a continuous face-on encounter with my own country, moving from a time where things were very unequal between the sexes, to one in which they are less so. Typical of attitudes in the early 1990s was the response to my first novel, *The Light-Makers*, which became an Irish bestseller after my appearance on the Gay Byrne morning radio show. During the interview, Byrne referred to the novel as 'erotic', a term I wouldn't have ascribed to the book. But I was very glad he did. The book remained a bestseller for some time. In those days it took very little in terms of language and situation to have a book described as erotic. In fact, the novel presented the story of a couple who are childless and who want to be otherwise. The protagonist Hanna Troy is a photojournalist and her husband Sam is an avant-garde architect. But the issue of childlessness in the 1990s was one of those subjects about which so many assumptions clustered. I suspect they still do, despite more liberal attitudes to matters of personal choice.

The *Field Day Anthology*, published to justifiably agitated discussion in 1991, neatly bookends the state of the literary nation, because female writers saw, in the three volumes that initially emerged, of what little importance their work was considered to be when *Field Day*'s all-male editors made their selections. Given that our population now includes people of many different nationalities who might like to be counted as Irish, it is interesting to speculate how they would fit into an updated Field Day anthology. How will the work of immigrants be received when the current generation of children grow up and turn to art? This, after all, is a country in which the term 'Irish writing' has carried certain associations, among them whiteness, maleness, family dysfunction and sexual repression. Nowadays most of those associations have been supplanted by secularism – but it's still quite a 'white' kind of secularism. White men must realise they are no longer the default group and that they must move over and not only make space for women, but learn how to hear, read and participate in the work of black people, gay people, and nationalities and races from all over the planet. Just as this is no longer a mono-gendered society, so too is it no longer mono-racial in its definition.

Social diversity is already visible in our fiction, and hand in hand with love, birth, death and landscape, we have embedded themes that include suicide, poverty, prostitution, ghettoisation, the hardship of emigration and the hardship of immigration. Ireland is a grimy place of distortions, it seems, as depicted by Colin Barrett and Kevin Barry, both of whom use the fairground mirror method of reflecting today's social undercurrents. They distort, and the distortion is deadly accurate. And yet we also have room for a different milieu, and at last have ceased to apologise for it. Anne Enright's *The Green Road* stages a fed and clothed middle class, replete with its family alcoholic, gay man, workhorse daughter, and a complex and interesting mother. In a fiction set twenty-five years ago, the whole narrative would have revolved around how people might come to terms with the fact that someone was gay.

But how did we make the journey from a world of pious sensibilities I felt bound to oppose in 1991, to one in which there is room for characters and attitudes that acknowledge the transformations in Irish society? Social exclusion, as it existed back then, was experienced differently, particularly if you were a woman. Take this excerpt from my early story 'After the Match', with Helen, the wife of a schools rugby trainer, in conversation with an older man at a post-match celebration in south Dublin. She has just been presented with a bouquet of flowers and considers this patronising:

The McElligot man cut in. 'They're saying thank you for putting up with this,' he said in a wavering voice, his eyes moist.

'Yip. It's a lot to put up with, isn't it?' said Helen.

'But my dear lady, you've sat here all evening on sufferance. Mean to say, what are you, some sort of feminist or something?' he spat the question. She swallowed hard.

'Of course I'm a feminist,' she responded, not knowing whether it was true or not. 'And I don't resent rugby. I just think it's given too much importance.' She was hamming it up. Sounding resentful.

'In what way, my dear?' he asked, taking a puff from the cigar, his lips making a wet smacking sound as he inhaled. She could have shoved it down his throat.

'To enhance careers. Old boys' network, that kind of thing.'

'I see. But you're a feminist too – I don't meet too many of those – thought all that kind of thing had faded out in the early eighties really.'

'No.'

'Thought they were all lesbians too if you don't mind my saying so. You're not one of those, are you?' he chortled.

Arguably, my fiction has mirrored the society I have taken part in all my life, but the reflections have been deliberately in the manner of a hall of mirrors that pull and distort. I remain more interested in misfits, in people with misshapen lives, who struggle with identity and its expression, who, despite appearances, provide depth of field and unconventional contouring. I believe that they are the people who bring the collective group forward and into the future, because deep down they are rarely passive.

Today, with the lessening of divisions between urban and rural, it's as if dysfunction, violence, and addiction, are equal maladies, insofar as they occur nationwide and indeed globally. The upside of this, may be a world that half accommodates variety of experience, which welcomes it, and which is gradually getting the message about cherishing all our children – meaning *people* – equally. As it stands, writers are engaging with the world in different ways, with women – it appears to me – focusing strongly on the present (and the speculative future). My story 'The Space between Louis and Me' (2012, uncollected) depicts a near-at-hand future in which one solution to social isolation is explored, that of a working woman who orders a bespoke 'virtual' man as her beautiful and compliant companion in a Dublin in which the real thing has proven unsatisfactory.

But there are many kinds of social isolation, and many immigrants who arrived in the nineties are now citizens who have struggled to be part of our culture whilst retaining their own cultural values. Their stories are no doubt already being written by the artists among them, new narratives which will augment our nation's evolving story. In my own writing, the displacement of people and their struggle to inhabit new space and be acceptable within that space, is an ongoing area of interest. My short story 'Little Africa' (2008, *Storm Over Belfast*) details the situation of a war-traumatised African boy as he comes to terms with the newness of Ireland and his mother's relationship with an Irishman:

> 'Sometimes, Angela's new man Colm stayed over at the flat. Mosi tried not to suspect him. He was white, his features as vague and unformed as most white people's. The only thing that distinguished him was his hairy nose. Mosi would peer with dislike at the small gingery hairs that grew inside his elongated nostrils and wonder if his mother had lost her mind from too much death and thinking.'

Our cultural environment needs to support artists' engagement with such matters, remembering that we too once limped into a new world in the hope of being accepted, when our mother-country could not nourish us.

Also worth remembering, is the historical and political experience that immigrants bring to our culture. It's not necessarily a blessed one, or a constructive one, because like the rest of us they are flawed humans, some of whom have committed atrocities, and some of whom have had atrocity done to them. I was reminded of this when I read Edna O'Brien's risky, provocative novel, *The Little Red Chairs*, which raises questions about a host country's potential for gullibility when confronted by cultural difference. The book has much to say about the presence and comforts of the multi-cultural, when the protagonist finds solace in London after being exploited by one of the new migrants in Ireland. O'Brien is among the first to question the complexities of global migration, as she obliges the reader to consider a Slobodan Milosevic-like character who manages to charm the pants (literally) off the local Irishwomen who swarm to him like bees towards honey. It is interesting also to note that O'Brien has lived through and witnessed – even if at a remove, from London – several upheavals as Ireland has created and recreated itself. That she continues to respond with such scrutiny and vitality to the society we inhabit, is a challenge to the rest of us.

Our kith and kin experienced so much exclusion and, like O'Brien, some of our best writers depicted this during the sixties, seventies, eighties and nineties. But in 2016, Ireland has been turned inside out. It seems essential that we consider the issue of inclusion with a questioning eye, which moves beyond openness yet at the same time does not exclude. If so, in twenty-five years' time, when we reconsider the year 2016, it's possible we will be looking back at the birth of a writing culture that has fewer O's and Mcs, Ryans, Johnstons, Meehans and Banvilles – one in which names such as Abioye, Wang, Dawidek and Kovačić will also represent what is known as 'Irish writing'.

Mary O'Donnell is a poet, novelist, and short-story writer. Her fiction includes the novels, *The Light-Makers, Virgin and the Boy,* and *The Elysium Testament.* Her fourth novel, *Where They Lie,* was published in 2014. Her seventh poetry collection, *Those April Fevers,* appeared from Arc UK in 2015. She is a member of Aosdána. www.maryodonnell.com

Only Slagging: Some Observations on Irish Satire and Satirists

Éilís Ní Dhuibhne

Writers dislike being labelled. 'Folklorist', 'Feminist', 'Woman', 'Realist' 'Gaeilgeoirist'. These are some of the labels I wear, some with more pride than others. What about 'Satirist'? An image of a mocking nineteenth-century pamphleteer, with long pointy nose and little wiry spectacles, leaps into my mind. Who would want to be known as a satirist, in these kind and compassionate days? But indeed I am that, among other things. I have a mean streak. From the beginning of my writing life I've written satire – as well as the other, non-satirical, serious straight-forward stuff. For example, my first published short story, 'Green Fuse',[1] is a poetic, romantic, serious, sad, layered, tearful, account of a doomed love affair. The kind of thing nineteen-year-olds who have been reading too much D. H. Lawrence tend to write. My next story, 'The Duck-billed Platypus',[2] is a satirical report of an interview for a civil service job – the kind of thing twenty-year-olds who are doing interviews for jobs they don't really want – or get – tend to write. The third was a fantasy, and the fourth, 'The Postmen's Strike', another satire. And so on. This pattern, of veering from the romantic/poetic to the scolding/slagging was nothing I controlled or was conscious of. Apparently I sometimes wanted to write compassionately about deep emotions and on other occasions I wanted to write cruel satires. And

---

[1] *Irish Press*, 1974.
[2] *Irish Press*, 1975.

there was always plenty of material for the latter. Events in Ireland cry out for a satirical response, and occasionally I have answered that call – as in the case of 'The Postmen's Strike'. Or 'Fulfilment'. The list goes on.

After all, we are a nation of oral satirists. In the vigorous popular Irish tradition of 'slagging', irony and humour combine in a form of teasing which is generally good-humoured, although always seasoned, however lightly, with the vinegar of malice. Satire in Irish written literature is harder to locate. The pure satirists I'm aware of are predominantly journalists, stand-up comedians, and radio and television performers: Miriam Lord, Kevin Myers, Mario Rosenstock, Frank McNally, and Paul Howard (who of course also writes books and plays). The butt of the satire for many of these artists are politicians – one of the few groups who accept being targeted by satirists as an occupational hazard, and who, to their great credit, do not sue (unlike other worthy targets, such as right-wing religious organisations). Paul Howard writes cutting social satire directed at the Dublin bourgeoisie. He is arguably an heir to Jonathan Swift and Flann O'Brien, although his reputation as a columnist tends to blur the literary dimension of his writing. It's worth bearing in mind that Flann O'Brien too was a columnist, and Swift a pamphleteer. The satirist is probably always a kind of journalist, observing life with a critical eye: a stinging fly in the hide of the state.

The origins of Irish satire lie deep in pre-Christian history. In our culture, as in others, satire was used by poets and others to injure enemies – who could be anyone who had displeased the poet in some way, for instance, by being niggardly in the dispensation of food and drink, or otherwise failing to meet the poet's high standards of acceptable hospitality. The Irish word for satire, *aor* (or *aer*) originally included the meaning of spell, or enchantment. Satires, which damage the reputation of the targeted individual, were accredited with magical power. And they could damage more than your reputation.[3]

An example of this kind of satire, having the force of a black spell, is recounted in *The Second Battle of Moytura*:

Once upon a time the poet came a-guesting to Bres's house, even Corpre son of Etaín, poet of the Tuath Dé. He entered a cabin,

---

[3]Vivian Mercier, *The Irish Comic Tradition*, Oxford, Clarendon Press, 1962. p. 106.

narrow, black, dark, wherein there was neither fire nor furniture nor bed. Three small cakes, and they dry, were brought to him on a little dish. On the morrow he rose and was not thankful. As he went across the garth he said:

'Without food quickly on a dish:
Without a cow's milk whereon a calf grows:
Without a man's abode under the gloom of night:
Without paying a company of storytellers, let that be Bres's condition.'

Nought save decay was on him [Bres] from that hour.[4]

In early Ireland, as in the Ireland of today, poets apparently had occasional cause for complaint, and did not hesitate to express their dissatisfaction when patronage fell short. In those days, injury, blemishes, or even death, could result from the satire or curse.

In other countries, such as Iceland, poets were similarly powerful. The Icelandic *nid*, or satirical poem, is still employed, most recently against bankers and politicians during the economic collapse. But who in Ireland has inherited the power of the poet? Do we have satirists among us? And what exactly, or approximately, is satire?

Vivian Mercier, in his book *The Irish Comic Tradition*, describes it thus:

Satire … besides employing a great variety of other comic devices, wit and humour among them, usually depends in some degree upon that fundamental satiric device, irony. I expect that most of my readers will agree that irony, in the basic sense of saying one thing and meaning the exact opposite, demands a more complex intellectual response than wit does…[5]

Mercier points out that the unlikely heir of the *aer* in Anglo-Irish literature is one of our greatest satirists, Jonathan Swift. The malice, crudity and visceral qualities of the Old Irish *aer* were certainly present in Swift's

---

[4] *The Second Battle of Moytura*. Ed and tr. Whitley Stokes, Revue Celtique, xii (1891), p. 71. Cited in Mercier, p. 112
[5] Mercier, op.cit. 2

juvenile invectives against people he disliked in, for example, Trinity College. His later essays and fiction are less crude and more ironic, but retain that energy of excess: the wild exaggeration which is characteristic of early Irish satire. 'A Modest Proposal' (that Irish babies should be eaten), or the chapter in *Gulliver's Travels* which likens the human race to Yahoos, combined cruel and some would say distasteful humour of exaggeration with true irony, wit, and general social and political criticism.

Just because you combine the distasteful humour of exaggeration with irony, wit and social criticism, does not make you a Jonathan Swift. But I have always felt that I possess a fair share of his *saeva indignatio*. Some of us express our savage indignation on *Liveline* but the short story is a convenient alternative if you can't get through to Joe Duffy. 'A Literary Lunch', appearing in 2008, was a humorous account of how committees operate, in particular examining the way in which one dominant personality on a committee can overrule all other voices. This story is a pure satire insofar as the situation described borders on the absurd: the humour of exaggeration is employed in describing, for instance, the food and drink consumed by the committee, the placing of members at the table strategically by the wildly domineering chairman, and the way the whole meeting is conducted. Like all satire, the story has roots in real life. I happen to sit on several committees, most of which are conducted in perfectly democratic and harmonious ways. But I have observed, with a writer's interest, power struggles, and in particular the power of certain types of personality to influence decisions. It's possible that I have sometimes been that personality myself – but not often because mostly writers perch on the margins, slyly watching and hatching satires, while other types of human being rule the roost from the podium or the chair. What I find particularly interesting is the way in which people in formal situations – on committees, in institutions, in houses of parliament – try to disguise plainly emotional motives in the politely beguiling garb of rationality.

I followed 'A Literary Lunch' with another satirical short story, 'City of Literature', which is even more fictional and exaggerated, and which I visualised as being located in the Irish Writers Centre, although I don't name it in the text. The first story satirises the literary scene during the economic boom in Ireland, and the second deals with literary affairs during the recession. It was to some extent inspired by the appalling treatment the Irish Writers Centre received in the economic downturn, when its *entire funding* was cut by the Arts Council, in an extraordinary decision. This was the equivalent of a letter saying 'Fuck Off', and, one suspects it had an emotional root lurking somewhere in the mysterious woodlands of Merrion Square. My motives in writing these stories were not personal, to my knowledge. I have always been treated extremely well by the Arts Council and by the literary establishment in Ireland – and I am delighted to live in a democracy which allows me to satirise the hand that feeds me. This is a real privilege, given that there are innumerable examples of countries that imprison, torture and execute writers who dare to speak out. Our tolerance for 'slagging' (and criticism) is far from universal.

Here, we do not get tossed into prison but even in this land where motley is worn – thank goodness – not everyone appreciates satire. Some people can't stand *Father Ted*! I suspect that it is a mark of strong satire that it inevitably provokes some negative reactions; it hurts feelings, it is iconoclastic, it touches raw nerves. It makes you laugh, but it disturbs. If it did not, it would be blunt – which is the death knell of satire. It is not coincidental that the early satirical spells could cut victims' faces, literally (how precisely this was achieved is not explained in the commentaries). Adjectives such as 'biting', 'sharp', 'cutting' are applied to all kinds of satire. If it does not cut somebody, it fails.

And that's the problem for satirists.

My 2007 novel, *Fox Swallow Scarecrow*, parodies Tolstoy's *Anna Karenina*, while simultaneously using that novel as its template. In *Anna Karenina*, Tolstoy criticises in a mildly satirical tone the aristocratic society of St Petersburg and Moscow in his day – a society which well-deserved censure. In my novel, I satirised the literary scene in Dublin in my day, possibly a less deserving target, but one which in its snobberies, conventions, cliques and rivalries, is every bit as interesting as the salons of St Petersburg. At least to those who are in it.

The quick stab of the satirical short story caused little harm, but the reaction to my novel was mixed, to put it mildly. Some people, including reviewers, loved it, acknowledged the humour and the fun and the satire. Others simply did not 'get it' and it garnered some of the most vituperative reviews I have ever received. (Some, I thought, clearly fired by emotion rather than reason. And they didn't grasp the *Anna Karenina* reference: if you are parodying a classic, you must spell it out on the back of the book, or in lots of pre-publication interviews, because some reviewers are, well, not very well-read.) Satirists may sting the hide of the state but they, even more than other writers, need thick skins.

One could make the rejoinder that, as Vivian Mercier points out, it takes a certain level of intellectual sophistication to appreciate irony and not everyone has it. Senses of humour differ also – a joke told to the wrong listener falls flat. Comic fiction is, ironically, the least marketable of all genres, probably for that reason.

This is one reason why writers who can, don't – or don't do it very often. Vivian Mercier points out that among twentieth-century writers, many had a real talent for satire but indulged it only occasionally; he mentions W. B. Yeats's 'September 1913', Joyce's 'Gas from a Burner', various poems by Patrick Kavanagh and Austin Clarke. One could add Frank O'Connor's short story, 'Soirée Chez une Belle Jeune Fille', and Sean O'Faolain's 'Childybawn', as good examples of satirical short stories, the one satirising civil war politics and the second sexual puritanism. All the above examples occur in the large oeuvres of writers who are better known for their more compassionate writing.

On the slopes of Parnassus, the stinging flies of today's Ireland are the playwrights. The straight among them, like Sebastian Barry or the late Brian Friel, have occasionally written satirical plays – notably Barry's play *Hinterland*, about Charles Haughey, and Friel's *The Mundy Scheme* – both generally regarded as heavy-handed and unsuccessful. It is easy to strike false notes in satire; however lugubrious the feeling which inspires it, the work must be delivered with a light touch. But several playwrights of the twentieth century and today have been primarily, and successfully, satirists, among them Hugh Leonard, Bernard Farrell, Martin McDonagh, and David Ireland – the last two among the most brilliant Irish satirists of recent times (although one is a Londoner and the other from Belfast). McDonagh's parodies of Synge's plays are outstanding; David Ireland's play, *Cyprus Avenue*, which satirises sectarian fanaticism, is a masterpiece.

Although there are exceptions, such as Paul Murray, most contemporary fiction writers who write satire fall into the same category as

O'Connor or O'Faolain. They are occasional rather than constant satirists. Evelyn Conlon is a good example. Her short story, 'The Park', which deals with the Pope's visit to Ireland in 1979, fits perfectly into the category of pure satire, and there is an ironic and satirical tone to almost everything she writes. But she writes straight fiction – such as the historical novel, *Not the Same Sky* – almost as often as ironic commentaries on Irish society. Celia de Fréine's poetry and drama have a strong satirical edge, but share space in her oeuvre with non-satirical work. Joseph O'Connor, Kevin Barry, Roddy Doyle, Anne Haverty, Anne Enright have written occasional satires – often in the form of short stories, as in the case of Roddy Doyle's brilliant satire on the new Dublin bourgeoisie, 'The Pram'. All of these writers have a comic or satirical genius, but it is not put to constant use (as it is by, for instance, David Lodge). Instead, the knives are allowed out at long intervals; more regularly, the velvet glove of compassionate humane writing is the garb of choice. In the land of Swift and Wilde and Flann O'Brien, one may scratch one's head and wonder what has changed?

In ancient Ireland, satire was triggered by acts of meanness and unfairness, pomposity and corruption. These are still the main incitements of the satirist's pen. Individuals who are, or perceived as, vain and pompous, are likely targets. Any institution, organisation, or social group, which has adopted rigid and unreasonable rules, is bound to excite opposition. When Salman Rushdie wrote about certain rigid and, to modern Westerners, unacceptable and outdated aspects of Islam in his novel *The Satanic Verses*, he employed an ancient and safe method of criticism: satire. This is the critical method employed by the cartoonists of *Charlie Hebdo*. But this satire fell on unappreciative and angry ears, and was met with an ancient and very unsafe method of criticism, namely violence – death threats in the one instance, death in the second. In ancient Ireland, as in many other places and cultures, satire was sometimes regarded as an actual death threat, since words had magical powers. But although words can hurt, and satire can hurt, it is not magic. Words cannot actually injure you physically, although they may affect you psychologically. Satire is a safer form of censure than bombs.

If compassionate literature is inspired by positive emotions – love, sympathy, empathy – satire finds its ultimate inspiration in negative ones: frustration, anger, indignation, but also the more ignoble bad feelings of malice and envy. Unfortunately these emotions are no less human than the nice ones and they too need to find expression. Literary satire is one of the art forms which provides a relatively civilised outlet for emotions we might prefer to ignore or dress up in sheep's – or emperor's – clothing.

The mores of our society today, which emphasise the need for respect for everyone, and decry any expression that may be received as bullying, is not an environment in which satire can flourish. There is nothing kind or nice about satire. This may explain why contemporary writers who are talented natural satirists produce satirical works only every now and then. They are simply too 'nice' to do it all the time.

'Most of the writers of the Anglo-Irish Literary Revival who seemed gifted for satire (Joyce, O'Casey, and Synge, for example) had too much compassion in their hearts to become pure satirists.'[6]

This observation is even more relevant today in the twenty-first century than it was when Vivian Mercier made it in 1962. Society has more compassion in its collective heart than it had even at the start of the decade of love. We may have reached a stage where making fun of almost any group or society or institution is regarded as distasteful. This may be a good thing for society. But injustice, lack of generosity, disrespect for artists, rigid institutions, corruption, and pompous individuals and organisations, have not gone away. Nor have the emotions of anger, indignation, and envy. It would be unfortunate if criticism could only be delivered in a serious po-faced fashion, rather than dressed in wit and laughter.

The poets of ancient Ireland directed harsh and dangerous satires at patrons who failed to feed them – or give them travel grants in the shape of horses. Over the past decade, the government of Ireland has failed to feed poets. The Irish Writers Centre continues to be underfunded. The Arts Council is crippled by lack of money while international conglomerates enjoy 'sweetheart tax deals' worth billions. Great Irish institutions, such as Aosdána, feel under constant threat from right-wing capitalist forces and from the Arts Council itself, which is in

---

[6]Mercier, op.cit, 186

danger of being perceived as just as mean as those medieval chieftains who did not value poets enough to give them a decent dinner, or a couple of horses.

> *I have heard*
> *He does not give horses in exchange for poems*
> *He gives what is natural for him:*
> *A cow.*[7]

Éilís Ní Dhuibhne was born in Dublin in 1954. She is a fiction writer, literary critic, and lecturer in Creative Writing. She has written several novels, collections of stories, plays and non-fiction works, and won many awards for writing, most recently the Irish PEN Award 2015 for an Outstanding Contribution to Irish Literature. She was inducted into the Hennessy Hall of Fame in 2016. A member of Aosdána, she is currently an Irish Writers Centre Ambassador.

---

[7]Róisín McLaughlin, *Early Irish Satire*. Dublin, Institute for Advanced Studies, 2008.

When Normal Isn't Normal

Martina Devlin

The sense of awe never fades. You can but wonder at this miracle which emerged from wasteland. Was it a mirage? Could it survive? Would it endure? It wasn't, it could, it did. That's why the peace process is the stand-out, shout-out event of the past quarter-century for me.

Even now when it's normal, I can't take it for granted. I trust I never will. One day in the future, I'm counting on somebody asking the wizened old lady I've yet to become, 'What sights have you seen in your long, long life?' And I'll answer, 'Peace. That's my marvel of marvels.'

A swathe of people has grown up for whom the Troubles are history – as remote as those grainy images of the first man walking on the moon, or newsreel of the concentration camps being liberated. A generation has emerged which can take the peace process for granted. But not me. My memory stretches beyond that 1998 breakthrough, slip-sliding into years that were ominous, jarring, alarming – a shadow across my childhood which absorbed a yardstick divergent from the standard issue.

Don't misunderstand me. It was a happy upbringing, as well, in my hometown in the North. The town is Omagh, since you're asking. Yes, that Omagh. The place where the centre was blown to kingdom come, with the ink barely dry on the Good Friday Agreement, by dissident republicans bent on subverting the peace process. But the place, too, whose Catholic and Protestant communities crossed the invisible tribal divide to support one another in the aftershock of carnage. The centre knitted up and held, Mr Yeats.

I've raced ahead of myself. I need to take you back some decades before that explosion, to my early years. I don't have much memory of a time before the Troubles. Yet children acclimatise to anything, even to a civil war waged around them while they swap comics, pore over Enid Blyton stories about midnight feasts and compute how to generate best value for their pocket money in Mrs Quinn's sweetshop.

They adapt to army foot patrols passing by the bottom of their garden: the casual sight of soldiers with loaded rifles glimpsed through the hedge, although there was nothing casual about the way they carried those weapons. They adjust to helicopters buzzing overhead, drowning out their lessons, to the blare of sirens interrupting their sleep, to roadblocks springing up without warning.

'Like bloody weeds,' grumbles your father, but he is polite enough to the military personnel controlling the checkpoints. You're on a journey, maybe to the seaside in Donegal, the car is flagged down, an armed teenager in a helmet inserts his head through the driver's window and – improbably – calls your father 'dad'. 'All right, dad, where you 'eaded?'

Such trimmings of a society operating under bizarre conditions become your benchmarks. Even so, buried inside the child is the instinct that this norm is wrong, quite wrong, and that other people don't live this way.

*

Here's a memory. It's a Sunday morning and I'm taken on an outing with some cousins to call on friends of their father's in Lurgan, an hour or so away. The family we're visiting has a nine-year-old girl, our birthdays a few months apart, and we two are sent to the playground. Outdoors, she hints at something more impressive to show me. There's a place, she says, where money is lying on the ground, waiting – no, begging – to be taken up.

Naturally, I follow where she leads. A few streets away, we begin to pick our way through shattered glass clumped across the pavement and road. Around us, the window of every building is demolished. I have never witnessed such destruction.

'What happened?'

'There was a riot last night.' She is blasé. Observing my astonishment, her tone shades into pity. 'Don't you have riots in Omagh?'

Ashamed on its behalf, I admit to Omagh's lack of riots.

She finds a stick and uses it to sift through the glass. 'Look, there's one!' She ducks down, and a fifty pence piece is held aloft.

The seven-sided coins are strewn through the wreckage. In the rioters' hands they became weapons, hurled pointed side out to break shop and office windows. I delve for some of this booty lying, literally, underfoot but fail to find any – handicapped by my lack of previous experience at scavenging. Not to mention my wariness of broken glass. Meanwhile, my guide rummages up four more fifty pence coins and, in a spirit of comradeship, gives me one.

By now, older children are gathering to forage, and she advises that we bail out – we've had the best of the pickings. I am overwhelmed by her worldliness. We'll be friends forever.

At home that evening, I display my loot to my parents, expressing the hope that Omagh might improve its game in relation to rioting. Or failing that, could we move to Lurgan? Tension quivers in the air. My father and mother exchange glances. I am marched into the sitting room to deposit the 50p in the Trócaire box and a lecture follows. Firstly, that metal disc represents ill-gotten gains and will not be spent in Mrs Quinn's shop. Secondly, Lurgan is out of bounds – the new friendship is about to wither. Thirdly, I am to thank my lucky stars I live in Omagh, where people have more respect for hard-earned money than to use it for smashing windows and causing disturbances. Fourthly, it's high time I was in bed.

Years later, I discovered that the twig held by Britannia on the reverse of a fifty pence piece is an olive branch. An irrelevant factoid. Except if you've experienced that same coin's use for rioting.

*

The effect of the Troubles on people in the North has been compared to life under the Blitz for Londoners. Both were traumatic. Both showcased the strength of the human spirit under duress. Still, I sometimes wonder about the two places being weighed side by side. I don't mean to advance a hierarchy of suffering – the we-had-it-worse-than-you complaint – but it seems to me to minimise the Northern experience. The sheer longevity of the Troubles is a critical element to bear in mind.

Bombs exploding, street disturbances, body searches, civilians (usually young men) detained in custody without charge for prolonged periods, and the constant, highly visible, presence of armed security forces – for thirty years, that was our reality. Outside our front doors lay a battleground. Watch towers, barricades and razor wire were our street furniture.

Even if today was quiet, no guarantees about tomorrow were possible. Research suggests such an environment had most impact on children and young people. The message absorbed by a child was that violence was random, some adults were downright dangerous and the world inherently was an unsafe place.

*

Here's another memory: Christmas shopping in Derry with my mother and sister. We're in Woolworth's, and I've wandered away into another aisle, drawn towards a shelf of ballerina angel decorations. Mesmerised by their glamour, I reach out to stroke a net tutu.

Having touched her, I long to possess her. I take out my blue plastic purse with a metal Scottie dog pinned to the front and count my spending money. I know to the last penny how much I possess, but I need to handle the proof. Just as I thought, but hardly dared to believe: I have exactly the right money for an angel. It's meant to be.

All at once, alarm bells shrill. Voices are raised. Feet pound on the floor. Goods are knocked over. I can smell the panic. I look about for my mother but can't see her. I open my mouth to call for her. But my voice is stuck inside my throat.

Just then, my mother dashes up, holding my sister by the arm. My sister is crying. My mother's nails scratch as she snatches at my hand and the three of us join the crowd straining towards the door. Grown-ups push past. I can hardly breathe in the crush. A sharp heel lands on my foot. I cry out, but the woman in the spikey shoes doesn't care. Her eyes flick down and away.

By the door, a man in uniform says two words: 'bomb' and 'evacuate'. I don't know what the second word means but the first is all too familiar, used again and again on the tea-time news watched by my parents. They shush us if we speak over it. Every day they switch it on and stare at the TV, their faces unsmiling. Even in the car, my father twiddles the radio dial, searching for news. How I dislike news!

Outside Woolworth's, people are running. Policemen are everywhere. Other shops are emptying. Our mother walks quickly to the bus station, my sister and me trotting beside her. We're catching the next bus home to Omagh. Without stopping in a café for the promised chips and fizzy drinks. Without the angel I chose but couldn't buy. We chance a whine but make no headway. 'Count yourselves lucky,' snaps our mother. Lucky? With our outing cut short? We have sense enough to stay quiet.

On the bus, I worry there might be people who didn't get out of the shop in time. I worry the shop will be blown up, and all the angels with it. I worry. I am still at primary school and I worry.

*

That was my reality. And not just mine, but the reality of many others. The trappings of everyday life were under constant siege. Supermarkets bombed. Cinemas bombed. Dancehalls bombed. Pubs, restaurants, hotels, museums, libraries, churches, offices bombed. A security state was the response. This is a small detail but it underlines the abnormality of life: bags were searched routinely before entry into shops or public buildings – even before people were allowed to pass from one street to another in their own town. Schoolbags were checked, too, because children were distrusted. The suspicion was mutual. My parents never told us to go to a policeman if we were lost or frightened; that wasn't an option in the community from which I came.

All-pervasive security and a feeling of being safe are mutually exclusive. But consider. That security state has been dismantled. All over the North, army barracks have closed down and the British Army no longer plays an operational role. The RUC has become the PSNI, the Police Service of Northern Ireland, and Catholic recruitment has increased as has Catholic support for its police-keeping. Devolved government at Stormont is working.

Nobody claims it is perfect. Not with peace walls, resistance to integrated schooling, dissident republicans waiting in the shadows and working-class loyalists feeling tangential. Peace doesn't mean justice for those who lost loved ones and saw their killers go free. But compared with children rooting for coins in the aftermath of a riot? Compared to running for your life in the course of a Christmas shopping trip? Believe me, this is paradise.

*

Are you ready for another memory? It's winter, and although it's a school night, I've been allowed to stay up because my mother needs company. She is fixated on the late evening news. The newsreader's voice is monotonous. I've learned to screen out those reports of explosions and deaths. I know they're real. Conversely, however, I treat them as unreal.

All at once, I realise my mother is behaving uncharacteristically. She's not overtly religious – my father teases her about her heathen instincts – but tonight a pair of rosary beads is twined between her hands. Round and round her fingers she twists the beads. They bite into her flesh.

'What's wrong, Mammy?'

'Your father's on a run to Belfast. He's not due home till the early hours.'

He works as a driver for Ulsterbus. And buses are being hijacked in Belfast. If only the bus is taken, that's a positive outcome. But sometimes drivers are forced to transport bombs in their buses.

The bulletin concludes without any mention of a hijacking, and I am sent to bed. I lie awake until the back door opens. That's a good sign but I'm not yet reassured. I strain my ears until the sound of my father's voice drifts up from the kitchen below my bedroom.

Next day, tired during lessons, I'm scolded for lack of attention by a teacher.

'Sorry, sister.'

*

Four months separate the Good Friday Agreement and the Omagh Bomb. Around the time of the agreement, in April 1998, Van Morrison's 'Days Like This' seemed never to be off the airwaves. We all sing along to his promise about magical days when nobody steps on our dreams … because maybe our dreams are theirs.

This was an upbeat time like no other – we Northerners, traditionally cautious folk, gave ourselves permission to feel optimism. To swell with it. To sense the world's approving gaze. We felt 'the hand of history' on our shoulders, as Tony Blair put it, until history reared up and took a whopping bite out of us.

It happened on a sunny Saturday afternoon in summer. August 15th, it's one of those dates I never have to double-check. That car bomb at the bottom of Omagh's lengthy main street was responsible for the single largest death tally of the Troubles. Those caught up in its killing spree encompassed so many groups. Mothers engaged in back-to-school shopping for their children. Spanish tourists on a visit. A group of schoolchildren on a daytrip from the Republic (the border is twenty miles away).

That explosion cost twenty-nine lives, plus the lives of two unborn babies – one of the victims was heavily pregnant with twins. Six children and six teenagers were among those who had to be buried. Some 220 people were injured: a litany of disfigurement and disability, people blinded, limbs amputated, skin burned and scarred. And for every person killed or hurt, an extended family suffered.

There hadn't been a bomb in Omagh since the 1970s. The town felt relatively safe and the Good Friday Agreement removed the last traces of doubt. The war was over.

Except it wasn't.

A red Vauxhall Cavalier, stolen from Carrickmacross in nearby County Monaghan, was on its way to Omagh. A 500-pound fertiliser-based bomb was planted in it. Car plus lethal load were parked in a busy shopping street. Three bomb warnings telephoned through by the Real IRA were confusing about the location. Inadvertently, the RUC shepherded people directly into the path of the device.

When it detonated, there was an unearthly bang, followed by a sense of eeriness – a great darkness fell. That's how survivors describe it. How well I remember the survivors. How well I remember the dead.

Almost as soon as it exploded, I was sent to Omagh from Dublin to cover the story for the *Irish Independent*. I clambered through rubble trying to make sense of it, trying to find words to convey the enormity of what had happened, trying both to comfort and interview the walking wounded – all the time not knowing if my brother was alive or dead. He had been posted among the missing. Fortunately, it proved to be a mistake. Meanwhile, I knew individually a number of those less blessed. How could you not know, coming from a compact town the size of Omagh?

This wasn't just a story. This was personal. But – why Omagh? Then again – why not? Why was havoc let loose in any town or village in that north-eastern pocket of Ireland in the previous thirty years? And how to square the circle of celebrating your family's escape when other families were marked out for bereavement?

Collateral damage is how accidental deaths are referred to in the course of achieving a military objective. Collateral damage has to be one of the most loathsome phrases in the lexicon of war.

As with other bombs in 1998, Omagh was a deliberate attempt by refusenik republicans to destabilise the peace process. That strategy failed – undermined by a tidal wave of revulsion at the slaughter unleashed. Political goals were meaningless in the face of such devastating human misery.

Omagh paid a steep price for the dissidents' tactical failure. Even so, *mirabile dictu*, the community grew closer. It refused to allow outsiders to shape its response to the atrocity, and people on each side of the tribal boundary lines reached out to one other. That first Christmas, clergy from all denominations in the town stood together at the altars of their churches, a tradition which continues.

For a long time, the international spotlight fell on Omagh. U2 wrote it into a song. A film was made about the bomb. Famous people walked the town's streets, including Prince Charles, and Bill and Hillary Clinton. I know those things happened because I saw them. Even so, they strike me as illusory. After three decades of violence, real and unreal tend to shape-shift.

People recalled that Benedict Kiely, the Omagh-born writer, had written a prophetic novella about a car bomb more than twenty years earlier. *Proxopera* recounts how a man's family is held hostage while he is compelled to drive the explosive into his town. Despite everything, the protagonist holds true to his conviction that the bombers must not be allowed to redefine Ireland. He says, 'Ireland, when I hum old songs to myself, is still Ireland through joy and through tears, a most abstract idea, and hope never dies through the long weary years.'

*

Here's a memory from that time: Ian Paisley's sermon at the funeral of Sunday School teacher Esther Gibson, one of the twenty-nine. Having heard some of his hellfire-and-brimstone speeches, I think I'm prepared for what will ensue when I squeeze into Sixmilecross's tiny Free Presbyterian Church near Omagh.

I anticipate invective and anti-Catholic hyperbole. After all, back in 1969, the Reverend Paisley stoked the fires of prejudice, telling a loyalist rally that Catholics 'breed like rabbits and multiply like vermin'. But today he rises above ancient enmities in a spirit of reconciliation. The congregation is reminded how people of all creeds have lost loved ones, and that a mother's grief is the same whether she be Protestant or Catholic.

Afterwards he leads the congregation in a lusty bout of hymn-singing. They take their hymns seriously in the Presbyterian community. Ladies in hats and gloves on either side of me, like characters in a Miss Marple story, lean in to share their hymnals. They point at the lines, nodding encouragement, until I surrender, clear my throat and join in. Their hymns aren't so different to ours, after all.

Would now be the time to tell you that older people refer to my hometown as 'Omey', which is also how you pronounce its Irish name, Omaigh? Catholics and Protestants alike call it that. Once, we were more aligned than we suppose.

*

In excess of 3,500 deaths have occurred as a result of the conflict. Nearly half of the total killings within the North took place in Belfast. Nine in ten of the dead were men, with younger age groups most at risk. Some 257 were aged under seventeen – they were children.

The 1970s were particularly bloody, with 480 people dying in 1972 alone. Between 1971 and 1977 a total of 1,867 people lost their lives, according to CAIN (the Conflict Archive on the Internet).

Figures can be anonymous. But behind each one of those numbers is a face.

*

One further memory, a recent one. I queue to buy a Christmas present in a Dublin shop. The Paris attacks of November 2015 have just taken place: a series of coordinated strikes by suicide bombers and gunmen on a stadium, concert hall, bars and restaurants. The death toll is 130 people, with hundreds of injuries. The shopkeeper and another customer are discussing it.

'The world has never been so dangerous,' says the customer. 'The random nature of those deaths – it beggars belief.'

'Imagine going out for a meal or to a sporting event and never going home again,' says the shopkeeper. 'It's impossible to get your head around.'

I listen, my mind looping back. 'Excuse me,' I put in, 'I couldn't help overhearing. I agree, Paris was shocking. But that's how it was in the North during the Troubles, particularly in Belfast. People went out to work, or for a drink, and didn't come home. They did everything the same as normal but one day normal didn't happen.'

They look surprised. They suggest I might be exaggerating. They propose that the scale of Paris puts it in a different league. Already they have forgotten, or maybe they prefer to forget.

But some things have to be held fast in our memories.

Some things should never be forgotten.

During the early years of the Troubles, the kids on my street played a chase game called tag. There was a rule that you couldn't be caught if you turned to your pursuer just before they touched you, crossed your fingers and said 'pax'. We didn't know what pax meant – just its effect.

Peace. That's my marvel of marvels.

Martina Devlin has written seven novels and two non-fiction books. Short story prizes include the Royal Society of Literature's VS Pritchett Prize and a Hennessy Literary Award, and she was shortlisted three times for the Irish Book Awards. A current affairs commentator for the *Irish Independent*, she has been named columnist of the year by the National Newspapers of Ireland.

Homesick for Poetry

Gerard Smyth

In a recent poem I begin with the line: 'Have I squandered a life writing poetry?' That question to myself is not in the least rhetorical but expresses the intended note of anxiety about a life that might possibly have been misspent. The poem does not go on to provide an answer, but then I believe that while poets might be obliged to raise questions there is no onus on them to find and deliver answers – that's for the philosophers.

I think most poets ask themselves this question at some point, particularly after a lifetime of writing – whether they do so publicly is another matter. Apart from my own endeavours as a poet, I have been an advocate for poetry, its value, and its necessary and central role in the cultural life of community, its capacity to show us ways of seeing. As a journalist I have been lucky in having a platform to proclaim and promote this advocacy.

As to why I plumped for poetry, and not another literary art form – the novel, short story or play (though as reader and theatregoer my life has been enhanced by all of these) – I can only surmise. In his poem, 'The Gift', Brendan Kennelly gives his own explanation for the arrival of poetry in his life: 'It was a gift that took me unawares / And I accepted it'. Neruda's 'Poetry arrived in search of me … I was summoned', is equally plausible. Summoned or not, the question remains: is it worth the syllable-by-syllable push and struggle, the incessant nagging demands and dictates of the voice that requires expression in metaphors and images?

To briefly return to beginnings, I could say that it was a matter of 'dabbling in words', as Kavanagh once coined it. This of course is the experience of most poets – an initiation process, playing around with 'the gift'. Poetry was then simply another activity of callow youth, but one in which I quickly felt 'at home'. I had no real understanding of the mechanics, rules, procedures or techniques involved in creating the work. I had a classroom awareness of what the shape and feel – and effect – of a poem should be but had not yet become conscious of its elusive quality.

I knew it to be a serious business, a secret art. Michael Hartnett warned me that the poet 'on the last sea he has to cross will have the rocks and sandbanks of art to cope with, here he may founder.' Another member of the senior ranks cautioned that the inexperience of youth 'is sometimes dangerously glossed with a deceptively tangible rhetoric'. The impatience and haste of youth also has to be reckoned with and young poets need to let their work settle and mature before releasing it into the world. That haste and impatience can lead to later embarrassment.

In that 'work-out' period I was cultivating certain imaginative attitudes and sensibilities but my journey was only beginning; what was then in view on my poetry radar was limited – the poets of the school curriculum being pre-eminent, all of them masters from bygone ages, and a few discoveries of my own. These were the foundations for what was to be, though unintended and unforeseen at the time, a life writing poetry, reading it and writing about it.

And so I settled into the habit of poetry and over two decades had the good fortune of finding both in Ireland and abroad outlets for my work and responses to it that sustained me. I was identified as a 'quiet voice' but you accept and work with whatever 'voice' you are given. The idea of the poet needing to find his or her voice might seem an outworn piece of advice but it is a necessary first step in the evolution towards the moment when you sound like yourself. Except in rare cases, time and practice is required to peel away the influences that keep a poet's unique voice and identity from emerging. In retrospect I now see my 'wild oats' poems as being tentative and hesitant, not quite sure of their voice or their purpose.

All of this – and it was intensive and consuming – ran side by side with another, different life in the service of language, as an editor on a daily newspaper, shaping and reshaping the news stories of the day. The work of the daily wordsmith was instant and urgent, in contrast to poetry's more reflective pace.

I maintained a clear demarcation, compartmentalising each of these activities, one of them an economic necessity, the other my access to an inner life. I considered the loftier moment of the poem as belonging to a far more superior order. In later years I came to acknowledge that journalistic practice and the job of editor had been a hugely determining influence on the form of my poetry – at least in how it aimed for concision, compression, economy. It taught me to seek out what is essential and discard all else.

In the late 1980s, after two decades of writing and publishing, my poetry life ceased. Often it's a case of a gradual two-way abandonment: the writer of his work, the writing of its author but mine was a sudden cessation. I do think, however, that I had been expecting it. To ease my self-esteem I created certain pretexts – the need for respite, the demands of other commitments, the desire for creative rejuvenation.

One contributory factor was my period of some years as poetry critic for *The Irish Times*. Whatever about the wearying effect of constant reviewing, this immersion in the work of others and making critical judgement on it, also led to a moment of self-doubt and re-evaluation of my own efforts which, I felt, were not finding their true direction. I was conscious of a disparity between goals and achievements.

And so I left eighteen years of writing poetry behind me. I felt no pang of loss or regret but bizarrely a kind of liberation, of release from the anxiety of waiting for the next poem to arrive, a sense of relief that the monkey was off my back. I assumed that this was merely an interruption, or adjournment. But after months and then years without a visitation, and not even a hankering to receive one, I accepted that there would never be a return to that particular writing life and got on with my journalistic career in *The Irish Times*. So convinced was I of poetry's permanent departure that on a winter Sunday in the mid-1990s I took out the copybooks containing my apprentice poems and drafts of my first collections and burned them – an act which later became the source of much regret.

What baffles me as I now look back is that the stoppage – which had nothing to do with writer's block – happened almost immediately after the publication of my third book (and my first with Dedalus Press) – a collection that achieved a broadening out of my themes as well as a shedding of influences that allowed me to finally sound like myself. If nothing else it had a confidence lacking in my first collection which was too self-aware and my second in which I seemed to be in experimental mode, wilfully opaque and sometimes far too rhetorical. In fact the 'surety and simplicity' of the third collection, as one reviewer called it, signalled the poetic strain I would later return to.

The life of the journalist took over and while my career, up to that point, had been concerned with daily events and the next headline, I had the opportunity to move onto the arts and literary side of journalism. I think that this may have provided a substitute for the disappearance of poetry from my life – or rather the practice of writing poems. The final poem in my last collection before the withdrawal into silence was called 'Interlude'. The interlude between that book and my next volume was to last sixteen years.

*

I agree with Frost's statement that a poem 'may not be worried into being' – but I do think that in some way I actually willed poetry back into my life. It happened like this: on New Year's Eve, 1998, it occurred to me that the year beyond the stroke of twelve marked the thirtieth anniversary of my first poems appearing in David Marcus's New Irish Writing as well as the publication by New Writers' Press of a debut small volume, *The Flags Are Quiet*. Waiting for the bells of midnight I was somehow overcome by a desire to ensure that my poems of the 1970s and 1980s were not going to be the last word.

On that particular evening I felt homesick for poetry. The sense of loss that I had failed to experience in the aftermath of ending my affair with poetry finally took possession of me. I felt an itch to try again, but also a resolve to try harder and do so in the form of a new mould. The old hankering was back.

What followed, in the first months of 1999, was a period of reacclimatising to poetry.

Not quite starting from scratch but almost. Nothing was unfamiliar but I sensed in myself a different way of seeing and seizing the material that was surfacing and certainly a different, less forceful, tactic in handling language.

I retrieved a handful of unpublished poems I had presciently, or instinctively, put aside twelve years previously. These reminded me of Pound's advice to use 'either no ornament or good ornament'. It seemed a good credo to begin with.

I am grateful for whatever prompted me to preserve those few poems because they became the building bricks for a new body of work and change of style. I can now see how those years when I was not directly engaged with poetry were productive in other ways that enabled the imagination to prepare for this moment of reconnection.

Other factors contributed to the different version of myself behind the new phase. Age-wise I was getting close to fifty – no longer tied to a younger man's emotional limitations. The 'awe of youth' had faded and the mid-life years were presenting a new set of complex everyday realities to contend with.

My own poetry shelves were better stocked – I had not altogether abandoned reading poetry in those intervening years but prose fiction, and quite a lot of it, had been my main reading fix. That this influenced the 'story-telling narrative method' that, for example, Thomas McCarthy noted in the new work is quite possible.

This time I was in possession of something that my younger self had been without: a memory bank, an archive from which to retrieve imagery and particulars; though I am familiar with the cautionary note in one of Linda Pastan's poems: 'How much of memory is imagination?' While Flannery O'Connor's belief that enough has happened to us by the age of eight to write about it forever may be true for some writers, we must reach a certain point in our lives to be able to fully understand and explicate those experiences. Austin Clarke was in his seventies by the time he could look back to his mental breakdown as a young man in his great work, 'Mnemosyne Lay in Dust'.

If the long gap between my early and late writing periods produced one significant change, it was the mood of the new poems. This shift of disposition and temperament was summed up by my then editor, John

F. Deane, when he wrote that the newer poems were 'suggestive of hope and generous living', compared to an engagement with 'the dismal side of modern living' in my first books. I could, and continue to, identify with Richard Wilbur's line about the poet being 'most surely called to praise'.

Place had been a preoccupation in my work from the beginning – reviewers have regularly been quick to apply the label 'city poet'. I have no issue with the appellation and gladly accept it as my 'calling card' as one friend suggested. I think my earlier attraction to the city as a subject came from a romantic sense of my haunts – according to a comment resurrected from an interview in the early 1970s those 'empty, crumbling streets' apparently had 'a sinister fascination for me'. By which I imagine I intended to suggest that they furnished me with images and metaphors.

I returned to my urban scenes and themes and rediscovered my roots. Poets I admired and had been reading more deeply, Kinsella, Kavanagh, Clarke and Heaney, had all demonstrated the value of locality and local reference and how the flavour and spirit of place can be made memorable. Our places of origin are where we first pick up the frequencies that leave their mark on us.

According to Kinsella memorialising places and their people is 'one of the things that art is for'. The fusion of place and memory ignited many of the new poems but I now had, I believe, a different foothold on my own places, and I emphasise the plurality there: my rediscovery of roots extended beyond the Dublin of my childhood and adolescence – I also have a deep and familial attachment to County Meath, my mother's home place and where I was the beneficiary of experiences quite different to those of the city boy who grew up smelling the Liffey and nearby brewery. The summers of my first two decades were spent in close contact with the rites and rituals of rural life. For me it is as much a place of origin and of first observations as my urban streets.

I have often pronounced myself twice-blessed in having two 'important places' grip my imagination: the realism of the inner-city and the landscape, scenes and nurturing ground of the country where my first poems were written during the summer of my seventeenth year. While place as a groove in my work unites the earlier and later poems, there is a significant difference between the work of those two periods: the naming of place is totally absent from the first, and vitally important to the second.

I hope that what also differentiates the 'new period' poems, if I succeeded in what I sought to achieve, is an exactitude in the language, a trust in plain speech as well as a far greater reach into myself. The novice poems could often be ambiguous, obscure, elliptical or, as one critic put it, 'hermetically sealed', resisting interpretation. There was too a dissonance to the melody of many of the lines – a reason perhaps why in retrospective editions of recent years I have attempted rewrites of a number of earlier poems: a course of action not always entirely advisable.

The new work moved in a different direction. Painting, cinema and especially music – all of which had been central to my life as a culture editor – as well as poems that came out of parenthood and family life, and that deeper retrieval from memory. Here and there history and its events are represented in recent work. The religious or spiritual themes I struggled with in poems of the 1970s and '80s resurfaced in a less conventional form.

I had new values to guide the way I should write. I took a different, less earnest, view on the distinction between my work as an editor and as a poet, readily acknowledging – with gratitude – that what I learned editing the words of others benefited my own poems: the refining of language to its most economic form.

In other ways too there was an interdependence between poet and journalist, between my newspaper job and the private moments at my writing desk. This is a notion that would have been anathema to me in my first poetry phase. A frequent topic of conversation with the late Dennis O'Driscoll (the only fellow-scribe who remained adamant that the muse would one day make a comeback) was the necessity of our daily journeys to the workplace as part of a discipline and routine that somehow helped to facilitate the poems. While most poets choose teaching as the adjunct to their writing lives – publishing, book-selling, librarianship are common too – it often baffled others that I could juggle the journalistic grind with poetry. Poetry, which mostly comes by stealth or intermittently anyway, depended on that other life keeping me connected to its sources.

As I began to publish again in various journals I was becoming aware that agents of change had moved in during my absence. An expansion and updating of the vernacular appeared with the emergence of a new generation that brought with it refreshed perspectives as well as new inventiveness and energy.

150

Finding new means of expression – making it new – is of course the challenge of every generation, none more so than the post-Yeats one to which I looked up: Kinsella, Montague, Hutchinson followed by Boland, Heaney, Mahon. Having come back to poetry, what shocked one day was the statement of a senior statesman of Irish poetry who, having noted my return, felt compelled to share his view that we were in an age that didn't care much for the lyric poet or the lyric poem. Momentarily the remark made me wonder had I made a mistake in my renewal of faith. But no, the lyric form remains for me the purest, most exalted form of utterance in how it transmits; it has retained and will continue to retain, its central role in poetry.

And so my last twenty-five years have been divided into three stretches: the exciting but unrepeatable beginnings when I discovered the sheer joy of poetry – even if many of the apprentice poems were quite downbeat. That was the time when what Ginsberg called 'the beginner mind' was at work but every poem up to the last requires its author to get back to that 'beginner mind'.

Then the prolonged arid years that left me feeling that I had been caught in a false seduction, before the business of getting back in step again: my rebirth, my second chance. Which is not to pretend that this third stage – still in progress – does not have its moments of doubt such as the one that produced the poem I mention at the beginning of this essay.

My younger self had the notion that poems magically materialise. According to Elizabeth Bishop the poet needs only intelligence, intuition and a good dictionary – though care needs to be taken with use of the dictionary. However, that is rather simplistic, it involves much more than that, as the poet who took twenty-five years to write 'The Moose' must surely have recognised.

Most poems require arduous effort and utter concentration to give substance to a thought, an idea, a random image; the magic that's needed is to make it all look effortless. On occasions when a poem is resistant and stubbornly unwilling to yield, I remind myself of what the Welsh poet Vernon Watkins once said: 'The parts of a poem depend on toil, but it is an accident which adjusts the parts to give a poem unity and make it move.' You have to wait for the accidents and be thankful for them.

If there has been any kind of motivation for my continuing fidelity, the steadfastness in coming back to it again and again, often after failure and rejection, it is my belief in Auden's insistence that poetry 'must praise all that it can for being and for happening'. The late James Liddy's suggestion that I was striving towards 'a life of psalms' sounds close enough to what Auden was calling for.

It may be only one of poetry's purposes but for me it is enough. Perhaps, too, it yields the answer to the question I asked in that recent poem.

Gerard Smyth's eight collections include *A Song of Elsewhere* (Dedalus Press, 2015), and *The Fullness of Time: New and Selected Poems* (Dedalus Press, 2010). He was the 2012 recipient of the O'Shaughnessy Poetry Award and is co-editor of *If Ever You Go: A Map of Dublin in Poetry and Song* (Dedalus Press). He is a member of Aosdána.

Under the Streets, the Forest

Sean O'Reilly

I wasn't long living in Dublin, after years as far away from Ireland as I could get, when the Good Friday Agreement was put to the people both North and South in a referendum in 1998. The Republic would also vote on changing Articles 2 and 3 of the Constitution, on whether to relinquish the territorial claim to the North and replace it with an aspiration towards unity based on consent, another way of saying that there would be no changes to the border until a Northern majority were in favour of it. Originally, the border was a temporary demarcation which came into existence when Northern Ireland chose to secede from the newly formed Irish Free State in 1922. The permanent shape of the border was decided in 1925 by the Irish Boundary Commission. All sides agreed that the Commission's final report should be suppressed, meaning that each could blame the other for the shortcomings. The Irish government at the time put up some degree of resistance until the British began to bargain with the young republic's debt obligations to the empire agreed upon in the Anglo-Irish Treaty of 1921, basically offering to waive liability for the debt in return for the border staying as it was. W. T. Cosgrave signed the agreement on behalf of the Irish. The Commission's full report was not published until 1969.

My short time in Dublin had already taught me that here, more than anywhere else I had been, I was first and foremost in any situation, a

Northerner. As someone trying to write, this meant that every word was partisan. Whether I liked it or not, I was bound to take a side. The act of representation itself was a political act. I began to envy those writers who could simply tell a story without having to pull their hair out about the rights and wrongs of political violence. It was said to me more than once, *You lot have nothing else to write about other than the Troubles,* a statement which could mean: you lot repeat the same old nonsense in the same old way, or, you lot have an unfair advantage over us down here in our quiescent democracy, or, even, when will you lot stop making us feel so bloody guilty?

In the days leading up to the vote, I was rereading Seamus Heaney's *Station Island.* This was Heaney's meditation on the role of the poet in society, and his own relationship to history and politics, and more specifically, the situation in the part of the island which he had left, and not left, stuck half-in, half-out. It is an examination of conscience, an inner courtroom drama, where the ghosts of his past get their chance in the box. In 'Away from it All', Heaney quotes the Polish poet, Czeslaw Milosz, and the lines,

> I was stretched between
> Contemplation
> Of a motionless point
> And the command to participate
> Actively in the present.

Contemplation versus the command to participate; that summed it up for me. Was fiction writing a means of engagement or a flight from it? Or, to put it another way, when so much fiction seemed to be about middle-class life and its anxieties, who could argue that writing didn't have a purpose in society? I didn't know the answer of course. When the result of the vote came through, the yes for peace and the disavowal of the historic belief that the island formed one national territory – and with it the rare feeling that here was a new magical beginning, fresh realms of time – a big part of me hoped I would now be spared the dogged command, the responsibility, and might be able to write freely, intimately, grossly if I wanted.

The appearance of Patrick McCabe's *Breakfast on Pluto* so soon after the Agreement was like finding another bottle of joy after the party has run dry. The foundling transvestite Pussy Braden sets off on a picaresque adventure to find his mother in London and on the way manages to make a mockery of every dominant narrative of Irish life, from republicanism to conservativism, from high to low culture, a linguistic drag act powered by a kind of innocence only desire possesses. At a critical point in the novel, Pussy is arrested after a bomb in a London pub. 'Why would he just not talk? …Why could he not just admit he had dressed up as a woman in an ingenuous scheme to disguise himself – for they would stop at nothing, these mad, fanatical bombers … ?' So thinks Detective Routledge of Scotland Yard. Pussy's reaction to the trauma of the interrogation is to retreat into a kind of 'outer-body experience' in her cell, a fantasy retelling of her life healed by the reunion with her mother. He imagines asking her if he is the way he is because his Daddy, a priest, has to wear a dress for work:

> Which would make her laugh and say: 'Of course not, silly! You simply wear them because that's just how you are!' And what would I say then? 'How's that for a mammy!' and rasp at all the snot-nosed urchins who now did line the road seething with unbridled jealousy. Mumbling to their tattered mothers: 'His mum's a lady!'

Pussy lives to tell her tale of shape-shifting border crossings, talking to us from her timeless exile on the doorstep of a house in Brixton. She survives on her story, the magic of her self-creation. In her platform heels, she has managed to outrun the narratives who want to claim and fix her. 'That's just how you are' – the dream of being beyond the reach of the discourses of power. Outside of language. Back at the origin. The traumatic loss of innocence and unity in order to separate from the mother is where each of us begins, psychoanalysis tells us. Then language gets a hold of us, mind and body, and disperses us into the grammars of identity. The body is half in and half out of meaning at the same time, neither brute object or simply reducible to a representation. Our bodies are not fully our own. Foucault thought the body had become almost invisible under the discourses which try to control it. We are made of skin and bone and law. Sometimes, when things get rough, when the borders are burning, we like to dream about a time before the soldiers arrived.

The actor Stephen Rea played the role of Bertie the Magician in Neil Jordan's film of the adventures of Pussy. She becomes his assistant in an amateur magic act. Bertie loves Pussy as though he has conjured her up himself, enslaved to her passivity, furious at any sign of independence. In an earlier film by Jordan, *The Crying Game* in 1992, Rea had the role of another significant and sentimental figure in this crisis of narratives in the Irish psyche. Fergus, an IRA volunteer, tortured by guilt over his part in the death of a black British soldier, tries to honour a promise and find the dead soldier's girlfriend in London. There she is one night in a bar, Dil her name is, singing 'The Crying Game'. Fergus begins to follow her, shadow her, creating his opening to be there at the right time when she is being hassled by an obsessive admirer. He removes the threat, unaware of where the real danger lies. His desire is disguised as guilt, a promise to a dead man. The time comes for Fergus to find himself in Dil's flat, stranded in her eyes, half in and out of the world, on the brink of her body and – this was the big secret used to promote the film – right then it is time for him, at the very last moment, to discover she is transgender. Dil has a cock.

We all laughed that bit too loudly in the cinema. Poor dopey Fergus, always getting the wrong end of the stick. The film managed to make radical connections between sexuality and politics, the body and nationalism, desire and violence – connections I had never grasped, not really, outside of my dreams anyway. After his traumatic glimpse over the edge, and into himself, Fergus resorts to a fantasy Hollywood world of violence and self-sacrifice, taking the fall for another murder and ending up in prison, another place where time is carefully guarded, and he is safe.

Pussy and Fergus: somewhere in the stories of these two characters was a hint of a resolution to the question of what I wanted to do on the page, what was driving me to write in the first place. Was I rubbing my nose in my own limits or was the act of writing itself some form of rebellion, a tout's confession or a honey-trap? Sartre had argued that 'to speak is to act: anything which one names is already no longer quite the same; it has lost its innocence.' He went on to say that the writer practises a method of 'secondary action' which he named 'action by disclosure.' The writer changes things by describing them, holding a kind of mirror up to a cultural elite so that they are forced to assume responsibility for how things stand. No one can claim to be ignorant of the law. To be unaware of the nature of their actions. The writer in this sense offers freedom through visibility.

A lot of this is on my mind as I stand in the sunshine in the Guildhall Square in Derry with a crowd of maybe 10,000 people. June, 2010. Like everybody else, I'm here for the public announcement of the findings of the Saville Report into Bloody Sunday. The families of the victims are inside the medieval hall with the powers that be. There's a good vibe in the Square, a giddiness scalded by the native sarcasm. They are testing the big screen on the platform; the rumour is there will be a live feed from Westminster. Every face in the crowd is meaty, naked, unbearably original. Time has stopped again, as it often has before in the Maiden City. We are a fairy-tale mob in the square, waiting to hear the royal pronouncement. We are waiting, and waiting is an enchantment as in Barthes' *A Lover's Discourse* "'Am I in love? – Yes, since I'm waiting'". The being I am waiting for is never real. But if I do not wait properly, in the right way, with the right intensity, if I am distracted, what I am waiting for might never occur. I may be punished, deprived. I must wait better.

The joy when the families appeared from inside the Guildhall, punching the air in victory, is hard to forget. So are the gasps of disbelief in the crowd as we watched and listened to the British prime minister announce that the killings were unjustifiable, and that the British government offered an apology. And there it was again, between the bouts of applause and the odd wisecrack, the awed silence and the tears, that same feeling of time flowing again, a release, a purifying surge.

Something that hadn't happened had actually started happening. A day that was never over had suddenly completed itself. Something had come true. The world was whole for a few hours. But as the elation passed, and the spell wore off, there were other difficult intuitions being discussed in the bars. Apart from the vague criticisms that the report had not gone far enough, that the top brass were let off the hook, some were finding the words to ask: Why were we so bloody grateful for this apology, this bestowal of time and innocence? Why did we need to be granted permission by this shower in Westminster to know what we already knew? Why did justice feel so like forgiveness?

Perhaps the same complicated emotions were experienced by people a year later when the Taoiseach stood up in the Dáil in the wake of the Cloyne's Report and attacked the Vatican not only for its failure to investigate child sex abuse in the Church but for 'an attempt by the Holy See to frustrate an inquiry in a sovereign, democratic republic.' All those people who had come forward with their testimonies, their memories of what had been done to them, were finally and officially believed and delivered from the shadows. The twelve-minute speech by the Taoiseach was described by Colm O'Gorman of One in Four as a defining moment in the process of Ireland becoming a true republic, a milestone in the separation of Church and State.

The sci-fi writer William Gibson commented that 'the future is already here, it is just not evenly distributed.' Well, the past is here now with us also, it is just not evenly believed. To change the present, you have to change the past; you must retell the story of how you got here, you and the other one you fail to keep out of sight. Your dreaded double fears story more than anything else; origin is a grave. Trauma – be it in the shape of Dil's cock, or Pussy having her fur collar felt, a priest washing his hands and warning you they will not believe your sob story or protestors shot in the back on their own streets – teaches us that external reality can be much less and much more than it is meant to be. The borders are not impregnable. The flags get bigger and brighter. The jails are empty. Invisibility leaks in everywhere. So much of the sky looks like your own handiwork. You need more and more injunctions to keep the show on the road, to keep them believing you. To be believed, isn't that what we beg from our parents, our lovers, from our lawmakers, our readers? The problem with laws is that they are both protection and incitement. The law creates the one who breaks it, Jean Genet showed us that, just as fantasy manufactures desire.

Think of Penteus, in Euripides' last play, *The Bacchae*. The young Theban king, appalled by the orgies staged by Bacchus and his followers, bans his people from worshipping the deity. Bacchus, in revenge, entices the king into the mountains to observe the revels. 'Would you derive pleasure from looking on, viewing something you find painful?' he asks the King. Penteus agrees. His own mother, Agave, is among the frolickers. Despite his own prohibition, he wants to see. Bacchus convinces him to dress as a woman for his own protection, a useless disguise as it turns out, false magic, because Penteus is torn to pieces in the mountains by his own mother and the Maenads. It's me, mother, your child, he cried out to Agave but:

> She was possessed, in a Bacchic frenzy.
> She seized his left arm, below the elbow,
> Pushed her foot against the poor man's ribs,
> Then tore his shoulder out.

We are all Penteus, laying down prohibitions left, right and centre, trying to keep at bay the stuff we can't bear to know, falling again and again for the call of Bacchus from the other side. How can I expect anyone to believe me when I know the point from which I speak is a division, a secret border, a pagan altar? On the page, I am tempted by my own desire to pervert the rules of visibility, thought and deed, word and image, to sneak across and listen to the hoofbeats on the bloodstained forest floor, wrapped in a cloak of fiction.

> There are telegraph poles to one side of the bog, wires sagging down, wires onto which birds fly and perch for a few moments and her whispering to them, 'Tell them, tell them where I am.'

This is the terrified voice of Eily Ryan in the novel, *In the Forest* by Edna O'Brien, published in 2002. Eily – the same name as Pussy Braden's idealised mother – is an artist living in rural County Clare who has been kidnapped along with her young son and taken into the forest by a disturbed young man called O'Kane. The novel caused a lot of fuss at the time because it was explicitly based on a real-life murder story and perhaps because any telling of the story would necessarily involve the creation of some kind of sympathy for the figure of O'Kane, and his actual counterpart, Brendan O'Donnell. After what was at the time the country's longest criminal jury trial, O'Donnell was convicted of three murders, Imelda Riney, her son, and a local priest. O'Donnell would kill himself in the Central Mental Hospital in 1997.

The novel attempts to show the dead end of a young man's fantasy, a violent ritual staged in the forest of his childhood, the murder of a mother and a child. The only account of what happened in the forest is the killer's. The author has to make sense of the event, find that extra touch which makes it seem real again. And believable. O'Kane is imagined to be driven by voices in his head, he has a gun, there is mention of a goat and a fox, weeds and toadstools, the trees sway and dance, the ground is so soft underfoot. As they push deeper into the forest, O'Kane tells Eily not to worry about her son, 'only an animal would hurt a child.' In a grove of saplings, he shows her a glass casket with the figure of the Virgin Mary.

> Next he takes out a bunch of withered lilies and scatters them on the ground, then a crumpled green dress, a scarf, an umbrella, a large white comb and a cassette with a tangled tape spilling out of it.

O'Kane orders Eily to let her hair down, to put on the dress – he produces a wedding ring. Goat girl, he calls her. They are to be married. Look at all the trouble he has gone to to prepare for the ceremony. Eily knows she is at the very 'rim of horror.'

After the real-life events there were the usual accusations that somebody or other, namely the police or social services, should have seen this coming. O'Donnell's mother had died when he was a child, he had been sexually abused, roamed the countryside like a dog, spoke in voices which included Satan's, stole guns, cars, spent time in prison, and basically terrorised the local community. In the novel, the fantasy tableau he creates in the forest, the pagan wedding, is dramatised as a violent fusion of all the disparate voices in him, an ending to all those voices, their fulfilment and destruction. O'Kane is one of the last anti-heroes of a collapsing tradition, a mytho-poetic eulogy – which may be what outraged people about the book. 'Magic follows only the few' are the highly ambiguous closing words.

Fantasies of return to the mother, of self-sacrifice and violence – this stuff is all very current in 2016, the year of the centenary of the Easter

Rising. Back when I first arrived in Dublin, even to mention the Rising was to be seen as a mad sentimental Provo. Many a year at Easter, I stood across the street from the GPO, and watched a handful of men try to enact an embarrassing salute. The Rising had been left behind; it was stuck back there in time, disowned, inert, timeless. Any anniversary, like a Halloween, opens the door to the ghosts of the past. The threshold is heavily policed. Not just anybody is allowed to pass. They are frisked and given a costume to wear. They will be celebrated, enshrined, visible salvage. But who knows what they are thinking behind those fiery eyes or whether it is really them?

The centenary of the Revolution breathed new life into many of these questions about the contemporary relationship, if any, between writing and society, whether the writer still believes in literature as a tactic of freedom, an interrogation of the meaning of freedom, whether there is any sense now to what Heaney called 'the demand to participate'. How many writers today are driven by 'a sense of injustice', as Orwell put it, about class, gender, race, war? Are those days gone, the questions now meaningless, defunct? With the collapse of the fatherly narratives of Church and State and nationalism, the country seems more than happy to be invaded by a new narrative of global capitalism which on the surface offers complete freedom to every consumer. The old prohibitions have been replaced by an even more tricky form of control dressed in the guise of permissiveness, a culture of self-denial transformed into a culture of self-expression. You must enjoy yourself or else. Visibility is the big brand. There is so much of it, nothing else seems to exist. Our beds are crowded. It is not the fact that we are driven by sex anymore that's interesting, Slavoj Žižek likes to tell us, but what we think about while we're doing it. Fantasy fills the space between us, a bridge and a hot tropic. The tanks shimmer out of existence in the sunshine. You can't see the drones but you can stare for hours online into the eyes and orifices of anybody you dare to dream up. You can't see the border either; after twenty-five years of crossing and re-crossing the barrier between North and South, watching the army dismantle the forest-green metal checkpoints, it is now no more than a text message on your phone to welcome you to a new tariff system.

More so than ever, it is an affront for a writer in this country to have a political agenda, to have anything critical to say. Writing in *The Irish*

Times in 1976, Francis Stuart complained that it is those writers who barely cause a 'ripple' who 'quickly become integrated into their society and serve a civic function in the same way as do lawyers, doctors or civil servants.' And he went on, that if 'one were pressed to explain their precise task, they might be said to preserve communal cultural standards and present the national identity.' The door-pushing ceremony of the centenary is a good time to ponder the relevance of this warning today. And to listen out for the scuff of the unshod hoof on the threshold.

Sean O'Reilly's published work includes *Curfew and Other Stories*, the novels *Love and Sleep* and *The Swing of Things*, and the novella, *Watermark*. He edited the special 'In the Wake of the Rising' issue of *The Stinging Fly* (Spring 2016). He teaches at the American College Dublin and in the Irish Writers Centre.

The Visitor

Belinda McKeon

March 7

Declan emailed this afternoon asking if I'd write something for an anthology the Irish Writers Centre is putting together; he suggested an essay about being an Irish writer in New York, where I've lived for the last eleven years. I'm on deadline with a new play – over deadline with that play, and not for the first time – so I don't want to get into writing an essay, I tell him, but would a diary do? Of the time between now and the deadline he's suggested? He hasn't replied yet, and maybe a diary isn't something he'd be interested in: too personal, too navel-gazing. Weaker, somehow, than the solid, gruff backbone of an essay. But I'm doing it anyway. I had this new Moleskine – bright green, Kelly green I think it's called here, given to me as a thank-you by one of the students who took my fiction workshop at the 92nd Street Y last October – and I've decided to write in it. To record these weeks, and whatever, within them, being an Irish writer involves.

Laundry, it turns out (I'm in my local park in Brooklyn as I write this, waiting for the clothes to stop spinning in the launderette down the block). Class prep for tomorrow, when I'm teaching a McCullers story ('Madame Zilenksy and the King of Finland'), as well as workshopping two student stories. Procrastinating on an essay I'm meant to have written weeks ago, for another anthology, something which should only take me a day, but which I've put off again and again so that it is now The Reason I Can't Get Anything Else Done. This is an old trick of my mind – allowing a doable thing to mushroom into an undone and seemingly undoable thing so that it forbids all the other doable-if-only-you-got-to-them things on the desk, and it's a bad habit I've long been trying to get rid of, because it causes no end of frankly unnecessary misery. The play, for instance; the play needs steady, daily, work, but something keeps getting in the way. This is an old story. I know how to change it. But.

Here I am, tucked into an alcove of a war memorial of some kind in McGolrick Park; feet up, writing in my diary like a teenager. In Dublin, I would never behave like this in public. Imagine if someone saw you? State of her, at four in the afternoon. Time on her hands. Looking for attention.

Two Irish writers do live near here, as it happens. John Breen, the playwright, lives just over there, in one of the houses on the park. Darragh McKeon has his studio a few blocks away. I see them once a year, maybe. We have good intentions, but time slips by. We're all in different circles as writers, and that all three of us are Irish writers doesn't bring us together any more often than any other circle would – and I like that, I have to say. The explicit ways to identify as an Irish writer in this city all tend to be Irish-American – there's a salon, a reading series – rather than having anything to do with writers who've actually come from Ireland. We might bump into each other occasionally at a reading in Ireland House, at NYU, or up at the Irish Arts Center, but, especially in the latter venue, the programming now is much more about putting Irish writers into conversation with their American counterparts, rather than about grouping them together and displaying them as a species all their own. That way, the conversation is about writing, and about fiction or poetry, rather than about Ireland, Ireland, Ireland.

March 9

Last night, Literary Death Match at The Bell House in Brooklyn. It's an odd event, slightly bizarre and pretty chaotic, but with a huge following, which Adrian Todd Zuniga has been running in multiple cities around the world for several years now. Authors read from their work, and are judged onstage on eccentric notions of literary merit by four non-literary, usually celebrity, judges. It's a lot of fun, really, but I wasn't in the mood, heading over there last night; *Tender* didn't make the Baileys Prize longlist, and I was hoping it would, and I know my publishers were hoping it would, and two Irish novels – Anne's and Lisa's – which I loved are on there, and I'm happy for Lisa in particular, but this stuff hurts, and it can seem never-ending during the publication cycle of a book, and it's a distraction of the unhealthiest kind where the creative process is concerned. Or, maybe it spurs some people on; maybe some people are so involved in the next project they don't even notice what's happening, or not happening, for the last one. Prizes shouldn't matter, anyway, but they do, these days, far too much. A book isn't a failure because it doesn't make it onto a longlist, but in this climate it can come, very easily, to seem like one.

Anyway. I wasn't really feeling the prospect of having my fiction dissected and judged live onstage, not even – or maybe especially not – by three judges who were out to get laughs: Wyatt Cenac from *The Daily Show*, the comedian Ophira Eisenberg and Michael Shannon, who was in that really quite good adaptation of *Revolutionary Road* a few years back. But they were extremely funny. They gave me extra points for having discovered a typo – 'riffled' instead of 'rifled', in the scene where my character interviews a senior male Irish novelist – as I read, and Shannon suggested Bill Nighy for the part of the novelist. The other novelist was Idra Novey, who read from her new novel *Ways To Disappear*, and at first the judges wanted to declare it a tie between the two of us, but then decided to give the (non-existent) prize to me, because I had 'come so far'. At which point, I, feeling mortified that anyone would think I'd flown all the way from Ireland just to read from my novel for four minutes, rushed to clarify that actually I'd only caught the G from Greenpoint, and they took the (non-existent) prize away and gave it to Idra.

There's a lesson in that. What is it? Know when to stop talking, as one of the other writers, Victor LaValle, suggested backstage afterwards? Milk your Irishness? (I got bonus points, now that I remember, for having an accent.) Something like that.

Declan said yes to the diary idea.

March 11

A piece on writer's block online at the *New Yorker*, by Maria Konnikova. Graham Greene was blocked in his fifties, and the dream journal he'd been keeping since his teenage years helped him out of it, because it was private, free; it was a place where nobody could see him. The Yale psychologists Singer and Barrios did experiments, in the seventies and eighties, with a large group of blocked writers, and found that they all had a reduced ability to daydream, to form pictures in their minds; some couldn't daydream at all, and some used their daydreams to imagine future, probably rivalrous interactions with others. The intervention consisted of a series of prompts asking them to come up with vivid mental images. Just demonstrating to them that they were still capable of creativity seemed to help them hugely.

I wonder a lot about daydreaming now and what the internet, the availability of the internet and its infinite daydreams, does to that faculty. My mind starts to wander now, and within seconds, if I'm online, I've clicked into something which will reroute that wander, or put an end to it, rather than allowing it to grow. Kids don't get bored anymore, we're constantly being told; they're overscheduled. I think the same could be said for the rail routes within writers' minds.

March 15

An Irish writer acquaintance emails, asking if I am involved in the Repeal the 8th campaign, if it has 'any crossover with Waking The Feminists', which is the movement seeking gender equality in theatre in Ireland. He's doing a radio piece about Repeal the 8th, he says. I give him the names of some people who are centrally involved – Tara Flynn, Róisín Ingle and others, several of whom have shared their own abortion stories online recently

– and he writes to tell me he'll look them up. Which irritates me; how can he be doing a radio piece on Repeal the 8th if he isn't already aware of these campaigners, whose work has been very visible in these past weeks online and in the media? And also, the assumption – or am I imagining it, am I being unfair? – that all these campaigns are somehow the same, lumped in together. Women giving out about things. Will they ever shut up?

No.

The Irish Arts Center sends around a van today to collect all my remaining galley copies of *Tender* for their Irish Book Day giveaway, when they hand out thousands of Irish novels at subway stations in the five boroughs. It's a great initiative. And also I'm glad to get rid of the galleys; what are you meant to do with fifty uncorrected copies of your own novel? (Give them to the right people before publication day, is the answer, but I never quite get around to that.)

March 21

I started something new last night. Unexpectedly, which hasn't happened in so long. A relief. I started it at the long kitchen table in the apartment where I go to work sometimes, ostensibly to cat-sit for my friends, but really just to be somewhere I can't get online. I didn't mean to write this thing – I meant to write an entry in this instead – but it came. So we'll see.

March 23

Leslie Jamison comes to Rutgers today, to talk to the students about her collection *The Empathy Exams*. There's a lot of Jamison's own self, her own past, in the essays, and as ever with a writer who puts lived experience into the work, there are questions from nervous students attempting, at the moment, to do the same; always the questions are essentially anxious darts into the territory of permission and of consequences. How do you do this; how do you go on, knowing you'll get in some kind of trouble, earn some kind of rebuke? How do you look at the people around you afterwards? There's no easy answer to this question, or maybe no not-uneasy one. Over dinner, we talk about the term 'vulnerable' and how it's applied to personal writing, especially personal writing by women, often in ways which seem to mean something other than vulnerable, or something additional: to mean unstable, teetering on some slightly embarrassing edge. 'I'm tired of female pain,' Jamison writes in the last essay in her collection, 'and also tired of people who are tired of it. I know the hurting woman is a cliché but I also know lots of women still hurt.' As in, yes, Sontag is right that literature romanticised the wounded woman, made her into a melodramatic trope, and yes, it's safer to pre-empt her territory with cool distance and sarcasm, but, sorry, these things are still happening to women. They don't get to have some other form of experience merely because their experience has come to seem a cringey undergraduate trope. 'It's always news,' Jamison writes of female pain. 'We've never already heard it.'

March 26

There's a sign on the door of the antiques shop next door: *Resurrection Sunday Closed.*

March 29

Easter weekend; the commemoration of the 1916 Rising, which actually took place in April, but religious sway seems to have won over again, or maybe the government just doesn't want to grant an extra bank holiday this year. The ceremony on O'Connell Street looks like an endless graduation at the Curragh or Templemore. It's ticketed; hierarchical, the audience sitting in stands neat as clipped hedges. A homeless woman had written online about staging a protest today, she and others who live on the streets, but they're somewhere out of sight. They all are. Enda Kenny isn't even the Taoiseach anymore – the parties are still squabbling like children over the formation of a government, weeks in now – but there was no way in hell he was giving up this day.

The Irish Times has replicated the front page of the 1916 edition. What strikes me is the image of Dublin the day after; the dead bodies on the streets, the horse carcasses, the buildings in rubble. It's hard to imagine, but then again, it's not. There's more than one city in the world from which images like those, and far worse, are being sent daily.

I've said no to almost every invitation to take part in commemoration-related events this year. There have been a lot of them; I imagine that's the case for every Irish writer in the US. Institutions and festivals have been offered extra funding for Irish-related events because of the centenary, and so they put together events with titles like *May the Road Rise to Meet You* and *Ireland's Green Hills*, and they approach Irish artists who, they seem to assume, are experiencing a year-long buzz of nationalist pride, and who will come along for evenings of charm and musicality, with a few joking-not-joking *Down with the Brits*-type asides thrown in to delight the second and third-generation audiences. In the 'literary tent' of an Irish cultural festival in upstate NY last autumn, myself and two Irish novelists turned up to find the reading podium flanked by huge portraits of the proclamation signatories. We shared the stage with a historian who was wearing some kind of improvised paramilitary uniform, and whose lecture seemed to be a lament for the waning of the IRA. At an event in the city earlier this year, *Tiocfaidh ár lá* was apparently declared from the stage as part of a poetry reading commemorating the Rising (I wasn't there; I pretended to be out of town when the invitation to read came). I wriggled out of other events, too, and I know I'm not the only one. The *Guardian* has pieces this weekend from Irish writers in response to the Rising, and as usual when I'm not part of something I feel excluded, even though I excluded myself – I told the editor, when she asked for a piece, that the centenary meant very little to me, but maybe that's not true. Maybe it's the opposite; that it has more meaning than I can deal with, especially as an emigrant.

March 30

John McGahern's tenth anniversary. There's very little about it; a few things in *The Irish Times*, a radio report from the archive in NUIG. He's out of fashion. Irish fiction at the moment is intensely excited about its own new energies and irreverences, and is extremely concerned to distance itself from What All Those Old Guys Were Doing In The Past, a.k.a. farmy/domestic realism, which is in itself a sweetly nostalgic reading of a literary tradition through which energy and irreverence, not to mention formal experimentation have actually been pulsing for a very long time. It seems that McGahern is equated more now with the TV adaptation of *Amongst Women* (headscarves and rosaries and soda bread) than with the visceral don't-give-a-fuckness of *The Pornographer* or *Getting Through*. Come away from the farm, we've all discovered the fragment!

To steal a way of putting things from Leslie Jamison, I'm tired of farms in Irish novels, but I'm also tired of people who are tired of farms in Irish novels. To write about the rural isn't automatically to write fiction mired in a past notion of experience, or to cling desperately onto a done-to-death stylistic paradigm. This is because in Ireland the rural, and indeed the agricultural, um, *actually exist*. 'McGahernesque' has been used as an insult in Irish critical circles, such as they are, for the last few years, and it's such a narrow way of framing not just his work, but the entitlements and potential breadths of Irish fiction.

That said, I don't love McGahern's work the way I did in my twenties, when I hero-worshipped him. My first novel was written too much in his shadow, and I feel embarrassed about that. I think he'd hate what I'm doing with my work now: too much of the self, my most recent short stories even overtly political, which he considered vulgar and unwise. We rebel, we kick back, whether as individual writers or as a scene; it's all painfully adolescent, really.

April 1

The *New Yorker* reviewed *Tender*. It's a good review, though it's only a Briefly Noted.

Never satisfied. April Fool.

April 2

This pregnancy – which I have not mentioned up to now, because if I started I would not stop, and I thought maybe it would not, anyway, be a big feature of these days, but a quiet one, but it is not being a quiet one, because the doctor has done the first scans and let us know that probably, again, this will be a pregnancy which will not succeed.

It is about waiting now. I am at work, seeing my students, and glad of the distraction. This morning, teaching Beckett's 'The Expelled'. They were into it. I thought they'd resist it. I was grateful to them: the way they dive in, and talk, and talk.

April 4

I have found myself not wanting to be alone – seeking out the company of friends during the day, which I never do. When I am sociable, talking – usually I am a loner, or at least a loner with internet – I do not think about it as much, the waiting, the prospect. Alone – but even then I am not alone, I realized this afternoon. Is that the problem? Is that the fear? That I don't want to be alone with this pregnancy, because I am afraid of losing it. Or because I am just afraid of it, because of how it can choose to leave.

April 5

My American editor sends me the paperback cover for *Tender*. It's a photo of Front Square in Trinity, taken from the side. I'm worried the square looks like some anonymous square in a European city, that it won't evoke anything of what they're hoping it evokes, and I say this to my agent, but half-heartedly.

In the morning A and I have another ultrasound. I wrote *another us* there at first. Which it will be. It will be one us that goes into that room and another us that comes out.

I am not writing.

April 6

At the ultrasound this morning, the doctor said nothing, and we both knew. He kept his gaze fixed on the screen. I tried to think, what does he look like, to what could I compare him, in a sentence? A boy playing a video game? But no. That didn't fit. He must be very skilled at keeping his poker face. Still, we knew. Beside me, I heard A sigh, and I knew he was thinking the same.

The nurse who took my blood had pink gel nails. Hoops in her ears. The CDC travel warning about Zika was up in the corner. She didn't need to tell me to make a fist; I know by now. The 'tiny sting', or whatever it is, is always tiny, yes, but it always hurts. She wiped the spot with alcohol and then wafted it away. Apply pressure, she said.

In Irish writing-related news? I don't know. This is what being an Irish writer is like for me right now.

April 7

Last night I dreamed of having to sing soprano, experimental soprano, in front of a load of Irish writers. Muldoon and Joe O'Connor were among them, so it must have been a 1916 dream, because they both wrote poems for the centenary. I was really panicked because I did not know the songs, lists of things, and because I could not read music.

Which I can, actually.

Reading *Margaret The First* by Danielle Dutton. *This time they tried, for him, crystals taken from wood ash and dissolved in wine each morning; for me, a tincture of herbs put into my womb at night with a long syringe.*

April 10

I'm visiting a class who have been studying *Tender* as part of their syllabus. One of the national papers does a mock-up cover this morning, imagining a front page with Trump as President: *Deportations To Begin* is the headline, *Curfews Extended in Several Cities* the sub. It's hard to believe that the actual front pages of the papers are not mock-ups these days.

The bleeding has just begun. So strange, to have this secret, this parallel reality. Visiting Irish writer and her visitor. This is what I discovered, when this started to happen; everywhere, on the subway, on the streets, in office buildings, there must be women who are going through this as they walk through their days. It comes when it decides to; usually, you are doing whatever you are doing when it decides to arrive, and you cannot cancel everything. Yes, there is pain. Yes, it is a problem, logistically. Should I use the word 'mess'? I don't know if I should use the word 'mess'. Oh well, there it is. You walk around, a secret mess. You can schedule it: you can take the pills, but the pills mean days off and heavy painkillers; you can get the surgery, but online women talk about the surgery costing anything up to $16,000 even with insurance, and anyway maybe the surgery is not safe.

I look at women sometimes on the train now and think, is she cramping? Is she going through – I did not realise this actually happened, but it does – the contractions? Is that why her face looks the way it does?

This morning at brunch with the professor who invited me and his older colleague, who runs an Irish Studies department elsewhere. The older professor tells me he has had many Irish writers at a series he runs: Kevin, Paul, Colm, Ferriter, Foster. 'Important people,' he tells me, and I look sideways, because I cannot, at that moment, look him in the eye. It would not be polite to say something, I tell myself. They have brought me here. They are buying me brunch. Should I be an 'awkward cunt', as Gina Moxley put it at the Waking The Feminists gathering last November, and ask him why the 'important people' he has named are all male? But I must have betrayed something, because now he talks, quite passionately, about wanting to bring women. Oh, and he has brought one – and he names the brilliant Catriona Crowe, and then calls her the 'travelling companion' of one of the Irish male writers, but then seems to catch himself again, and pronounces her 'a powerful woman'.

She certainly is, I say carefully. We go up to meet the students. They are wonderful. They discuss the unlikeability question so well, which always comes up with my central character, but with adult audiences, or whatever non-student audiences are, often seems like the end of a conversation rather than the beginning of one.

April 14

The literary manager from the Abbey writes to wonder how I am getting on with my long-languishing play. How indeed. I cannot use the miscarriage as an excuse, because the last time she wrote, six months ago, the same thing was going on, and while I know she would be very understanding, I don't want to be Miss Miscarriage. I write and ask for another six weeks; by June 1st, I will be done with teaching, I tell her, and I will have time to finish it up.

Anyway, it is just another version of the same email every writer writes to everyone chasing their material; a fake excuse instead of the real excuse, which is better, probably, for everyone. June 1st it is. I have been working on this play too long. I want it to come into the shape of itself.

April 28

Anne Enright gives a lecture on Maeve Brennan at NYU. About how, for a new generation of female writers, she says, Brennan is 'a casualty of wars not yet won'. About how, for an Irish writer's reputation to hold abroad, it has to have that balance between home and abroad. In Brennan's case, home faltered, so the reputation fell. That is changing now, but not before time. About how, on the pages of the *New Yorker* back in Brennan's time, and the time of Kiely, O'Connor, Macken, maybe even Lavin, 'Irish' was a sort of code for 'endearing'. And about how, 'despite the lack of surface charm', Brennan was very, very Irish.

It is impossible to be an Irish writer here, in the US, and not think about charm, all the time; about the realities of how we use it, and about how much of a lie that is, how much of a bribe to get the easy laughs and affection from an audience who might otherwise frown at us, not with hostility, but just with puzzlement. I am thinking more and more, is it not better to puzzle them, or leave them uncertain, than to lean back on the old switch of the accent and – it comes so naturally, here, with the accent – the charm. Jokes about the kinds of thing the Irish do, about the weather, about, for fuck's sake, booze. Stop it. Stop looking for laughs. Stop looking for comfort objects. You came here to be here. Now, eleven years later, can you not be here?

April 29

This was my deadline. I am writing past it now.

Belinda McKeon is the author of two novels, *Solace* (2011) and *Tender* (2015). She is also a playwright. She teaches at Rutgers University and lives in New York.

Luck and Storms

Nuala Ní Chonchúir

People say to me, variously: 'You have a great life, a great time.' 'Another book?' 'Travelling again! Where are you off to now?' 'Aren't you so lucky?' And I often think, what's luck got to do with it? I didn't arrive here by accident. The concept of luck interests me, the notion of it – is it something real at all? It seems wrong-headed to suppose that some people are lucky while others are simply not and, yet, things often seem to fall that way. We all know the fortuitous people as much as we know the ones whose luck never seems to rise.

When it comes to building a life as a writer does luck really play its part? Or is it more to do with working hard (that is writing a lot and reading a lot); learning to thicken your hide against disappointments; and mastering the art of stick-with-it-ability? Is it more about being tenacious, staying open to opportunities and putting yourself in their path, and keeping your ear tuned, than bald luck? I do think luck can jump into a writer's life in terms of timing: things like securing the right agent early on; or the right book being published when there is a hunger for just that type of story. But your book needs to be written in order for those things to happen so, really, it comes back to putting in the hours and getting the work done.

I moved to Galway, from Dublin, in 1996 to work for Punchbag Theatre Company, not with the idea of becoming a writer but to bring up my two-year-old son in a less frenetic, more cultured environment. I was suffering heart shrivel in my hometown; after returning from living in the Scottish Highlands, Dublin felt crowded and demanding to me and I wanted a quieter life for us. Also, things like Galway Arts Festival and the prevalence of spoken Irish in Galway city acted as lures to the west. My last job in Dublin was with an IT company; in Punchbag I was surrounded by artists. A normal day in my office – which was actually the theatre's lighting box, accessed by a ladder – saw me dealing with actors' queries, chatting on the phone with John B. Keane about our production of *The Field,* or sorting through unsolicited manuscripts.

There were two writers on the staff and, when I tentatively told them I wrote a bit, they were encouraging. One said, 'What's the point in hiding what you write? Share it.' He suggested I join a writers' group, something, oddly, that hadn't occurred to me before; he mentioned Galway Arts Centre as a place that held workshops. I attended those writer colleagues' book launches and saw them take off for literary festivals and readings in Europe and all over Ireland. I envied the variety of their existence, and their freedom, and wondered if I might one day have that kind of life for myself.

Though my writer colleagues' lives seemed charmed, all I saw then was the gloss, the trimmings – the outward evidence of what being a writer meant: books, appearances, launches, readings. I probably didn't fully realise the sequestered nature of it all, the long hours of writing and rewriting, the struggle to live on small amounts of money. And the absolute need for three things above all: time, space, and perseverance. I knew nothing of 'success' and its various meanings to writers – one woman's successful career is another's failed attempt. I hadn't a clue about the business side of publishing, or the different experiences offered by small versus large publishers; the publishing world to the outsider is a mysterious place. I didn't know either about jealousies and factions, writerly cliques and gossip, and that you can be isolated even within a group.

I may not have fully realised back then the importance of connecting with your peers, the value of mentors and champions, and the necessity for networking. But I learnt soon enough that if the writer is a lone fish for most of her activities, she also needs to swim with the school occasionally. That presented a small difficulty for me. Though I'm sociable, I am essentially an introvert and I prefer my own company above anyone else's.

Good news for someone who wants to write, in many ways, but part of the bargain of being a writer is going out and meeting your peers and readers. It is often, also, the only way to earn money – you have to leave your desk and your writing to one side in order to be able to come back to your desk and write.

Was I lucky to walk down Quay Street to the Claddagh to work each morning, stopping off to meet the theatre's director for a planning chat in Café du Journal? Was I lucky to have writers as colleagues and, through them, to realise that being a writer was not some slippery chimera attainable only for the rich, the well-connected, or the exceptionally gifted? I certainly was. But had luck got me there? I don't think so; decisions had, and the upheaval of my tiny family that pursuing a life better suited to me entailed. There's a Japanese proverb that goes, 'The day you decide to do it is your lucky day.' I am more inclined to think that action brought about my luck.

The job in Punchbag Theatre lasted a year; I married a colleague and we had a baby boy. Over the next few years I worked variously as a translator, in a bookshop, in the university library and in the Western Writers' Centre. I attended writing workshops at Galway Arts Centre out of which grew an all-woman poetry group, Garters. I had poems accepted in the local literary magazines – *Burning Bush, west 47, The Cúirt Journal, Crannóg* – as well as national ones. I took part in readings in Galway and beyond.

My first poetry collection was accepted by local feminist press Arlen House and published in 2003. But my real interest was in fiction. Separate to Garters, I began to write short stories and submit them. I had a string of 'hits' in short story competitions: I won the Cathal Buí prize judged by Carlo Gébler, then RTÉ's Francis MacManus Award and the Cecil Day Lewis Award. When I won the inaugural Cúirt New Writing Prize and the Arts Council awarded me a bursary, I decided to give full-time writing a go. This was 2004 and Arlen House published my first short story collection the same year. My husband had a job and, though life would be frugal, we decided to give it a go. We moved to the countryside near Loughrea, but sadly my marriage ended shortly after that; it was a difficult time personally but, creatively, I was a-buzz. I had completed a novel, secured an agent, and published another short story collection with Arlen House.

A new relationship, with a childhood friend, saw me move myself and my two sons to Ballinasloe, twenty miles from Loughrea. In our new house I had a study to write in, with everything to hand: desk, books, printer. My new partner – now husband – is a gentle, generous man. A good, easy-going father, he is supportive in work and family life. At that time, he worked one day a week from home, otherwise commuting to Dublin. There were long days for both of us. Money was tight. We pared things back; got rid of one car. We had a welcome baby girl. A year after that, we eloped to New York and got married. Once our girleen was out of our bed and the cot, she needed a room of her own, which meant I no longer had a room of *my* own. Instead, I wrote in a dark corner of the dining room; it was gloomy but adequate. I completed my second novel there.

We all know that writing can be a lonesome pursuit. For curbing that isolation, the internet has been a real boon for me. In 2007 I set up a literary blog – Women Rule Writer – to connect with people and combat the detached feeling of living in a place where I knew few people and no writers. Through blogging I met other writers, readers, and I connected with all sorts of bookish people and organisations. I found blogging really suited me – I could communicate with people from the comfort of my desk and enjoy the kinds of conversations I relish: those that involve books. The blog has been a great way to make real-life friends and to find work (teaching writing classes, securing commissions, as well as guest-blogging at other blogs like The Anti-Room, etc.). And the conversations that take place in blogland and more so, nowadays, on Twitter and Facebook, have been really empowering for me as a writer and as a person. I feel I have gotten to know myself through the writers I have met, and friends I have made, on social media. Through books and sites they recommend, and the in-depth, thoughtful conversations we have had – the sharing of ideas – I have a better understanding of who I am and where I belong in the writing, and wider, world. Social media is social, no matter what the naysayers may think – there is a give and take there that I find enriching every day. I don't always love the freneticism of the internet, and I'm not always in the mood for its constancy, but overall it has been a great help and comfort to me as a writer.

When I was pregnant with my daughter, I began to feel the lack of the support of a real, live writing community around me, so I decided to set up a writing group. I contacted fourteen other writers whose writing

I admired; all published, though not all with books out – I wanted this to be an earnest endeavour. I bought a big table and invited them to my home in Ballinasloe for a meeting to see what was what. All fourteen came and seven years later that group, The Peers, still meets once a month to workshop fiction, poetry and memoir. We are serious about the work but we have such a great time at those three-hour sessions. My husband often commented on the raucous laughter that emerged from our dining room in the years the meetings were held at our home.

When my second novel was published, I remember attending a panel at a literary festival, peopled with commercial fiction writers. What sunny, optimistic women they were. They talked of bright, light-filled writing rooms. They talked of *views*! They seemed buoyant and happy. Maybe bestsellerdom makes writers extraordinarily content, I thought. Or maybe it was the bright, light-filled writing rooms. When I got home, I moved my desk upstairs to my bedroom, hoping the sunny aspect of the room would shine a positive light on my new project, a novel about the poet Emily Dickinson and her Irish maid. It appeared to work. I had spent a number of years agentless so I had begun the search for the right agent for me. I wanted someone communicative, female and, preferably, Irish. It took two years to narrow it down and find the right one. And it was she who took on *Miss Emily* and sold it well to publishers in the USA, Canada and the UK. Since I was a little girl I had dreamed of being published by Penguin – my name and that iconic penguin were now on the same cover.

My husband managed to secure a job that lets him work four days at home most weeks. This meant that I was freer to travel, freer to accept invitations to read at festivals and conferences from Croatia to Lisbon, to New Mexico to Brazil. By attending more festivals, I was invited to do more – one invitation often leads to another, and readings and appearances are a welcome, if small, income stream. I also mentor on the BA in Writing at NUI Galway – virtually, as my students are usually abroad on Erasmus schemes – so that provides a link to beginner writers as well as being a modest source of income.

George Lucas said, 'Good luck has its storms.' There have been plenty of storms in my writing life, lots of frustrations. There were seven years between writing my first novel and getting it published. I have been with publishers who published books and then did no more for them, so that I had to do every ounce of promotion which, inevitably, breeds dissatisfaction. Money is difficult to come by on the literary fiction side of things – advances have been small for the most part, which means I do other time-consuming work to earn even a modest income. And I didn't find the right agent for me until I met agent number three.

I think the beginner writer in Ireland now has a lot more opportunities than when I started to get serious about writing in the late nineties. The internet, and access to ready information, is part of that. But there have been a lot of good movements in this country that provide platforms for beginners: literary magazines like *The Stinging Fly*, *The Moth*, *The Penny Dreadful*, *Banshee* and *gorse* have appeared and stayed. There are more agents operating here now and more interest in Irish writers from UK-based agencies. The Irish Writers Centre has asked writers for their input and, between the work of the great staff there, and a sharing of ideas with the wider writing community, great initiatives have been born, like Mindshift and the Novel Fair. There is now a dedicated group for mid-career writers, so often neglected in favour of debut authors who are perceived to be more exciting. The website writing.ie has staged date-with-an-agent events and is a great one-stop resource. Words Ireland is doing good work at bringing organisations and writers together to have necessary, business-like conversations. There are writing degree programmes springing up in all the universities. Perhaps if such a range of opportunities had existed when I first got serious about writing, my path would have been less bumpy, less gappy and frustrating.

But then, I think, maybe if I had had the good fortune early on to have a hit book, a bestseller, I wouldn't have had the freedom I've had to write the kind of books I want to write. Maybe I wouldn't have worked across genres and got so much pleasure from wandering between poetry, short stories and novels. Bestsellers have a way of bringing insane amounts of away-from-the-desk work into your life. They bring expectations and pressure and disappointments, too, though not many will acknowledge that. I have met successful writers (lucky writers) who are haunted, exhausted and burnt out. At least with my modicum of success, I have managed to (mostly) keep a rein on my workload and spend a lot of time at my desk.

I often wonder, 'Where do I fit in?' And if there even is such a thing as fitting in, as belonging? Do I need a niche at all, or is out here on my own, on Introvert Island the best, safest, most productive place for me to be? I live in East Galway, essentially in the Midlands, on the border with Roscommon. Though I am a member of Group 8, an artists' collective here, I don't hang around with writers except at literary events and festivals. And, to be honest, my favourite place of all is at my desk, deep in the work, in the meaty fairyland of the zone.

Unlike being social, my writing is not mood dependent. Five days a week I go to my desk. Whether I am happy, or down, tired or energetic, in mourning, or content with life, I go to my desk and write. Weirdly, the work produced on a bad mood day is no better or worse than that written on a good mood day. Which is why I always go to my desk and write. It's my sanity, my happiness, my joy.

Bob, a writer friend, talks about providence in his writing life as opposed to luck. He is fortunate – he has won several of America's major fiction prizes – but I understand that distinction he makes and why he makes it. Luck has not made him the successful writer he is; talent, incredible commitment, hard work, and a spark of providence has. The Oxford Dictionary's first definition of providence says it is 'the protective care of God or of nature as a spiritual power'. I much prefer its second definition: 'timely preparation for future eventualities'.

Do I feel lucky to lead the life I lead, with its emphasis on the imagination, on moulding words, and travelling to converse with other writers? Yes, I do feel lucky, of course I do. Are the storms inherent in the writer's life worth it? Yes, on balance, they are. If other people want to say that luck brought me here, let them. I will take Bob's lead and think of it as providence – I did a whole lot of timely preparation for the future eventualities that had me land right where I belong.

Nuala Ní Chonchúir, a.k.a. Nuala O'Connor, has published four short story collections, three novels and three poetry collections. Her third novel, *Miss Emily* (Penguin USA & Canada, & Sandstone UK), about the poet Emily Dickinson and her Irish maid, was shortlisted for the Bord Gáis Energy Novel of the Year 2015. www.nualanichonchuir.com

Poetry's Unintended Consequences...

Sarah Clancy

I hate misery memoirs but because this essay has some of those ingredients in it I want to let you know in advance that I am writing about something much different to misery. If it wasn't plagiarism I would steal the title of poet and activist Audre Lorde's searingly honest essay 'The Transformation of Silence into Language and Action' as the title for this one. In that essay Lorde, on being diagnosed with a life-threatening illness, realises that what she regretted most about her life was her silences or the times she waited for some other person to speak:

'I was going to die, if not sooner, then later, whether or not I had ever spoken myself. My silences had not protected me. Your silences will not protect you.'

I have a theory that writing poetry has taught me how to speak in the way Lorde is talking about. In this essay I want to examine that personal–political process of transformation that beginning to write creatively and to perform my work in public, during a time of recession, social change and personal trauma ignited for me.

I better give you a few details about myself so you know who you are dealing with. I am forty-three now, from an urban, middle-class, West of Ireland family. I left school at seventeen without really having any qualifications and spent a decade working on farms and at horse fairs buying and selling horses in rural Ireland. Eventually, afflicted by wanderlust, I travelled for a few of years working in various low-wage roles before returning to an Ireland that was beginning to improve economically. In this new Ireland I got some better paid work, in a factory to begin with and later in a travelling cinema where the manager encouraged me to start some evening courses. Eventually at thirty-five I managed to wrangle my way onto an MA course in university. After completing these studies I worked for a variety of human rights or social change organisations including Amnesty International. I didn't begin writing with any degree of seriousness until I was about thirty-six. Although I had written things like diaries, letters, song lyrics and bad adolescent poetry all my life and had always been a voracious reader, I had never really made any efforts to become published or to learn about how I could improve my writing. I had never taken any steps to 'become a writer'.

In 2009 I enlisted in the Over the Edge writers' workshops in Galway and since then I have written three collections of poetry and have also performed my poetry around Ireland and abroad at various types of events that include poets: readings, slam competitions, radio programmes, protests, academic conferences and the like. Now before it starts to sound like I am writing some form of very tedious and lacklustre literary CV, I want to tell you that during the same seven years the following things also happened and had a direct bearing on my life: because of the devastating recession that hit 'boom time' Ireland I ended up without work for the first time in my life. I found myself unable to cope with the things I needed to do in order to hold on to my house. I was luckier than most to be able to sell it in the collapsed property market but it did leave me with nothing to show for years of work and a small-ish debt which I haven't yet managed to pay back in full. All of this resulted in me having to move indebtedly and sheepishly back to my family home to live with my long-suffering parents and as the spiritual teacher Ram Dass quipped – 'If you think you are enlightened, spend a week with your family'. While I did find bits and pieces of work to do during this time (including working as a tour guide taking tourists around Ireland and extolling the virtues of our culture to them) for the first time in my life I became dependent on

Ireland's social welfare services. This was an education in itself, and one I wouldn't care to repeat, though my circumstances are still precarious enough to mean that it is far from out of the question.

> if I can't write about real things why bother?
> If I can't mock the signs on the wall at welfare
> that say after two decades of working
> now I'm likely to drink in the daytime
> to have poor personal hygiene
> or to spit and swear at the people who work there
> and are only paying their bills same as anyone

During these years too, like most people in Ireland, I had to negotiate the particularly poisonous atmosphere which was created when so-called austerity policies and the good old-fashioned Irish tradition of shame were combined. Countless friends and acquaintances' circumstances fell apart so much that they plummeted into trouble with homelessness, with their mental health, and several people in my immediate circle even took their own lives.

> And I remember Cuba Nightclub
> you dancing to the Jackson Five
> and us fizzing out into Eyre Square later
> with you telling me no day trippers need apply
> not some Month's Mind notice on a shop window
> in the rain a few short years later
> insisting that you've died.

At the same time as the recession many of Ireland's cultural certainties were eroding. The Catholic Church in particular was in freefall. While I worked at Amnesty International, the CEO there, Colm O'Gorman, released his book *Beyond Belief* which documented the sexual abuse he had experienced in his youth and his monumental effort to confront the Catholic Church in Ireland in pursuit of justice for himself and others. This coincided with or helped to provoke a period of intense media focus on childhood sexual abuse in Irish institutions. Revelation after revelation emerged demonstrating how widespread the sexual and physical abuse of children had been within our culture. The spotlight was also turned on our history of anti-woman practices such as the incarceration of women and children in mother and baby homes and Magdalene laundries.

Against this backdrop I began to come to terms with the fact that I too had been meticulously and thoroughly groomed and then abused when I was a child and adolescent by a much older man. Despite my own misgivings about doing so I became embroiled in an attempt to have the offender prosecuted which was eventually successful. Now I can hear you all thinking *mis lit* to yourself so I will get to the point which is to tell you that it was through writing creatively that I began to understand that I had, probably as a result of these damaging early experiences and the ones that followed, constructed an intricate and almost impermeable sort of smoke and mirrors series of feints and half-truths that allowed me to operate at some distance to reality and from any real knowledge of myself or of the culture I was living in. I know now that the psychoanalytic term for this is disassociation and that it is a very common effect of abuse. In fairness I probably could have explained exactly what it meant if you'd asked me in 2009 too, but the tricky thing about disassociation is that even if I was talking about it then, I would not have known it applied to me or that I was doing it.

> … and I am on the air now whinnying,
> I'm twanging like a string plucked and echoing,
> here I am my own doppelganger. I am listening.
> Can you hear me listening and don't I sound just like myself?

About writing though, despite my own very determined internal resistance to any unravelling of my defences, through the agency of putting pen to paper and creating something, I inadvertently and totally by accident started to break the silences I held that were damaging or limiting me, and these were silences within me that I honestly hadn't even really known existed. Somehow in whatever I wrote I found that I was poking monsters with sticks so they could not and would not go on sleeping.

Cold Cases
Some doors should stay shut
not all are portals
some conceal sleeping things
that are less ferocious
left undisturbed behind them
let's whisper this time can't we?
Let's not go in there
sharp stick poking
turn now with me – this time
let's keep on walking.

For me writing has been an ongoing process of personal de-colonisation. It is fascinating if simultaneously unnerving; every time I think that I have explored as far as I am going with the de-colonisation of my mind something happens to trigger or trip me into another new phase of it. I started out by writing smart alec poems, almost picaresques, little risk-free snapshots which were much like the types of conversations I had been accustomed to hearing in rural Ireland. My whole first book of poetry *Stacey and the Mechanical Bull* is taken up with a series of poems which are character sketches designed to make the reader and myself as the writer laugh. Alongside these though I was also writing really dark and strange poems, poems of love and loss and longing which I kept myself at a distance to. I can remember arriving at poetry workshops and reading these poems which I thought were not any way anchored in my personal experience only to find myself upset by them and to find my companions either embarrassedly silenced or gazing at me sympathetically. Strangely too though I experienced a kind of compulsion to share these exact poems, I began a habit – a bad one which I still have – of posting just-written poems on Facebook. Publish and be damned, I thought, but at the handy remove that social media gave me. Buried deeply amongst some of the other things I was learning at that time, the greatest surprise for me now is how deeply ashamed I felt after sharing these poems. Not only was I ashamed of sharing them, I was ashamed of writing them, of appearing to think that I was a writer and at even seeking the type of attention I was obviously looking for.

As I went on writing, I discovered that it was not possible for me to engage either my imagination or my subconscious without in the end being forced to confront or own up to a whole variety of things about myself and my place in the world that I had never previously given attention to. I discovered that I had been colonised in all sorts of ways. I'd been colonised by the conservative merchant prince type society I grew up in, colonised by religion, colonised by the power of others which was wielded in ways that were extraordinarily harmful to me. I was then re-colonised by my own need to appease or incorporate these experiences. Later on I was colonised by the need to be seen as 'reasonable', competent and not damaged. No matter how hard I tried to avoid the personal/ confessional, out it came in everything I wrote. Fictional characters that I created expressed things that I thought but hadn't realised, and even more scarily than that, every time I took my eyes off them they went off uninvited to revisit my own personal and formative experiences in ways I'd never been brave enough to do without them.

> ... so I can say Lazarus get up out of that
> because I want to talk to you about how I'd resolved
> to be only one person all of the time but then a woman came in
> to my ninth floor hotel room and stood at the window
> looking down at some city or other beneath her,
> I or the me I was using stayed at a distance
> with my back to the wall and across those great acres
> of room space and bed space and sheet span
> I watched the light burnish her edges;
> her ribcage, her jaw and the fine hairs on her arm
> and as the evening grew gentler I watched the rise and fall
> of her breath while the day itself melted and Lazarus
> I wanted to go to her but this I that I've chosen to be
> all of the time now didn't know how or where to begin,
> I didn't believe that my static-filled fingers could touch her
> and that she might welcome it and I wanted to tell you
> that I mightn't be able to stay being me in situations like this
> where I have all the ingredients gathered and measured
> and then I forget how to cook them and I'm saying this

because I've learned that staying one person isn't straightforward
and sometimes being truthful is less accurate
than having the courage to act the part beautifully,
and Lazarus I want to tell you whenever you get up
that I might not be able and I know you'll know what I mean
because we are each other's others and we know things:
Lazarus, it's high time you were up.

So far I have been focusing mostly on how the act of *writing* poetry has affected me in my life, but there has been another whole aspect to the affair between poetry and me that has been at least as important and that is the performance in public of my poems. Despite the fact that I have published three full collections of written poetry in a very short time (I am not commenting here on their literary merit or lack thereof, just that they have been written and published), if I am referred to anywhere in literary circles it is usually as a slam poet or a performance poet. I began this 'performing' of poetry at the now defunct North Beach Nights Slam Series in Galway. I don't think I'd had any great awareness that there was such a thing as performance poetry before that. I had already tried to read my poetry in public at a couple of more standard type readings, those ones where everyone sits quietly and the earnest poet reads their sombre work to the assembled audience who often give no appearance of being alive at all. Each time I had tried to read poems in public though I had been overwhelmed with nerves and I mean the whole hog: sweating, leg shaking, dry-mouthed nerves. These nerves came as a shock to me. By that stage of my life I was well accustomed to speaking in public for my work; I had been the spokesperson or rabble rouser for many a campaign and was often called on to go on radio or appear in public and so it took me entirely by surprise that I could be so debilitatingly nerve-struck just from trying to read a poem of my own. I know now that the problem was more than just nerves. When I was reading poetry without performing it, I was publicly dismantling various protective personas that had served me well and that I desperately wanted to cling to. For some reason which I still don't quite understand I was determined to keep going with poetry even as its effects unsettled me.

Back then I was less forgiving of myself and so, irritated with my own nervousness, I determined that I would read my poetry at every available opportunity until I got over the stage fright and this is what led me to North Beach Nights and other similar performance poetry events around the country. In the end, even though I had come to page poetry first, performance poetry took over. For someone as deflected and full of defences as I was there was something spectacularly liberating about taking up public space and using it to communicate emotionally charged poems. I think the best way to explain it is that I was acting out parts that I had written for myself in order to try them on and see if they fitted. Without a doubt too all sorts of things were at play for me in the spaces I got to occupy because of poetry: this is where a lot of the de-colonisation that I mentioned before happened. I was belatedly learning to recognise issues of gender, particularly of what type of woman was allowed to occupy what type of public space and how they were expected to behave there. Defiantly at first I was learning to feel entitled to take up space and attention without apologising for it, and I was without a doubt trying on aspects of my own sexuality in public. I had been 'out' as being queer, and mostly interested in women for a number of years before that but from the viewpoint I have today, I had never really taken any ownership of my own sexual identity and in fact was only really provoked into doing so finally during the marriage equality referendum in 2015. Bit by bit it seemed like I was test driving my own personality. While on one level my poems had exposed me to myself, on another level they became devices that provided a safe enough distance for me to role play some of the new discoveries I had made before I actually took real ownership of them.

> It began from fear of the moment sleep hits
> that unbearable inescapable loss of everything
> convinced me to undertake an occupation
> of the half deserted cities of the world at night time,
> I took to night walking that year in darkness
> I occupied the fear of falling, of sleeping
> I occupied the equal terrors of waking or not waking
> I escaped from lying in my stacked box apartment fearing
> the horror of sounds seeping from other people's radios,
> from the sheltered ughs of their futile attempts at lovemaking

One of the things about our contemporary human existences under the type of neoliberal precarity forced on us is that any sort of personal crisis has to happen against a back drop of frenetic twenty-four-hour-a-day activity, something is always happening somewhere and this was certainly true for me. Very often, unless a person is very secure financially, and has a strong support network, staying still is not an option. It seems at times that we are all swimming ferociously because if we stop we will drown. For me all this writing, publishing, performing and self-realisation happened while I was also trying very hard to actually just exist – working, paying bills, relating to other humans, losing a house, losing defences, confronting an abuser, dealing with the horrendous justice system and trying to keep the truth straight in my head for the guards who at one point wondered if I would not be better off just to 'forgive' my abuser. In this turmoil and difficulty though, I really benefitted from having begun to write and from having the outlet of public performances to deal with it all in. One great benefit of poetry for me other than the joy of actually writing it has been that whilst everything was apparently falling apart in other aspects of my life, somehow the poems that I wrote were finding audiences and connecting with people and this connection was rebounding in my direction. Bits of good news kept arriving on bad days. I would hear that a poem was being published somewhere, or that I had been placed in a competition, or I would get an invitation to read at a festival in another country. Even more importantly though from where I am standing now, I was largely accepted and welcomed and offered friendship by my fellow writers.

In a great example of fraud syndrome, it often occurs to me that my own engagement with poetry has had very little to do with literature. I have not really been consciously striving to write 'literature' or even wanting to be perceived as writing it. I noticed this quite strikingly on one occasion when I was invited to read at a festival with a renowned and highly talented poet. I was in weird dislocated humour the day of the reading, I felt like I was watching myself and her, and it became clear to me that other poet and I were doing completely different things. The other poet was inviting the audience to engage with her poems, with their skillfulness and erudition whereas what I was doing was standing there reading my poems and somehow through the medium of the poems saying, this is me, I am here and entitled to exist.

191

In a very perverse way during the last few years, whilst I found it difficult to talk about what was going on to the people I probably should have been talking to, I was able to excavate my own experiences in really public ways including national radio and at public events – memorably on one occasion to an audience of about 80,000 people at an anti-water charges protest.

Cherish the golf course
and its sprinklers, sure
Irish Water will save us,
cherish piece work and internships
and zero hour contracts,
aren't you lucky you have a job at all
do you not remember the coffin ships?
and are you not grateful
yea, cherish your own exploitation.

As well as the more customarily overt political-statement-type poem, from reading in political contexts I learned just how private and inward-looking the content of a populist poem can be. I learned that sometimes it is the act of making something unspoken public that makes poetry 'political', and I learned too that to do this I had to stand my ground and be willing to be associated with what I was saying. In doing that I think I have begun to learn to speak in the way that Audre Lorde meant in her essay. Like a lot of writers I often don't know exactly what I have written about until someone else interprets it or until there is a fair span of time between the writing of it and my own re-reading. In looking over my experience as a fledgling writer in Ireland over the last few years for the purposes of this essay, I think I have been writing against the culture of shame. Despite the severe indoctrination we experience under our catholo-capitalist regime which seeks to make us individually ashamed of what it perceives as failures – unemployment, poverty, abuse, emotion, childlessness, pregnancy, needing help, (the list is endless) – I seem to have been writing against this, in a way writing to say that people are not inherently shameful, that we, that I, am plenty good enough to stand up for something better than this overwhelmingly destructive economy-as-society existence. My experiments with writing and performing creatively showed me that I had been misunderstanding my centrality to my own life. It was only by freeing a sideways non-direct part of my brain that this façade of misunderstanding started to crumble. In lots of ways this has been terrifying and disorienting and I am not writing this from safety, although my circumstances have improved enormously. You'll have to take this as a message from the rubble, from the creative and mostly welcome devastation caused by the power of poetry in my own private and public life.

> In the cause of silence, each of us draws the face of her own fear … But most of all, I think we fear the visibility without which we cannot truly live.
>
> —Audre Lorde

Sarah Clancy is an award-winning page and performance poet from Galway. She has published three collections of poetry with the most recent being *The Truth and Other Stories* published by Salmon Poetry in 2014. She is on Twitter @sarahmaintains.

The Paradigm of Nowhere: Literature and the Suburbs

Rob Doyle

When the French novelist Michel Houellebecq moved to Ireland as a tax exile some years ago, he chose to live in a nondescript housing estate in the hinterlands of Shannon airport, rather than, say, in a Georgian townhouse in the heart of Dublin, or a windswept cottage looking onto the Atlantic. In interviews, J. G. Ballard mocked anyone who still thought that the 'real England' was to be found in the grand imperialist structures in the centre of London: Buckingham Palace, Tower Bridge, and so on. All of that, he argued, was little more than a museum display documenting a bygone period. He insisted that the *real* England was now to be found in the satellite towns, commuter belts, peripheral mega-malls, and the sprawl of the suburbs. Living by his own rhetoric, Ballard moved to the suburban town of Shepperton, outside London, in 1960, and stayed there until his death in 2009. Nowadays the myth of Ballard as inner-space visionary is inseparable from his Shepperton address. The narrator of his lysergic novel *The Unlimited Dream Company* describes Shepperton as 'the everywhere of suburbia, the paradigm of nowhere.'

Houellebecq and Ballard, two of the most original writers of recent decades, both wilfully opted to live and work in the kinds of place that many of us automatically think of as bland, soulless and boring. There are no doubt many aspirant writers growing up in the suburbs, satellite towns, and commuter-belt housing estates of Ireland, who long to get out as soon as they can and never look back. Probably there are fewer established writers determined to move to the suburbs and the new estates, and make that the material of their literary endeavours. Despite the Ballards and Houellebecqs, here in Ireland there seems to be a lingering sense that (to narrow our focus a little) the suburbs in particular are 'not literary'. If you write novels, it is generally assumed that you will write either about the countryside or the city, and not the seemingly faceless, characterless, ahistorical zones which are neither one nor the other and where, as it happens, so much of what now constitutes the 'real life' of Ireland takes place.

Sometimes in our assumptions we forget to move on, forget that we *already have* moved on. The suburbs are, of course, as 'literary' as anywhere else. They are as strange, eerie, rich with life and enigma, and as ripe for mythologisation, as anywhere else.

As is true of so many things, in the twentieth century it was the Americans, in particular the great alpha male novelists and story writers, who were ahead of the pack in exploiting the literary potential of the suburbs. Think of Richard Yates's *Revolutionary Road*; the copulative fictions of Updike; Cheever; Carver; Franzen; the DeLillo of *White Noise*. These writers helped to define how we think about life in the suburbs: dissatisfying, conformist, empty, desperate. Everyone sleeps around and everyone drinks too much. To locate the purest vision of existential desolation, look not to the Left Bank in Paris, nor the urban nocturnes of an Edward Hopper painting, nor the anguish of the avant-garde, but to an American suburb in the 1950s. In *Revolutionary Road*, a harrowing examination of the agonies behind suburban curtains, one character puts it thus: 'I guess when you do see the hopelessness, that's when there's nothing to do but take off. If you can.'

In laying bare the sadness, the boredom, and the hopeless emptiness, these pioneers of suburban literature helped to aestheticise, even glamorise the suburbs, to make it seem that some kind of poetry was feasible there.

I myself grew up in the suburbs of south Dublin, and I got out as soon as I could. I don't particularly want to move back. While it's possible that I may never again feel compelled to write about the suburbs, I have done so. After years of false starts and abandoned typescripts, I finally found myself writing about bored, disaffected, angry, hard-drinking suburban youth. In other words, I started writing about my own background, in fictional form.

For the first twenty-three years of my life I lived in a semi-detached, two bedroom, Corporation-built house in Crumlin. My parents still live there. They bought the house as a young couple in the early eighties, on my father's postal worker salary. The house is about seventy years old now, and had only one previous owner before my parents bought it. It's on Kildare Road, the same road where a young Brendan Behan once lived and, allegedly, caused an explosion while making bombs for the IRA in the bathroom. I'm one of those people who enjoy visiting the former homes of eminent writers, but I don't recall ever seeking out the plaque that I'm told adorns Behan's house at 70 Kildare Road, despite living just a couple of corners down the road for so many years.

The suburbs made me, for better or worse, as a man and as a writer. I did not enjoy growing up in Crumlin. The suburbs in general, and Crumlin in particular, didn't suit my temperament, or so I liked to think. I wanted the expansive and the sublime, but what they gave me was the cramped and the banal. I distinctly remember thinking, as a caustic teenager, that no one of any note could possibly have come from Crumlin. A Google search now tells me that all manner of celebrated people, from Gabriel Byrne to Fintan O'Toole, not to mention Paul McGrath, did grow up in the area. There have even been a few writers, including the aforementioned Behan. Evidently, hailing from Crumlin doesn't automatically mean being a raging malcontent, doomed to obscurity. Nonetheless, there are many truths in life, particularly where strong emotions are involved, that we only figure out in hindsight. When I say that the suburbs of south Dublin made me, I can see now that much of this can be related to a single concept: space.

A year and a half ago, my then girlfriend and I spent some time travelling around Ireland where she, being French, had never previously been. For the last couple of nights, we stayed at my parents' house on Kildare Road. Alice, my ex, looked about the place in wonderment. It must have been very difficult, she suggested, for a family with three sons to live together in such a small house. As soon as she said it, I could see how perfectly true it was, yet it had never occurred to me before. Growing up, I hadn't thought that I lived in a small house: why would I, when it was the only one I knew?

In the light of this simple revelation, a lot of things made more sense to me. *I* made more sense to me. My writing, that too made more sense.

In 2014 my first novel, *Here Are the Young Men*, was published. That is the book I produced when I finally decided to stop trying to write about exotic, far-flung places, and turn my attention to the south-Dublin, suburban existence I'd known growing up. Although I like to think it's funny, pacy and energetic, the book is also bleak, brutal, feverish and anxiety-ridden. Perhaps the best adjective with which to capture its tone would be 'claustrophobic'. The summer of its publication, I did a long interview with Olaf Tyaransen of *Hot Press*. The issue went to print while I was in the south of France with my ex. I read the interview online, and found that Tyaransen, an admirer of the novel, had described *Here Are the Young Men* as 'the product of an obsessive, if not downright disturbed mind.' This made me laugh. It also made me wonder.

As many other writers before me have learned, you cannot really choose what you write about: like it or not, everything you produce is a self-portrait. I hadn't necessarily intended to write a novel that twitched with obsessiveness and claustrophobia: that's just the way it came out. Nowadays, I would say I'm a more or less serene person. I like silence, my own company, long walks in the city, browsing in bookshops, watching the world from a café table. Every time I return to the house where I grew up, though, I can feel the old neurosis kick in pretty much immediately. There's just no *space*. You can hear the people in the other rooms; you have to keep your voice down on the phone unless you want everyone to hear what you're saying; back garden conversations must also be muted if you'd rather the neighbours weren't privy. There is too much proximity and this breeds irritability, malcontentedness, neurosis. A few days there and your eyebrow starts to twitch. Twenty-three years there and you end up writing a novel that even a sympathetic interviewer calls the product of a disturbed mind.

What Roberto Bolaño called 'the literature of desperation' tends not to emerge from the countryside, nor from the townhouse, and certainly not from the Big House. Writers who grew up in such environments as those – in other words, the producers of most of the Western literary canon – tend to have more capacious, reasonable, reflective, serene inner worlds than the multitudinous children of the suburbs. Naturally, there are exceptions: the misanthropic rural rants of Thomas Bernhard come to mind. Still, I think we can make the generalisation without too much hazard. The literature of desperation used to come from the inner city; now, by and large, it comes from the suburbs. There are no Virginia Woolfs in Kilnamanagah, no Thomas Manns in Finglas, no William Blakes in Blanchardstown. Or are there? I think again of J. G. Ballard, and his celebrated exhortation for science-fiction writers to forget about outer space, and turn instead to *inner* space, the new enigmatic frontier. Perhaps the very drabness of the suburbs will yet prove a suitably pressurised site, for those who can hold their nerve, to blast away from the outer world and embark upon the psychonaut's voyage.

I am proud of what I write, in all its rage, madness and long pent-up frustration. When I spend time in the serene and spacious homes of friends in the countryside, though, I occasionally feel uneasy about it all. Friedrich Nietzsche, surveying the contemporary scene with its Christian, egalitarian morality, frequently lost his cool: 'Bad air!' he exclaimed. 'Bad air!' A virulent anti-liberal with a loathing for socialism, anarchism and the democratic spirit, he insisted that nothing noble, beautiful or worthwhile could come from origins that were cramped, ugly, confined, and proletarian. The working class suburbs of Dublin, or Crumlin at least, could be described as most of those things, especially if one were hungover. If you come from the working class, if you come from the suburbs, and you take someone like Nietzsche to heart, you might come to lose pride in your origins. And who needs that? For all my occasional moments of discomfort, I am essentially at ease with the fact that the fictions I write portray characters who are closed in, frenzied, and prey to extreme nervous agitations – just like the troubled, addled young men and women I knew growing up in suburban Dublin. Writing that is forged in such an environment will always be irate, pent-up, and finally explosive. Freedom resides in determining what form the explosion will take.

Rob Doyle's first novel, *Here Are the Young Men*, was one of *Hot Press* magazine's '20 Greatest Irish Novels Since 1916', and was selected as a book of the year in *The Irish Times, Sunday Times, Irish Independent* and *Sunday Business Post*. His second book, *This Is the Ritual*, is published by Bloomsbury. Rob is the editor of the Dalkey Archive's forthcoming anthology of Irish literature.

On Breaking the Silence of Immigrant Voices

Dominique Cleary

'My mother says you can only really be brave if you know you will lose. And the silent negative is not like any other silence either, because one day you will say what you are thinking out loud with your arms folded, like Marianne. You can't be afraid of saying the opposite, even if you look like a fool and everybody thinks you're in the wrong country, speaking the wrong language.' – Hugo Hamilton, *The Speckled People*

I was a teenager when my family moved to Ireland in 1984. Spanish is the official language of Ecuador, but I grew up in a bilingual household. My father was American and I had his accent. My spoken English was reasonable, but my written English needed work.

Within days of landing, I was sent to school on a bicycle. To add to my disorientation, I had to travel on the wrong side of the road and negotiate roundabouts in reverse. I struggled to remember the names of the girls in my class. Sinéad, Aoife, Naoimh, Gráinne, Siobhán were all new sounds to my ears. And even when I finally conquered the phonetics, they remained an enigma in their spelling.

I discovered how few of my classmates had heard of Ecuador. Being so far away brought my country and all that I had taken for granted while living there into sharper focus. I wanted to share it and in my enthusiasm I probably came across like a geography tutorial. I was often met with that thin line between boredom and mild interest when I described that it was on the equator of South America; that it had some of the highest peaks and volcanoes in the Andes; that it was partly covered by Amazonian jungle and that Charles Darwin had developed the theory of evolution on our Galápagos Islands.

My new friends teased me that I lived up a tree and wore a loincloth like a 'savage'. I was afraid to over-explain myself, so I didn't say that I had left behind a modern capital city in a relatively prosperous oil and coffee producing country. And I certainly didn't mention the bananas. That would have compounded the ridicule. It was easier to stay silent, to smile and swallow my memories, and to avoid conversations that would touch the homesickness nerve. It was easier to try to disappear into the crowd.

We were frequently asked how long we would be staying. There was an inherent suspicion in the question. No one in their right mind would come to live in Ireland, especially from a better climate. The 1980s were depressed years of high unemployment so the quizzical looks abounded. It was a time when air travel was expensive, Europe was still referred to as 'the Continent' and Ireland felt like a faraway outpost.

The obvious outsiders at the time were mostly diplomats or refugees who had come from Chile and Vietnam in the 1970s. We had tourist visas until my mother became the Consul of Ecuador. When I was no longer her dependant, my status in Ireland became vulnerable. I learned not to draw attention to my foreign origins. I was lucky to be white and that my surname was Cleary. A connection with Ireland, though not traceable, was generally presumed.

I am an Irish citizen now, I have Irish children, and after thirty years I have absorbed the Irish way of life, acquired some turns of phrase and developed a stoicism towards rain. I will never really know how much Ireland means to me unless I have to leave it. But even after all this time, I have yet to feel fully integrated. I skirt pronouns like 'we' and 'you' when referring to my life in Ireland.

I identified with Molly McCloskey, an Irish-American writer, in her essay 'These are my floods' when she describes, I paraphrase, how, even though she never felt unwelcome in Ireland, she knew that Irishness was very narrowly and historically defined. Even if she lived here forever, she would never possess the collective memory. And because she couldn't *feel it*, she will always be excluded at an emotional level from the 'national conversation'.

My Ecuadorian maternal grandfather died in 2008. I went home to Quito for his funeral. Amid the heartbreak of losing him and all that he symbolised in my past, I found I was also grieving for my divided self. He was a writer and when I read his final book, a memoir, I felt the need to map my own experiences. Writing became my way of making sense of the cultural abyss between my past and my present. When I started to write, I tried to ignore the niggling feeling that my themes all evolved from my disquiet at being a perpetual outsider in Ireland, and after thirty years, in Ecuador too, and I worried that my memories of a faraway place in another time would not have value or relevance in modern Ireland.

When I began to look for outlets for my stories and essays, I came across the term 'Irish Writing'. I observed how it dominated the literary landscape and I tried to figure out whether I fell within its boundaries and how I was going to relate to it, if at all. I discovered it to be an elastic term with no concise definition. It holds the greats like Joyce, Beckett and O'Brien, Elizabeth Bowen's big houses, J. G. Farrell, the outward vision of Aidan Higgins, and the multitudinous contemporary scene. And it includes books by Irish authors in Ireland, London, New York and all over the world, written from a myriad of perspectives: the diaspora, the return, nostalgia, religion, sexual repression, the economic boom, post-crash Ireland. I searched for people like me, the non-Irish, the new Irish.

A book with a difference and one that recognises the cultural diversity of Irish writing and Irish life and speaks to me as an outsider, is Hugo Hamilton's *The Speckled People*. It was published first in London by Fourth Estate in 2003. At its simplest, it tells the story of children dressed in Lederhosen and Aran sweaters growing up in a household where only Irish and German are spoken. English, the language of everyone else, is prohibited within the home. The children inhabit a crossroads between the father's idealised hope for the future and the mother's private haunting by her lost past. The father is an authoritarian Irish-language-speaking figure who yearns for an Irish culture free from Anglo-American contamination. Hugo Hamilton says of his family: 'We are the new Irish. Partly from Ireland and partly from somewhere else, half-Irish and half-German. We're the speckled people, he says, the "brack" people, which is a word that comes from the Irish language…. [it] means speckled, dappled, flecked, spotted, coloured.'

Gerald Dawe, poet and academic, in his article 'Breaking the closed shop of Irish Writing', said the memoir challenged 'the standard critical categories which operate, both internally and externally' to the phrase 'Irish Writing'. When used liberally without cognisance of the effect of its narrowest definition, it can marginalise, repress stories and stunt writers struggling to integrate and who feel insecure about sharing their family's 'non-Irish' past. It can narrow the scope of 'our' literature. *The Speckled People* asserts that 'Irish' is no monolithic cultural or political entity.

Hugo Hamilton, in his piece 'A right turn out of silence', written for the launch in 2010 of an anthology of sixty-six immigrant poets entitled *Landing Places: Immigrant Poets in Ireland* spoke of the silence of immigrants. I recognised my own hesitancy and doubts at self-expression in his description of it as 'the inability to trust what you feel. The fear that you will not be understood in this country. The suspicion that your memory as a newcomer is of no relevance here and that only Irish memory and Irish achievements and Irish cultural landmarks are worth talking about.'

According to Hamilton, the anthology was evidence of inclusion, the message being that 'the experience of immigrants matters to us, that we value their words and their views and the impressions they have gathered of this country. It is also saying that we value their memory, the stories they have brought with them, the joy and the pain and the homesickness they have for the places they left behind.'

Gerald Dawe believes that the diversity in Irish social life has always been 'anecdotally recognised but officially ignored' and that to 'draw attention to a different way of lifestyle and/or history was conventionally seen as drawing attention away from the big picture of the achievements of an Irish Ireland, or, in Northern Ireland, the cause of Unionism and the cherished British connection'. Irish history has been underscored by migration in both directions. The Huguenots came in the eighteenth century and among their descendants were literary geniuses like Samuel Beckett and Stewart Parker. European refugees, including Jewish and other minorities, have also settled in Belfast, Dublin and Cork. They blended into the background when the struggle for independence became the main narrative.

Dawe was not entirely optimistic that *Landing Places* was likely to change the terrain of the Irish literary landscape. He said we have only to observe post-Celtic Tiger Ireland and its political and cultural landscape, where the general feeling is of having lost one's bearings, to wonder 'whether the opportunity has not already been missed, along with much else, in generating a genuinely vibrant multicultural civic society rather than the often pietistic homilies that often stand in for thoughtful and actual planning ahead or resources and educational opportunity.' Racism, Dawe says, is 'etched under the surface of Irish life' and what has emerged post-crash is self-obsession.

My first experience of submitting work in the hope of being published and therefore my first interaction with the term 'Irish Writing' was with 'New Irish Writing' in the weekend section of *The Irish Times*. Every month, I read the featured story and poem and carefully studied the biographical notes about the authors. I was aware of the influence and importance of the Hennessy Awards for New Irish Writing in launching careers and shaping the literary landscape. Indeed so many of the best Irish writers today broke through on the page. I believed my first hurdle was one of eligibility.

The submission guidelines asked the question 'Are you a new Irish writer?' I wondered whether I could seek comfort in the fact that the origins of the page were in the literary quarterly *Irish Writing* founded in 1946 by David Marcus, a grandson of a Lithuanian immigrant. I even wondered whether I could make a fanciful interpretation of 'new' as qualifying 'Irish' rather than 'writer'.

I should not have felt so insecure because the guidelines were clear in that submissions were accepted from Irish-born people and Irish residents. However, I felt the need to explain my provenance in a covering letter, the fact of my Irish citizenship and the number of years I had lived in Ireland. I received an encouraging reply to my submission and I have submitted one or two more stories since then. I have seen worthy stories published by Irish citizens living in South Africa, Canada and Scotland. But nothing yet has been published by a non-Irish person resident in Ireland.

I found a ready welcome from the editors of two journals to whom I submitted my essays: the *Dublin Review* and *gorse*. I had read their back issues and perceived their openness to international voices living in Ireland. And through further exploration, I was pleased to find other journals showing a similar interest.

The feature *Writing Home*, edited and compiled by Nessa O'Mahony, appeared in the Summer 2009 issue of *The Stinging Fly*. O'Mahony discovered that her cultural identity or Irishness seemed heightened when she moved to the UK for postgraduate studies. She sought out writers who, like her, shared the distinct quality of writing through 'the prism of displacement'. The contributions represented the tension between 'home of origin' and 'home of choice'. Among the nineteen contributors were writers like Ozotu Rosemary Abu from Nigeria and Christina Aguilera Arias from Argentina, both poets not prose writers, living in Ireland at the time.

As my writing output began to increase, I became interested in the requirements of Irish publishers. I scanned through the list on the Publishing Ireland website. With the exception of international presences that have worldwide markets, such as Dalkey Archive Press, Hachette Books Ireland and Penguin Ireland, many Irish publishers are specialist and have clear statements on their websites about the type of writing they support.

Some state that they are 'Irish publishers' willing to publish books 'that appeal to the Irish market' (North and South), and require 'Irish interest material', 'Irish interest books' on 'broadly Irish interest themes'. Phrases like 'if you or your book don't have a connection to Ireland, we probably aren't the right publisher for you' or 'please don't submit to us if you're not an Irish or Irish-based author' appear. Others urge those submitting to ensure that their work is in line with their current list.

These phrases are not exclusionary on purpose. A practical reason for the requirement of Irish residence or an Irish connection is to limit the deluge of unsolicited submissions from abroad. But a difficult requirement for a non-Irish writer resident in Ireland is the need to fall in line with publishers' current listings where there is a dearth of immigrant literature. It is a circuitous argument along the chicken and egg cliché, but it is difficult to see how a new immigrant voice might be encouraged.

Tramp Press, run by Lisa Coen and Sarah Davis-Goff, breaks the mould. Their website states 'if you are a brilliant fiction writer of any description at all, we're looking for you.' In fact, Tramp launched itself into the publishing world in 2014 with *Flight,* a novel by Oona Frawley, a Joycean scholar born in New York to Irish parents. The novel is set in the run-up to the 2004 Irish Citizen Referendum which changed the law for children born in Ireland with foreign parents. (It took away their automatic right to citizenship.) Frawley had lived in Ireland since 1999 and was well placed to write about the Irish attitude to 'foreigners' or the 'new Irish'.

Until Tramp Press came along, she had searched for a publisher for ten years. Others were unsure if they could sell the book. It was suburban, the characters were cosmopolitan and a black Zimbabwean protagonist proved a stretch at the time. It was not considered the 'right kind of Irish'. It was suggested to Frawley that she take out her black character or make her Polish. Furthermore, marketers wanted to make the most of Frawley's family connection to Wicklow in order to ensure sales.

We need only to look at the recent results from the Central Statistics Office census to see how vital it is that Ireland embrace a more open and dynamic culture, one that enjoys being part of the greater world outside itself instead of reverting to tired ideas about identity and narratives of the past. Only preliminary results were available from the 2016 census at the time of writing. However, the census taken prior to that, on 2 April 2011, shows a total of 544,357 non-Irish nationals living in Ireland, an increase of 143 per cent in nine years, and that figure is likely to have increased again. The average age was 32.6. Almost 48 per cent of non-Irish nationals who spoke a foreign language had a high standard of English. And 344,929 non-Irish nationals had completed their education. All these factors point to a mature, literate, and English-speaking pool of potential creativity and expression.

The question of nationality was asked for the first time in the census of 2002. The top ten countries of origin out of 199 listed in the 2011 census were: Poland, United Kingdom, Lithuania, Latvia, Nigeria, Romania, India, Philippines, Germany and the United States. If Ireland is to become a centre of creativity and progress, these voices and others should be at the very heart of what shapes Irishness today.

Dominique Cleary is from Ecuador and lives in Dublin. She has published essays in *gorse* and the *Dublin Review*. She has worked as a solicitor and a mediator. She recently completed the MPhil in Creative Writing at Trinity College Dublin.

Seize the Means of Publication
(Hard Lessons Learned as a Working-Class Writer)

Lisa McInerney

MY LIFE IS NOT NEWS

In 2006 I had a blog called *Arse End Of Ireland*. This title referred less to a geographical point than it did to a state of mind, because everyone in Ireland thinks their corner is the arse of it. The blog functioned mostly as an outlet; it sharpened my wits and obliged me to learn to work to deadline, but it also gave me a place to waffle, because coming in at the wrong end of a huge family, no one listened to me in real life.

The blogging software made a writing platform available to all manner of chancers. I was living in a council estate in a small Galway town; I was surrounded by chancers. I was typically up for a bit of chancing myself. I wrote about life as I experienced it: boy racers, dealing with the County Council, feral terriers, cans, setting wheelie bins on fire, Supermac's and, on dark occasion, how the decisions taken by the government in Dublin affected those of us clinging to the margins. The working class, or the welfare class. I come from somewhere between the two.

I wrote with some degree of lurid intimacy; I changed names and edited rambling conversations, but otherwise I was personal, political, vulgar and plain. There was an element of anarchy to *Arse End*, in that it depicted a panorama different to the one detailed by mainstream media, where Ireland was affluent and cosmopolitan and populated with tanned and sartorially prudent counterfeit Americans. My Ireland (I am told even now) seemed a refreshing counterpoint to this national campaign aimed at convincing us we were very swanky altogether.

'My' Ireland was common as muck but portrayed uncommonly.

After megajoules spent trying to distance myself from my blogging beginnings, it occurred to me that I should wonder why. There was nothing so ignominious about it. Blogging felt far too egalitarian a method, populist rather than hard-won. I was being very hard on myself. Harsh. Apologetic. Ashamed. And why? We talk so much now about the arts being closed-off to working-class creatives that I should be making more of my way in. I suppose one far too easily falls in with the fever dream of workable meritocracy. There is no meritocracy, only graft and grift.

Defining the working-class writer in an Irish context is a difficult thing, so sure are we all that we're at least a little bit working class, or that if we're middle class we're once-removed from working class, that there's a shadow of hard work and ballsiness there somewhere and don't you dare doubt it, like it is an outrage that an onlooker might imply privilege or accident of birth had a hand in one's success. 'Of course I'm working class,' a friend once exclaimed to me. 'My father was a *dentist*.'

It is much easier to see through this with artists from the United Kingdom, where class seems to come in definitive strata; accent, address and schooling history are that much harder to belie, as plenty the Mockney scamp has discovered. For so long in Ireland class seemed so immutable that it was hardly applicable in the everyday: there were Protestants and there were Catholics, the aristocratic Anglo-Irish and the shifty, spitting natives. One hundred years into our nationhood and the notion of social class pervades but is porous; it is easily obscured or transferred. A handy trick, when the populace wishes to be seen as affluent and cosmopolitan but also scarred by circumstance and tough as Connemara goats.

This class permeability is especially true of rural Ireland. I went to the same school as the children of bank managers and doctors simply because it was the only school available, and outside of the odd sneering altercation about the provenance of a pair of jeans, we all mixed well enough. Certainly no teacher or parent or more economically advantaged student told me I couldn't be a writer; I didn't know there were class obstacles most insidious and sly on all paths to the creative careers. I just set out, as a person sets out on any excursion, not knowing whether there's a bus coming around the next corner ready to knock her into the middle of last week.

But then this is the crux of class: the clash between individual goals and the restrictions of this social construct – the personal versus the communal, a constant struggle between what you want and the reasons you cannot have it. If I started out writing now, I would be far more certain of the likelihood of failure than I was when I started posting gonzo meanderings online from the box room of my state-owned three-bed. Perversely, in acknowledging the class barriers in the arts we can unintentionally strengthen them.

MY LIFE IS NOT LITERARY

The creative sorts I met growing up tended to be bohemian refugees from the capitalist class, people who wore loud prints and didn't brush their hair and spoke with English accents. The kids who took Art at my school were their children; they were into pottery and asymmetric hairstyles. They were othered, or I was othered; we othered each other.

The biggest stumbling block for potential working-class creatives in Ireland is education, but not just in the sense that we might not be able to afford it or do not have access to it or need a particular kind of it for scribbling yarns. Education, in my family, was a block concept: study, in a general sense, and get general points to put towards a third-level course. Scholarly knowledge was something you were expected to acquire but sit on until exam time – you didn't share what you'd learned, in the way you did not share the details of your bodily secretions. Correcting an older family member was likely to get you a dead leg. *We are so very proud of you, vaguely, please do not give us the details.*

'Does she read a lot?' my Leaving Certificate English teacher asked my mother.

'She does.'

'I could tell. You can always tell which ones read.'

This pleased my mother greatly, because it meant I was educating myself, quietly, in another realm altogether.

No one read literature in our house. There was a shelf full of novels visitors had brought through Shannon airport. The paperback spines were fanned and tearing; there were colourless slashes through names like Alistair MacLean, Catherine Cookson, Judith Krantz, Erich Segal. I played with these books as if they were action figures. Moved by this display of tragic oddity, family members started bringing me age-appropriate books, memorably a misprinted Bible with pictures that I coloured in (to my mother's horror) and half a dozen Brown Watson classics, all of which I still have, all of which are mangled. I wandered from Narnia to Kirrin Island to Wonderland, stockpiling the tools of an eventual trade. I joined the library and withdrew the same books over and over. I amassed facts and opinions. I became a pain in the arse.

In a house in which the most-read publications were the *Sunday World* and *The Puzzler*, writing was an incongruous hobby, pleasant in small doses in a fool's leisure time. Writing to be read was an alien concept. Art was a corruptive thing. Having too much of it was warping. One distant cousin swore blind he'd been offered seventy-five thousand euro for his novel, a thing of which he spoke often, but a thing no one had ever seen. He was also an alcoholic and a deviant, and no one liked him.

When education is of arm's-length importance, you may educate people, but rarely will you educate them to the point of their being sure-footed in a creative realm. The romantic slant is that art is better when the artist is near breaking point, which is nonsense, of course. Writing requires comatic bloody-mindedness. Anxiety is bad for it; real life is bad for it; guilt is a killer altogether. Working-class writers experience the same drag towards the written word as anyone else; the problem, for us, is that even if we adequately manage the guilt inherent in arsing with allegory we haven't learned the poise to handle the professional side of it. The grant applications. The pitches. The negotiations. It is so very hard to escape the feeling that you're being self-indulgent, hiding from responsibility, playing pretend.

Now add to that the holes in your reading when you come from a house without literature – when you would have read Nabokov and Proust and Conrad and bloody Joyce and bloody Beckett if only someone had said you were supposed to – and an inability to explain the hidden machinery in the craft because you'd never come into contact with those who'd studied it. *How do you write?* I don't know, I just do. *But put that 'do' in the context of this greater literary world, this national history.* I can't. I never really knew it.

There is the chance of creative writing instruction. When this is structured as part of an academic degree it can seem preposterously unattainable to the working-class writer, expensive and ultimately unprofitable, and therefore – again – self-indulgent. Part-time evening courses are easier to get one's guilty head around. These can go no short distance towards assuaging a writer's fears about isolation and legitimising her ambition. Access is often the problem. Courses are usually held in urban centres, well and good only if you correlate working class with streets and suburbs. Even if these courses and their associated creative communities are physically accessible, the writer who needs them most is not guaranteed to find them, or to acknowledge that these spaces are open to her. Self-indulgent, you see. A waste of time and money. A hobby class for bored and bratty beatniks.

MY LANGUAGE IS NOT LITERARY

The fewer published working-class authors who speak for their craft, the more compartmentalised by class the world of literature becomes, the more insular it becomes, the narrower its definitions. The fewer working-class writers we have, the greater the chance of middle-class leitmotifs defining literary themes. Fewer working-class writers try to get published. More books appear about mid-life crises, disillusionment with the self, ennui, ominously large houses, brooding affairs with pert protégées and literal voyages of discovery. And these plots and themes become interchangeable with literature, shorthand for human experience.

There's some small overlap between working-class fiction and transgressive fiction, particularly in fiction from this north Atlantic archipelago. If a character's merely being working class is edgy, any attempts to escape the confines of class will be transgressive. Nihilistic rebellion, mob rule, heists, assorted violent escapades, moral compasses askew. In transgressive fiction, middle-class characters act out to save themselves from spiritual stagnation. Working-class characters do it for fiscal advancement.

Whether their arcs are transgressive or entirely non-combative, middle-class characters enjoy moments of reflection, great epiphanies, and love affairs for the ages; working-class characters fight, fuck and spew great wads of colloquial imprecations. There's often humour in the sweary, working-class rejoinder. Without humorous intent, that language becomes 'challenging', wilfully anarchistic rather than indigenous.

In real life, sweary comebacks are not always entertained. I am admonished now and again for my use of swearwords – usually by middle-class people. This policing of language, sorting words into levels of legitimacy, is more than mildly silly. As you benefit from language, so you have the duty to force its evolution (perversely, a writer's job is to freeze lexicon and make it permanent; writing is a contrariwise, regressive act, really).

It's a more than mildly silly thing too in literary fiction, where the odd fuck is held as delightful, especially when applied in the context of a spot of pseudo-savage lovemaking, but too many fucks and the writer's work will be affixed with the prefix 'urban' to warn those about to receive that it's a journey down the seedy streets of argot and patois. The logic here is rickety: 'literary' fiction applies to those stories that have transcended storytelling to become art, and making art too accessible is anathema, for how can something be art if any chancer can make sense of it? Ergo, can it be art if it's written in the vernacular, which is so full of fucks and bollocks? And so the challenge to working-class writers is to sufficiently elevate their vocabularies and cease being so bloody earthy.

But someone's got to be earthy; middle-class fiction isn't guaranteed to accurately demonstrate the realities of working-class life, but if working-class authors want to be taken seriously must they be more middle-class? Must they engage in the war on salty language, and send their fucks to the frontline?

Or can they get around this by writing their working-class characters' dialogue phonetically, so that readers can tell they sound like slack-jawed yokels, and so remain safely deviant? *Wha'? Ya blaydin' thick, ya.*

MY LIFE IS NOT FEMININE

How dare you use the word 'cunt', a woman on Twitter flung at me, *when it's so misogynistic?* I hadn't realised it had but one meaning. It had bent away from Middle English and wasn't at all a gendered word in my side of the country; I'd heard it applied to sneaky men long before I'd realised it had something to do with genitalia. *Young feminists!* howled my rebuker, in the manner of someone bemoaning the congregation of damn kids on her lawn.

There is something about a sweary working-class man that's legitimate, fetishised. There is something male about swearing, and something male about being working class. All that struggle, you know. All that sweat and block-laying and emigration and stout-drinking. When one thinks of working-class communities one thinks of men in white vests, young lads in hoodies. In the manner of Terry Pratchett's dwarves, the feminine is there but no one seems to want to think too hard about it.

When first people started comparing my writing to that of other authors writing fiction about working-class characters or set in dirty cityscapes, they were almost exclusively male examples: Irvine Welsh, Kevin Barry, Joe Orton, even Dickens. The first point of reference is usually male; the literary avatar is usually male. 'It's such a male book,' I was told of *The Glorious Heresies*, more than once – a book with themes like sex work, motherhood, gender roles, predatory femininity, abortion and revealing Halloween costumes. In gendering it, some readers found it easier to digest. 'Working class' evokes aspects of violence, roughness, rolled-up sleeves, drunken banter and inopportune expectorating, all traditionally mannish pursuits. When one is asked to consider 'working class' only in its feminine aspects, one comes up with mouthy pregnant teenagers or mouthy pregnant fishwives. Maybe the no-nonsense single mam with a heart of gold. Tropes they may be, but even as tropes they take second billing to their masculine equivalents. They are supports against which masculine motifs can holler and flail.

Outside of the context of motherhood, working-class femininity is rarely celebrated, either in fiction or reality. Certainly, being a working-class woman writer has its own challenges, its own peculiar clash between duty and safety. As a novelist it is my duty to accurately portray whatever side of life I'm writing down. As a woman it's my obligation to stay out of trouble.

The physical world is no place for a girl, apparently. The woman novelist cannot always walk the streets and feel what it is she's meant to capture. She cannot take off into the wild, listen to the wind, touch the ground, eyeball the malcontents. Even in her own neighbourhood, in the world she's passionate about getting right, she is frequently unsafe. She cannot walk at nighttime, she cannot talk to strangers, she must never be alone outside. Working-class fiction is, by glorious definition, writing about reality, but reality isn't safe for a woman. What a dichotomy! Imagine the worst from the safe indoors. Write about serial killers.

MY LIFE IS NOT GENUINE

In the spitting fire of strife the worst input is a wordy one.

'Here comes McInerney with all her fucking logic!' my friend T screamed in a defensive rage, then smashed his phone off the footpath. He'd lost the rag because he'd been caught doing something he wasn't supposed to be doing in the toilets of an underground club in Cork. I'd made an error in trying to reason with him; he was agitated and I was too fond of the reasonable gab. T was a fella that in jocular moments appointed my privately educated husband the title of 'lord', in that kind of edgy waggishness most susceptible to splintering. 'I thought he must have been a prick,' he admitted, years later. 'He knew so many words.'

I've found that my version of reality as a working-class author is automatically suspect because everyone assumes me to be middle class. It is a bizarre thing to be supposed to be appropriating your own background, forging patronising parables from your own truth. I've been frowned at for allowing my working-class characters vocabularies that are surely beyond the plebeians, and asked about why the middle and working classes mix so well in my writing (they weren't mixing; the person asking had just assumed one character was middle class because she wasn't quarrelsome and attended university).

It's an Ouroboros of misdiagnosis: the characters aren't thick and taciturn enough to be working class, even though they're directed by a working-class creator, who is not quite thick or taciturn enough to be authentic, and so therefore must have flayed a peasant to wear her hide.

Earlier this year I was scolded for writing a brief piece about social issues. The presumably working-class complainant, believing me bloated of bank account, was very put out that someone so la-di-dah was allowed to venture an opinion about the state of the nation. That's problematic in many ways, but mostly I was annoyed that someone thought me middle class (an outrage, you will recall). Erased by my own! It's too ridiculous, I thought, and stewed for longer than was reasonable.

I'm suspicious of writers who do not come from working-class backgrounds but who choose to write about the working class. They may do a fine job portraying lives different to those they've known, or their own circumstances may have brought them close enough to the facets of working-class life they're describing – the big, squabbling family; the mistrust of authority; perhaps they've been kicked a few rungs down the ladder and now occupy spaces beside the rest of us, their only elevations their accents. After all, it's the job of the writer to put themselves in the heads of others, and what a boring literary landscape it would be, if we only ever wrote about writers (there are far, far too many literary novels about writers). But I am fearful of the bourgeois creative – a horror of the *haute bohème* – portraying the proletariat as colourful entertainments, people so lacking in social grace that they're liable to say or to do absolutely anything: get arrested, get pregnant, get smashed, get killed.

Which is why the working-class writer is obliged to steel herself to ignore the class barriers in the arts.

MY NARRATIVE IS MY RESPONSIBILITY

The otherwise crucial discussion about the proliferation of privately-educated practitioners in all areas of the arts has a sour kicker; like those monsters urban legends say live in mirrors, when you talk about it too much you make it real. There are those of us that assume Writing is a gentrified neighbourhood, where the minted meet in reclaimed tenements to laugh at how they stripped the proletariat of their authenticity, in a kind of peasant hide free-for-all. When novels are published featuring working-class characters or themes, we assume they were written by appropriating poshos who, as Jarvis Cocker so succinctly put it, think that poor is cool. We assume that blue-blood blowhards think working-class people are more alive because we're unmannerly, too ill-educated to hide our passions, like zoo animals, riding and ranting. We become disillusioned. We convince ourselves it's not worth claiming our own narratives.

I can propose no snappy solution to class imbalance in writing. Class is a construct designed to compartmentalise, to sequester: class *is* imbalance. But as a construct it suffers from its own vastness; as a structure it has points at which it is too thin and rusts and buckles and snaps. I do not know if it would occur to me that there are platforms available to chancers, not just in online writing's teeming realm, but in the many literary journals and magazines published in Ireland. That there are spaces in which I might not feel the need to rein in my literary ambition, in which writing has worth as a form of expression, and is not condemned as self-indulgent. Writing groups. Courses facilitated by those compatriots a little further into their careers, but compatriots nonetheless. Libraries … Oh Jesus, that we might save our libraries. That we might always maintain those meditative places, those little monuments to myth and cant and science.

I wonder often why the middle class aren't much more worried about giving arts-based careers a lash in the first place. After all, there's rarely money in art; being able to make a living in the arts is the glorious goal, whereas being able to make a living from any other profession is a rational starting point. People raised to expect that they'll make a reasonable living in adulthood should surely baulk harder at the penury involved in making art full time. So here, maybe, is a notion of my station, a proposal not of solution, but a radical perspective: working-class people are better suited to the arts. Living in the now, totting up desperately in the Lidl queue. Close to the earth and to the edge, outsiders, transgressors. And the associated economic deprivation is, after all, nothing new.

Lisa McInerney's short stories have featured in *The Stinging Fly*, on Granta and BBC Radio 4 and in the anthologies *The Long Gaze Back* and *Town and Country*. Her debut novel *The Glorious Heresies* won the 2016 Baileys Women's Prize for Fiction and the 2016 Desmond Elliott Prize.

Notes on Desperation – A Writer's Apprenticeship

Kevin Barry

1

Twenty-five years ago I was living at 2, Pery Square, in Limerick city, in the basement of an old Georgian house that was then owned by an aunt of the politician Des O'Malley; the house now operates as a kind of *Angela's Ashes* museum. I was paying a rent of twenty-five Irish punts a week for the dark but rather characterful flat, or rather I was supposed to be paying this amount – in fact, the arrears had somewhat gotten on top of me, a situation that culminated in my being chased through the streets of the city by the auctioneer who managed the building; I was on a mountain bike, he was in a car. He eventually cornered me in Todd's Bow, behind the eponymous department store, and I raised a placating palm and insisted that I would pay what was due, though in fact I wound up moving to Cork instead.

I had been working as a reporter on the *Limerick Post*, the weekly freesheet newspaper, busily covering the courts and the council meetings, and also gathering research materials for my novel *City of Bohane* (2011), though I had no idea I was doing so at the time – in terms of writing fiction, the best research is the research you don't know you're doing at the time. I was also running house music club nights in local discos and organising one-off raves, on account of which the Henry Street branch of the Garda drug squad would sometimes park outside 2, Pery Square, and they would aim significant little smiles at me as I passed in and out of the place, paranoid as a goat.

I was reading Jonathan Raban's hybrid travelogue/essay books, Don DeLillo novels and early James Ellroy slasher-fests, and I had very firm plans to myself write stories, novels, plays and screenplays – some weekends I would haul my Apple MacIntosh desktop computer home with me from the *Limerick Post* precisely for this purpose. But as is the way when you are twenty-two years old, life kept getting in the way.

2

In 1999, I was living in Cork city, freelancing for the *Examiner* and *The Irish Times*, but increasingly feeling rather haughty and put out by the fact that I was wasting all my writing energies on journalism. So I chipped in with a pal and we bought a tiny *Father Ted*-style caravan for four hundred Irish punts and agreed a timeshare on it.

The caravan was hauled out to the far end of the Beara Peninsula and situated in a field beside Ballydonegan beach at Allihies. My timeshare friend used the caravan maybe twice ever, so I more or less had the run of it to myself, and I spent the best part of the summer of 1999 living there – my address was c/o Allihies Post Office – and attempting to write a novel.

The novel focused on a migration that had occurred around the 1880s; workers from the played-out copper mines at Allihies had moved, en masse, to Butte, Montana. I was at this point reading a lot of Cormac McCarthy, and I was determined to have scenes with wolves. I spent months spacing out around the derelict old tin mines in the Caha Mountains, making plans, drafting long, elaborate paragraphs in a notebook held open against the sea breeze, and muttering to myself darkly.

I still have the notebooks containing this novel – they are in a box in the far room here in County Sligo – but I cannot bring myself to look at them. I know that there are something like 70,000 words in there. I'm pretty sure there is occasionally a line of sparky dialogue, or a half-ounce of decent description, but I'm certain that the great bulk of it is pastiche.

Still, the fact of that 70,000 words achieved in pen and ink was enough to keep me going, and I had vague plans for other novels, and maybe some stories.

Every Thursday morning I would cycle or hitchhike the twenty kilometres into Castletownbere and from an internet kiosk I'd file my column for the *Examiner*. This was a 500-worder that could be about anything under the sun, and the writing in it was far superior to anything in my novel; I was writing in something like my own voice, and I had discovered that I could at least to some extent handle the intricacies of comic timing.

On August 13th 1999, I went for a walk along the headland cliffs past Ballydonegan beach. At a slipway leading down to the water, I crouched on my heels and made a very solemn vow to make a go of this fiction-writing business. I was so earnest that I imagine my lips were moving. But I believe that mad ritual gestures like this are very necessary for emerging writers, and I still hold to this date as my writer's birthday – I was about to get fucking serious about things.

I planned to make a trip to Butte, Montana, in the autumn. I would soak up the reverberations of the place, and then I'd go to Spain early in the new year and write a second draft of the novel. I can't remember what the novel was called.

3

In late October 1999, at a room in the Capri motel, in Butte, Montana, I tearfully decided to pack in the Butte, Montana novel. I could sense that my abilities at this time were just not up to it. In fact I was years away from it. I had dutifully filled notebook after notebook at the Butte, Montana library with nuggets of Butte, Montana lore. I even met a ninety-nine-year-old man who had been brought up on the Beara Peninsula, and who played me some Irish songs on his fiddle; his name was Yank Harrington. Big old lunks in cowboy hats paraded the Butte, Montana streets, and they had boiled-ham farmer heads on them straight out of Beara, and the phonebook was full of Harringtons and Sullivans, but I couldn't get any purchase on the material. I didn't know how to bring it down, to reduce it; it kept opening out, and expanding, and eventually it just floated away, into the blue, blue skies above the Rocky Mountains.

4

I was living for a few weeks in a *pensione*, in a former convent, in the city of Alicante, in the south east of Spain. It was late January 2000, and I was writing a short story. It was set in Cork city. It was about a man living in a bedsit who became dangerously obsessed with a mouse who had taken up residence behind his fridge. Going by the prose on him, this fellow appeared to be a Corkonian first cousin of Vladimir Nabokov. The story was called 'The Linoleum Years' and a print-out of it is probably to be found in a box somewhere in the far room in County Sligo but I can't bring myself to go and root it out. I'm sure it's not up to much, but I do know that when I was writing it, I heard a kind of resounding click – for the first time, a character seemed to come fully to life on the page for me; however wonky its construction, or predictable its denouement, this story contained a character who seemed to live and breathe.

I had saved enough money to avoid freelance work for a few weeks at least. I spent all of those warm winter days writing fiction. I lay on my belly on the bed in the *pensione* and I scrawled the sentences on a pad – I had read that James Joyce used to work in this way. I was obsessed with the sound of the sentences; I tried to put as much vitality and music in them as I could. I was also obsessed with the fact that James Joyce preferred white wine to red, saying that white wine was like electricity, red wine was like the blood of an ox. I was trying hard to drink white wine rather than red – I was buying it in cartons at the *supermercado*. '*Supermercado*' was about the extent of my Spanish.

Even at this relatively early stage, I knew that I would never have a quiet, unshowy prose style. Sometimes I yearned for one, for a clean, brisk, pared-down style, clear as glass, unobtrusive … but my style wasn't like that at all; my prose behaved like an hysterical step-dancing ginger-haired child leppin' up and down on the page looking for attention. I discovered that winter in Spain that there is nothing mysterious about prose style – your style is merely a direct projection of your personality. And after a certain period of time has elapsed – I was by now thirty-one years old – there isn't much you can do about your personality; mine was composed of hysterical nervous energy and I was just going to have to go with it on the page.

After I had finished a writing session, I would walk the streets, aiming for the *supermercado*, walking in a cloud of distraction amid the happy babble of the voluble Spanish city and, as I didn't have the language, I was entirely entrapped within my own, but now happily so.

5

I have carried over a kind of guilt complex from the 1990s and early 2000s – I don't think I worked as hard as I could have at my writing; I was going at it in an occasional (and, just occasionally, in an ecstatic) way. Now, to counteract this guilt, I work like a dog.

For the past nine of these twenty-five years, I have been mostly based in an old RIC barracks, in south County Sligo, and seven days a week I perform the three-step commute across the backyard to the former turf shed that is now my office. Or the Black Lizard Studio, as I have dubbed it, because one day a black lizard walked across a print-out of my novel *Beatlebone*, then close to being finished, and I immediately got down on the floor and wrote a black lizard into the text. I did so because I believe that a kind of sympathetic magic should occur around the edges of one's writing projects; if it doesn't, the project is probably fucked.

I write stories, novels, plays, film scripts and essays in the shed, and maybe on one or two days of the seven, it seems to be going well. But most days are sluggish, and the brain feels dull, and I'd rather be doing other things. But I persevere, and now and again, just for a while, the hand feels guided across the page.

I feel like I've earned the good days, because if I have not always worked as hard as I could have, I have stayed true at least to the idea of this practice, to this strange occult business of making fictions come alive in the world. I have stayed true to it for a quarter of a century now and sometimes writing no longer seems like the thing I do, it seems like the thing I am.

Kevin Barry is the author of the novels *Beatlebone* and *City of Bohane* and the story collections *Dark Lies the Island* and *There Are Little Kingdoms*. His awards include the IMPAC Award, the Goldsmith's Prize, the *Sunday Times* EFG Short Story Prize and the Rooney Prize. His stories have appeared in the *New Yorker*, *Granta*, *The Stinging Fly* and elsewhere. He also writes plays and screenplays. He lives in County Sligo.

From a Yellow Room

Anne Enright

Twenty years ago I lived as an Irish writer in France for a month. I was given a flat on the ground floor of a house in Douarnenez, a Breton fishing town, where I was welcomed by the people who ran the annual film festival there. The town had a sardine factory and a working port, and a small swimming beach where I sometimes went, though it is hard, on a small beach, to be all alone and Irish white. The film buffs of Douarnenez were very hospitable: they drank a fair amount and cooked terrific food but they also thought I had no table manners and that I was a bit mad. 'I read your book,' one of them said, and I saw her circle her temple with a forefinger as I turned away. Culturally it was a strange mismatch. I did not feel solidarity with the Breton Celtic 'thing', I barely felt solidarity with the Irish Celtic 'thing', but that was something they could not understand: that the Ireland they loved – yearned for, indeed – was not, for me, a real place. The flat they provided, meanwhile, was covered with sixties', yellow flowered wallpaper. When I say 'covered' I mean that the yellow wallpaper went up the walls and then across the ceiling. There was a differently patterned yellow floral wallpaper in the bathroom, and another one again in the small kitchen, and on the ceiling of the kitchen. We are talking geometric, here, more Twiggy dress than Van Gogh. The shower curtain may also have had yellow flowers on it, or I may be imagining that.

I did the same thing in that yellow front room as I have done ever since. I sat down and wrote, or tried to write. Progress was slow. Progress is always slow, but I did not know that yet. My first book, a collection of short stories, had been written at weekends while I worked as a producer/director in RTÉ. It proved a small success, and in 1993 I left the job to Become A Writer. By the time I arrived in France, I had managed one intense and fractured novel, ignored by the Irish papers (I had to look that up online just now – my goodness how depressing) until the paperback came out, when it got a brief paragraph from Helen Meany. I had no money, but that was neither here nor there. In 1996 I was free, and a bit mad, and there was still plenty of time in which I could write, very slowly, my next novel, which was reviewed (hurrah!) and condemned (oh dear) four years later in *The Irish Times*.

When I check my files, I see that I was working on a film script of that first novel with the help of some money from the Irish Film Board, who failed, some months later, to read the thing. At least the guy who made decisions didn't read it. He got to page 41, he said, and gave up. The contempt of the film industry for the writer is well known. It was an attitude I recognised from my time in television, where literature was considered a thing of the past. I had been hired by the national broadcaster – or so they told me at the time – as one of the 50 per cent of the population then under twenty-five. I was paid to be young. In the *Picador Book of Contemporary Irish Fiction*, which came out in 1993, Dermot Bolger described my work as 'belonging to the future'. It was not an easy brief – to move from the imagined past into the fantasised future of an entire nation state. One, moreover, that did not seem to give a shit. I learned, very quickly, to send my work out of Ireland, where it might be read free of mythopoetic fuss. Or just beyond page 41. Which would also be nice.

During this painful first decade of my writing life, the books started to do well elsewhere: going into French and German, finding a publisher in America, garnering praise in the UK. Dermot Bolger's agent was also my agent, along with Hugo Hamilton, Éilís Ní Dhuibhne and Colm Tóibín. Imogen Parker played Pokémon Go with Irish fiction before anyone was interested in Irish fiction, and she placed her authors with UK publishers during the boom in publishing there. The fact that I had a

London agent must have seemed quite worldly to some older writers, the way social networking makes the next generation seem worldly to mine, but I was, by my own recollection, just blundering about. There were some letters from London, but really not many. I got a fax machine and it transformed my life: it meant I could make a few quid writing columns for BBC Radio 4. I relied on the writer's retreat at Annaghmakerrig for nutrition, and on parties jammed into Colm Tóibín's small house in Stoneybatter for drink and urgent literary connection, much of which was, fortunately, forgotten the next day.

And then there were strange opportunities: a Radio 4 producer took me to Senegal. A pal lent me a cottage overlooking Glencar where I sat and spoke to no one for three weeks straight. And, Doireann Ní Bhriain wrote and asked would I like to go to France. Yes, I would. I would love to go to France. Thank you very much.

If you look at the list of writers Bolger took for his 1993 Picador anthology, you do indeed see something like the future: Colum McCann and Joseph O'Connor were then practically unknown. Roddy Doyle won the Booker Prize that same year, for a novel ignored by the Irish papers – not to fetishise reviews or reviewers, but there does seem to be some unease or reluctance here. The book went straight into the Irish bestseller lists when it came out that spring.

Other gaps were opening between some official sense we had of ourselves and what was happening in the country around us. It was in 1994 – earlier than you might expect – that the phrase 'Celtic Tiger' was used for the first time. If you check the graph, you can see house prices began to rise about then, and they did not stop rising for another thirteen years. Ireland was getting younger all the time. In 1996, the country was the selected focus for the Frankfurt Book Fair, and three million pounds, split between the Irish and French governments, was spent on L'Imaginaire Irlandais, a festival of Irish theatre, music, visual arts and literature that took place across France.

The programme was notable for being open to emerging voices. Jennifer Johnston, McGahern and Banville were already known in France, but they were joined by people like Deirdre Madden, Glenn Patterson and Eoin McNamee who were closer to the beginning of their careers. As well as residencies like the one I did in Brittany, there were festivals, conferences and group events. The French thought we were wonderfully *sauvage*. The Irish, as a man in Caen explained to me, were not split by Descartian dualism. We were ontologically different, he seemed to imply: fresh, primitive, natural. We were possibly also, by his standards, quite badly dressed.

At a festival in Saint Malo, Colm Tóibín took photographs with a little cardboard camera and talked everyone into a great sense of themselves. A rumour went around, as we piled into the minibus, that John McGahern was in a limo. And indeed, when he appeared, McGahern was guarded and ushered about by his French publishers. I do not know if I was looking at the past or the future when the black car slid past but it was, for me, something entirely new.

The high point was a series of solo readings at the Pompidou Centre, that icon of the modern, which manages the trick of being high-minded and subversive at the same time. The place was important to me, the way the Louvre was not, but it might as well have been the Louvre, I was so pleased with the way my life had turned out as I rode the external elevators up to the fifth floor. I tried to imagine the space where I would read – a white room with a splash of green, perhaps, where I might stand behind a podium made of perspex. Or it would be much more interesting than that, I could not imagine what it would be like. I arrived to find an Irish pub – just as fake as the refurbished pubs at home – beautifully rendered and solid, it was stuck, like a cube of raw Rathfarnham, up against the glass wall. So I read with the rooftops of Paris behind me and people buying crisps and Guinness in front of me; tills ringing, stools scraping along the faux-flagstone floor. Many in the audience could not really understand English, and others could not hear. A few of the writers in the series got quite upset, apparently, but I did not. I thought it was a great joke.

It was sometime in the mid-nineties, I think, that Irish writers stopped hating one another. If there was one thing we learned by going abroad, then and many times after, it was to agree with foreign audiences that Irish writing in general was wonderful, which is to say to praise each other, whether we wanted to or not. Tóibín and Bolger made great mischief by sharing information about book deals. English writers never talked to each other about money, an agent told me – not ever. I got the impression there was little communication between English writers about anything, compared to the Irish who were increasingly a force, corralled as we were into hospitality rooms and tents around the world. We kept our rivalry to the page, for the most part, and the show on the road.

The next ten years were full of opportunities for Irish writers abroad, while the critical culture at home remained uneasy. If you wanted to be loved, you got on a plane. Ireland Literature Exchange helped to fund translations and Culture Ireland helped with promotion and travel, especially to those countries deemed important to the Irish economy. Irish writing is a successful brand. The government was happy to use writers as calling cards, blithe to the fact that some of us painted a pretty grim picture of the country we were supposed to represent. The writing, meanwhile, was done at home – at least mine was. I wrote in an Irish accent and on Irish soil with the paradoxical feeling that I was trapped in the country and writing my way out of it, both at the same time.

If you ask me, it was not until the crash in 2007–2008 that the future actually arrived in Ireland. Or that we stopped hanging on to the past. Or that the difference between inside Ireland and outside dissolved. What collapsed along with the economy were all those false futures, as well as the false authority that had inflated not just the property bubble, but some idea of the national 'self'. I think of Ireland at the end of the boom as a great bubble of narcissism that, when it popped, exposed us to the wide world again: exposed, too, the envy and misogyny that besets ambitious minds in a self-enclosed and self-reflecting space. Poor again, foolish, shamed, we were left back where all ladders start, back in the creative muck that writers love and that authority, perhaps by definition, dislikes.

(Whatever that is. I mean 'authority'. The voice in our heads.)

The last few years have brought a new wave of voices, sometimes lyrical, sometimes outraged or transgressive, from a generation of people who were badly wronged by the boom. If the future is finally here, then it is wonderfully various. Some things are the same as when I started out. These writers have very little money. They are praised abroad. They have a complicated relationship with the home place. But they move from Irish to international publishers with great ease. Exile itself is not what it used to be, and it seems to me that new voices find a welcome not just with the Irish reader – the silent partner in all our sorrows and our joys – but with academics, critics, funders, journalists, the whole charabanc.

In 2016, twenty years after L'Imaginaire Irlandais, the government spent tens of millions on centenary funds for the commemoration of the Easter Rising. Much of the money went on community projects and local celebrations, which involved thousands of people across the country, with a major input from RTÉ. A few individual artists (very cheerfully) adopted the correct posture for the day that was in it, and picked up a cheque, and it all went splendidly, actually, it really felt like something happened there. Between that Easter Sunday on the 27th of March, and the Brexit result on the 24th of June, nationalism felt good; it felt grown up and right. Everyone sang from the same hymn sheet. It was culture, alright, but it sure as hell wasn't art.

In 2014, I ran around Oslo with a mixed bunch of writers, many published by small presses, most of them on their first book: Donal Ryan, Eimear McBride, Paul Lynch, John Kelly, Belinda McKeon. I watched them watching each other, drinking Tullamore Dew out of plastic glasses in a town where no one knew how to get back to the hotel. These writers were already, almost instantly, known – which makes some things easier, and some things not – and I wondered how they would proceed and what they would do next. What will the future bring? Good things, no doubt. Nothing you could name. The unforeseen.

Anne Enright is an Irish Writers Centre Ambassador and the first Laureate for Irish Fiction. An award-winning novelist and short story writer, her work has been translated into over forty languages. She lives with her family in Dublin.

A Note from the Irish Writers Centre

Founded in 1991, the Irish Writers Centre has long been a hub of literary activity, supporting established and aspiring writers throughout Ireland from its base in the heart of Dublin's cultural quarter at 19 Parnell Square. The Centre has been described by our Patron, President of Ireland, Michael D. Higgins, as 'a vortex of creativity'.

As the national resource centre for Irish literature, our mission is to support and promote writers at all stages of their development. We offer a diverse programme of writing courses, professional development initiatives, literary events and information services on all literary matters in Ireland.

All of this is made possible through the engagement of suitably qualified writers and facilitators who deliver our programmes with a zest and enthusiasm that has secured our reputation for delivering high-quality supports and initiatives for Irish writers. Increasingly, we are broadening our reach to provide these supports across the island and internationally. We have partnered with many organisations to do this and have been especially supported in this endeavour by Words Ireland.

This year, 2016, is an auspicious one for both Ireland and the Irish Writers Centre. While it is twenty-five years since the opening of our Georgian doors, Ireland has been commemorating its centenary of the 1916 Rising. We wanted to celebrate both occasions and our response was in the shape of a stylish, evocative film and app entitled A Poet's Rising, which enables the viewer to engage with the history of Ireland through the work of some of our most eminent contemporary poets. We asked Theo Dorgan, Thomas McCarthy, Paul Muldoon, Eiléan Ní Chuilleanáin, Nuala Ní Dhomhnaill and Jessica Traynor to bring the people and events of 1916 to life at iconic Rising locations through newly commissioned poems, accompanied by original music from Colm Mac Con Iomaire. The viewer can access the poems via the app, either in situ or in the comfort of their own home.

We wanted to create something equally splendid to commemorate our own continued existence, something to mark our resilience and relevance, something that would celebrate the writers whom we seek to support. Writers often express their thoughts through their characters or situations, but it is equally important to hear writers' voices unvarnished, upfront and telling it how it is – and there are scarce opportunities to mark a prose writer or poet's true voice in print, in one collection.

This anthology intended to allow writers from a wide range of ages and persuasions, and with as broad a palette as was required, to offer a view – a personal, direct, unambiguous perspective – about any aspect of life or literature they have observed in the last quarter century. We hope the reader has found that the resulting essays provide a compelling snapshot into the ruminations of some of our best-known contemporary writers – in their own words.

As our anniversary year draws to an end, on behalf of the team here at the Irish Writers Centre, I'd like to acknowledge and thank Irish writers everywhere for the significant contribution they make in enriching our lives with their writing on a daily basis. A book is a source of flight, knowledge, growth, a wonder and a haven. Words matter, and we need our writers to keep nourishing us with them.

Valerie Bistany, 2016
Irish Writers Centre Director

Acknowledgements

Lines from 'The Journey' by Eavan Boland are reproduced by kind permission of the author; lines from 'Archaeology' by Katha Pollitt are reproduced by kind permission of the author; excerpts from *Proxopera* are reproduced by kind permission of the Jonathan Williams Literary Agency as agent of the author; excerpts from *Seeing Things* and 'Away from it All' by Seamus Heaney are reproduced by kind permission of the Heaney Estate; excerpts from 'The Kings Are Out' by Patrick Galvin are reproduced by kind permission of the Jonathan Williams Literary Agency as agent of the author; lines from 'The Man Who Was Marked by Winter' by Paula Meehan are reproduced by kind permission of the author; excerpts from *The Speckled People* by Hugo Hamilton are reproduced by kind permission of the author; excerpts from *The Irish Comic Tradition* by Vivian Mercier are reproduced by kind permission of Eiléan Ní Chuilleanáin and Cormac Ó Cuilleanáin as agents of the author; excerpts from *Breakfast at Pluto* by Patrick McCabe are reproduced by kind permission of the author; excerpts from *In the Forest* by Edna O'Brien are reproduced by kind permission of the author. With thanks also to Martina Devlin, Kathy Sheridan and *The Irish Times* for permissions.

*

The Irish Writers Centre wishes to thank Aifric Mac Aodha, Tom Murphy at the Law Library and the Irish Copyright and Licensing Agency (ICLA) for their time and support throughout the publication process.

We would also like to take this opportunity to acknowledge the following for their continued hard work, dedication and enthusiasm in helping the Centre to grow and evolve:

Irish Writers Centre Team
Valerie Bistany, Bernadette Greenan, Amy Herron, Pádraig Burke, Arnold Fanning, Helen Mulvany, Emily Cook, Paul Fitzgerald and Paul Rooney

Irish Writers Centre Board
Liz McManus (Chairperson), Martina Devlin, Hilary Fennell, Anne Larchet, Paul Moore, Luán Ó Braonáin, Mary O'Donnell, Rossa Ó Snodaigh and Christopher Pressler

Thanks also to our Patron, President of Ireland, Michael D. Higgins and to our Ambassadors: John Banville, Anne Enright, Roy Foster, Marian Keyes, Éilís Ní Dhuibhne and Joseph O'Connor.

A heartfelt thanks to all the team at New Island and, in particular, to Dan Bolger who was so enthusiastic about this project from day one. And to all of our *Beyond the Centre* contributors, editor Declan Meade and assistant editor Amy Herron for producing a book worthy of our twenty-five years – we couldn't have done this without your insights.

And finally, a special mention must go to Jack Harte, without whom the Centre wouldn't exist.

The Centre gratefully acknowledges the support of the Arts Council/An Chomhairle Ealaíon, the Arts Council of Northern Ireland, Dublin City Council and Foras na Gaeilge.